Material Insurgency

SUNY series in New Political Science
―――――――
Bradley J. Macdonald, editor

Material Insurgency

Towards a Distributed Environmental Politics

ANDREW M. ROSE

Published by State University of New York Press, Albany

© 2021 State University of New York

All rights reserved

Printed in the United States of America

No part of this book may be used or reproduced in any manner whatsoever without written permission. No part of this book may be stored in a retrieval system or transmitted in any form or by any means including electronic, electrostatic, magnetic tape, mechanical, photocopying, recording, or otherwise without the prior permission in writing of the publisher.

For information, contact State University of New York Press, Albany, NY
www.sunypress.edu

Library of Congress Cataloging-in-Publication Data

Name: Rose, Andrew M., author.
Title: Material insurgency : towards a distributed environmental politics / Andrew M. Rose.
Description: Albany : State University of New York Press, [2021] | Series: SUNY series on New Political Science | Includes bibliographical references and index.
Identifiers: ISBN 9781438484372 (hardcover : alk. paper) | ISBN 9781438484389 (pbk. : alk. paper) | ISBN 9781438484396 (ebook)
Further information is available at the Library of Congress.

10 9 8 7 6 5 4 3 2 1

For Mom and Dad

Contents

Acknowledgments ix

Introduction 1

Chapter 1
Climate Change Environmentalism and Distributed Politics 17

Chapter 2
H. D. Thoreau and the Practice of Distributed Knowledges 49

Chapter 3
Bacterial Insurgency in Karen Tei Yamashita's
Through the Arc of the Rainforest 79

Chapter 4
The Material Temporalities of Leslie Silko's *Almanac of the Dead* 101

Chapter 5
(Dis)intentional Politics and Its Limits: Crisis and
Innovation in Nathaniel Rich's *Odds Against Tomorrow*
and Chang-rae Lee's *On Such a Full Sea* 133

Chapter 6
The Unknowable Now: Passionate Science
and Transformative Politics in Kim Stanley Robinson's
Speculative Fiction 169

CODA   203

NOTES   209

WORKS CITED   231

INDEX   237

Acknowledgments

I am, of course, beyond thrilled for the opportunity to publish this work, the culmination of a decade of (material) intellectual labor. It is only possible, however, because so many other people, events, places, and things exerted their influences upon the project at the right—and sometimes even the not-so-right—time. The myriad assemblages that propel an intellectual project through its long and winding trajectory, as much as the unique writer, are the unruly partners of writing process. Writing a book that takes up distributed agency as its focal point, you begin to notice and become generally, though certainly not entirely, more cognizant of these less obvious partnerships. For my own part, I am privileged to have had the opportunity to see this project through its many phases and learn so much from the brilliance of the artists and scholars I have met, in person and word, during the research and writing of this monograph. Before going back to the beginning of the journey, I would like to thank the folks at SUNY Press, especially Michael Rinella, Diane Ganeles, and New Political Series editor Bradley J. MacDonald, for their consistent support of this project and professional and timely labor on its behalf, and to the anonymous readers, who provided detailed and immensely beneficial feedback. The commitment of the New Political Science series to innovative approaches and interdisciplinarity is truly remarkable, and I am humbled and energized by the opportunity to add this small contribution to its intellectual mission.

The earliest work on what would become this book project began during my PhD exams and dissertation process; and though it has developed in ways I could not foresee back then, it also would not exist without those earlier instantiations. More people than I can list here made my graduate experience at the University of Washington (UW) the profound life-altering (in a mostly good way!) experience it was, but I especially want to thank Edmond, Jay, Jane, Lee, Pacharee, Jentery, Brooken, Caitlin, and Erik for being fellow-travelers who continually made me smarter and laugh harder. For everyone who made Pub Night the special ritual it was over the years, may the College Inn live on in the memories we made in its depths. My eternal thanks to Marc for always having the best plans for a writing break, and to Curly for keeping my spirits up with reports from the river. While all of the names on this next list could also be on the former, I want to separately thank the intrepid members of our infamous dissertation reading group: Kate Boyd, Curtis Hisayasu, Jason Morse, Jed Murr, Christian Ravela, Suzanne Schmidt, and Simón Trujillo. Thanks for being wonderful friends, brilliant thinkers, and smart, generous readers all at once. Only hindsight can truly show what a special thing we had going there, just the right balance of academic rigor, good humor, and unconditional support is more rare in graduate school (and academia more broadly) than we knew at the time (even though we sort of knew).

To chronicle all of the ways this project, and my academic career, has been beneficially impacted by Eva Cherniavsky is beyond my ability, so instead I will simply thank her for the wise guidance and her uncanny knack for generative critique that leaves me so immensely indebted. This project would be something else entirely, and much lesser, without her guidance and example, and I remain fundamentally in awe of her intelligence, perceptiveness, and profound generosity. I am so very grateful for Tom Foster, my go-to for all things speculative and science fiction, and Linda Nash, for keeping me grounded in historical context to the best of her ability (any lack thereof in this book is all on me). It's always good to have some ecocritics in the fold, and Andy Meyer, Eric Morel, and Ned Schaumberg were always insightful interlocutors and great conference partners; and also to know a few who have blazed the trail ahead of you, so I thank Alenda Chang, Jill Gatlin, Erin James, and Jennifer Ladino for the bits of wisdom at critical junctures. The opportunity I had to teach and learn at UW's Program on the Environment while dissertating was priceless, where what were so often daily, evocative interdisciplinary discussions across the environmental humanities, social sciences, and environmental sciences with my colleagues and students made every day a new one.

I also regularly think back to the professors who sparked the first fires of my academic aspirations. At Lafayette College, Paul Cefalu and Suzanne Westfall inspired me to think big, and someday I know they will even forgive me for becoming an Americanist. And a grand thank you to Laura Walls for leading a certain presumptuous undergrad through an independent study that would launch my long-running and still burning fascination with H. D. Thoreau. And now that I realize independent studies are a form of essentially unpaid, and mostly thankless, labor, I am even more appreciative of her generous support, then and now; it means the world. The very first interdisciplinary environmental studies course I ever took, before I even knew that that was what we were doing, was taught with brilliance and passion by Robert Walls (I still have those books on my shelf, Bob, including *The Sacred Forest*). And my current colleagues at Christopher Newport University, who really all deserve individual recognition, do so much to make our English Department a stimulating and welcoming environment. A new faculty member could not ask to arrive to a better department chair and institutional guide than Jean Filetti, and then I lucked out again with Mary Wright, who cares about her department and colleagues in such a meaningful way that it makes us all better. And for advice on all things career and more-than-career related, a special thanks to my hallway pals Rebecca Barclay, Kara Keeling, and John Nichols.

Sadie, my partner in adventures big and small, from coast to coast, thank you for making this whole thing make sense; and for teaching me that when it does no such thing, that's okay too. And for Lila and Maisie my love is bottomless and enduring. They show me each day what it means to love with a wide open and trusting heart and to see the world through joyful eyes, not to mention their relentless training to make me a morning person (at least sort of, keep working on me).

My love and thanks to Brenda for keeping me humble, as I remain well aware I'm the second smartest sibling (of two); and to Aunt June, for all the books. And, finally, I dedicate this book to George and Elizabeth Rose for all the countless ways they have shaped and supported my life's path, along its many twists and turns, with a patience and unconditional love that seems beyond the realm of the possible. In summary, I am one lucky (post)human.

A similar version of chapter 3 was originally published in *ISLE: Interdisciplinary Studies in Literature and the Environment* vol. 26, no. 1, Winter 2019, as "Insurgent Bacteria: Distributed Agency and Political Subjectivity in Karen Tei Yamashita's *Through the Arc of the Rainforest*." Published by Oxford University Press on behalf of the Association for the Study of Literature and the Environment. And an abbreviated version of chapter 6 was published in *Science Fiction Studies*, vol. 43, no. 2, Summer 2016, as "The Unknowable Now: Passionate Science and Transformative Politics in Kim Stanley Robinson's *Science in the Capital* trilogy."

Introduction

Emerging postanthropocentric conceptions of subjectivity, agency, and knowledge formation practices contain substantial implications for currently dominant modes of environmental advocacy and social movement organizing. The nonhuman turn in environmental humanities scholarship has arrived at a critical juncture, and it is now incumbent upon eco-theory scholars to more seriously grapple with the political implications of the decentered and disanthropocentric human subject. The now prevalent concept of hybrid, or distributed, agency is central to this problematic, as it highlights the interconnected, overlapping, and dispersed nature of agency to suggest that agentic forces are always already an inextricable mixture of the human and nonhuman.[1] It is this more nuanced understanding of the complex relationship between human and nonhuman agency that is most fundamentally altering our understanding of political agency and, in turn, historical change more broadly. Undoubtedly, contemporary environmental movements will be impacted, and might well benefit from, this ongoing decentering of the human subject; however, posthuman and postnatural conceptions of matter, subjectivity, and agency also present serious challenges to our contemporary sense of political efficacy.

While critiques of anthropocentrism and liberal humanist subjectivity enable an integral step toward a more ecologically sustainable society, *Material Insurgency* aims to provide an in-depth and critical consideration of what—particularly in terms of political subjectivity and agency—comes after the decentering of the human subject. Therefore, the chapters to come investigate the ways in which a distributed, fragmented concept of agency (one that does not allow for the reassertion of a liberal humanist subject-actor at convenient moments) also raises a series of problematics for thinking human political subjectivity and best practices for social movement organizing. While hopeful about the transformative potential of posthumanist and new materialist theories generally, I also deem it necessary to explore the flip side of the coin: that is, what we might come to see as the crisis of the postanthropocentric and distributed human subject, as it relates to the efficacy of environmentalism as a social movement.

In the introduction to their influential edited collection *New Materialisms: Ontology, Agency and Politics*, Diana Coole and Samantha Frost turn productively to the concept of distributed agency to explore the potential for posthuman conceptions of knowledge formation practices and agency. They suggest the concept of distributed agency is based upon "a materiality that materializes, evincing immanent modes of self-transformation that compel us to think of causation in far more complex terms," and that moving beyond the traditional construction of the rational and intentional human subject-actor in this manner requires us to recognize "that phenomena are caught in a multitude of interlinking systems and forces and to consider anew the location and nature of capacities for agency" (9). Attending to the complexity of distributed notions of subjectivity and agency also then, and this is an integral point, necessarily impacts our understanding of intention and causality. The editors explain:

> Conceiving matter as possessing its own modes of self-transformation, self-organization, and directedness . . . disturbs the conventional sense that agents are exclusively humans who possess the cognitive abilities, intentionality, and freedom to make autonomous decisions and the corollary presumption that humans have the right or ability to master nature. (10)

Taking distributed agency seriously, it follows, has major implications for our understanding of the relation between human and nonhuman communities and the best practices for evaluating human society's impacts on the environment. The terrain of possibility is, quite truthfully, stunning in its uncertainty, complexity, and breadth, and the scholarship currently emerging from this new materialist and posthuman disruption of liberal humanist conceptions of the rational, autonomous self has been strikingly incisive and vital. The task ahead, though, is still more challenging. Given that these emergent theories of materiality "cast doubt on some of modernity's most cherished beliefs about the fundamental nature of existence and social justice but also because presumptions about agency and causation implicit in prevailing paradigms have structured our modern sense of the . . . dimensions of the ethical and the political" (6), Coole and Frost can only be correct in suggesting these "developments thus call upon us to reorient ourselves profoundly in relation to the world, to one another, and to ourselves" (6).[2] This emerging line of inquiry is fundamentally upending the long-held and comfortable humanist notions of intentionality, rationality, and autonomy; and environmental theorists and activists must now be careful not to underestimate the depths of this disruption.

The chapters to follow explore the theoretical challenges of distributed agency through a rereading of literary materials spanning two centuries of U.S. fiction and nonfiction. I suggest that turning our attention to environmentally themed literature facilitates a productive exploration of alternative and radically nonhierarchical visions of the relation between the human and nonhuman (each disruptively operating, to varying degrees of success, outside the binary constraints of Cartesian dualism). In particular, I focus upon literary fiction and nonfiction, including the works of authors such as Henry David Thoreau, Leslie Silko, Karen Yamashita, Chang-rae Lee, and Kim Stanley Robinson, which grapple with the implications of posthuman conceptions of nature for environmental justice and social movement organizing. The selected literary archive explores alternatives to humanist conceptions of the relation between human and nonhuman communities and, in varying ways, offers an opportunity to explore the possibilities for—and limitations to—a posthuman and distributed environmental politics. Each text, therefore, operates as a resource for imagining a kind of environmental actor whom we cannot necessarily study empirically, because she is still only a prospect, or potential, of our imagination.

The ultimate value in turning to literature, in this case, is that it provides a window into the possible constitution of an environmental politics (and a subject of that politics) that does not yet exist and that we do not quite know how to imagine. This study, as a result, reads environmental writing with an eye toward developing an argument that posthumanist scholar Rosi Braidotti might consider commensurate with her concept "dreaming forward," in which critical appraisals of past and present moments allow for radical and affirmative imaginings of a just socioenvironmental future beyond humanism.[3] Within this process, the "irreplaceable potentiality of fiction is that it makes possible the imagining of possibilities" (Ghosh 2016, 172). One of these possibilities fiction might help us explore, according to Amitov Ghosh, is how "to find a way out of the individualizing imaginary in which we are trapped" (181). In fact, the posthuman is best conceived as a "non-unitary subject . . . [with] an enlarged sense of interconnection between self and others, including the non-human," no longer held back by the "obstacle of self-centered individualism" (Braidotti, 49–50). And she is most likely to emanate from a "posthuman theory [that] is a generative tool to help us re-think the basic unit of reference for the human . . . [and] rethink the basic tenets of our interaction with both human and non-human agents on a planetary scale" (5–6). The relation of possibility between posthuman theory and the selected fictional texts galvanizes this project's search for a posthuman political subjectivity capable of effectively operating with, and within, the modes of distributed agency.

The new materialist theoretical work of Stacy Alaimo, Karen Barad, and Jane Bennett, to name just a few of the many influential scholars in this field, is also central to this project, as it has produced its own definitive critique of humanist models of subjectivity and agency (and their dependency upon anthropocentricism and human exceptionalism). My own thinking about what exactly postanthropocentric models of subjectivity and agency might mean for social movement organizing is deeply indebted to, and endeavors to expand upon, their foundational scholarship. The question of intentionality, first and foremost, is central. Distributed agency, as a particular expression of the broader theories of a postanthropocentric world, disrupts the humanist model for the rational, autonomous, intentional human actor. Intentionality, as a discrete property of the human individual, is no longer a safe assumption. While interpreting the radical significance of Danish physicist Niels Bohr's complementarity principle, which plays a foundational role in her influential theory of *agential realism*, Karen Barad finds that "intentions are not preexisting determinate mental states of individual human beings" (2007, 22–23). In fact, she goes on to suggest that once "agency is cut loose from its traditional humanist orbit," it is, in fact, no longer solely or entirely "aligned with human intentionality or subjectivity" (177). This ongoing destabilization of the assumed connection between human subject and intentional act, fundamental to her concept of "intra-action," compels us to consider its subsequent impact upon sociopolitical organizing strategies. Especially, as Barad argues, because "intentionality might better be understood as attributable to a complex network of human and non-human agents, including historically specific sets of material conditions that exceed the traditional notion of the individual" (23). Rather than a supposed intentional agent of change, Barad asks us to train our attention upon the complex materiality of agentic forces. This reorientation should then lead us to recognize "it is less that there is an assemblage of agents than there is an entangled state of agencies" (23). This is where Barad's work is especially integral. Her influential concept of intra-action eschews a more superficial understanding of distributed agency in which human and nonhuman agencies impact each other and eventually become intertwined, instead insisting that all phenomena manifest from the outset as fundamentally "entangled" agencies.

What then would it entail to organize political resistance to social and environmental exploitation within a world, in Barad's formulation, comprised of an "entangled state of agencies"? Recognizing agency as a coproduction of forces emanating from the human and nonhuman worlds requires, at the very minimum, an acknowledgment that political agency is always already partial and bound to produce effects not calculable in advance.[4] And once the assumed anthropocentric link between human act and result is severed, as it is by the concept of distributed agency, it is not so easily recoupled. That is, if we are to understand each human action as imbricated and complexly intertwined with nonhuman agency, then this necessarily impacts our understanding of the relation between the human political act and its result. I hope to explore these issues, in part, through some of the following questions: To what degree do a given social movement's actions in the present moment relate to its declared future goals? Or, even more provocatively, what would it mean to organize without intention? Is it possible, for instance, to organize an efficacious movement without a defined goal, or endpoint, in mind? Jeffrey Jerome Cohen suggests that distributed agency, what he calls "agentism," is a "form of activism" in and of itself because "only in admitting that the inhuman is not ours to control, possesses desires and even will, can we apprehend the environment disanthropocentrically, in a teetering mode that renders human centrality as a problem rather than a starting point" (2013, xxiv). From within this "teetering mode," what is it social movements look like? With these provocations in mind, *Material Insurgency* focuses particular attention upon the ways in which embracing the concept of distributed agency will necessarily change our understanding of causation, linearity, and futurity within environmental politics and beyond. In so doing, I hope to provide some insight into the challenges and possibilities disanthropocentric modes of subjectivity and agency present for environmental theorists and activists, as they search for viable sociopolitical pathways toward a more just and egalitarian world.

It is far from surprising that posthuman and new materialist conceptions of the decentered subject have captured the imagination of environmental scholars, as they articulate an in-depth theoretical structure for the long-standing and varied environmentalist critiques of anthropocentrism (and the nature/culture binary, more broadly). Additionally, distributed agency seems to align with environmental activism's longstanding contention that humans would be better served by understanding themselves as one member of the ecological community rather than as outside, above, and/or fully in control of the nonhuman environment. Understanding human agency as distributed across the human and nonhuman, as opposed to being the sole possession of an intentional, rational, and discrete human subject has therefore become tremendously influential in new materialist theory, and rightfully so. Despite its potential to revitalize existing critiques of anthropocentrism, I will suggest here that we should not be too quick to extol the decentered, posthuman subject as automatically a more ecologically aware citizen. There is a subtle but detectable habit of mind, among environmental advocates and theorists alike, that assumes the human subject, once made sufficiently aware of their more interconnected relation to surrounding nonhuman communities, will recognize their ethical duty to treat the earth more carefully and respectfully. Eco-theory scholars and green activists, in other words, might be guilty of, at times and to varying degrees, too confidently celebrating this newly decentered human subject as automatically better positioned to think and act in ecologically sound ways. According to this line of thinking, one might suppose the human subject will reconfigure their ethics and practice based upon this newly decentered worldview, while simultaneously retaining what seems to be their fully intentional and rational agency. This newly transformed, decentered, and ecological citizen will then *act* in a more responsible and ethical manner from their now decentralized (i.e., correct, or proper) relation to the world. It sometimes seems this conceptualization of the new materialisms' political impact attempts to claim that everything and, simultaneously, nothing has changed. That is, endowed with an entirely reconfigured subjective position and a newly minted disanthropocentric ecological consciousness, the distributed political actor can now act, in similar ways as (but to different ends than) the humanist political actor that preceded her, to improve society's treatment of a still surprisingly passive and malleable nonhuman world. This assumption, if unchecked, will limit our ability to successfully disrupt the traditional reification of the natural world in humanist thought. It may be much more difficult, but I think necessary, to admit that the materialist disruption of the rational humanist subject position also unsettles many of our assumptions about the political subject and her ability to organize and propel social movements.

For these reasons and more, the question of distributed agency's impact on social movement organizing remains an essential and animating concern throughout this book. Jane Bennett, speaking to the political consequences of the new materialisms, in her influential book *Vibrant Matter*, argues that if "an image of inert matter helps animate our current practice of aggressively wasteful . . . consumption," then further attention to "a materiality experienced as a lively force with agentic capacity could animate a more ecologically sustainable public" (2012, 51). The understandable, though possibly optimistic, desire to see theories of materiality and distributed agency as providing a pathway to a more ecological society is clear in this passage. Bennett's confidence that admitting more "actants" into our conception of agency will allow humans to devise "wiser interventions" is typical of new materialist arguments generally (2012, 4). If we allow that agency, however, is not the exclusive property of a presumed rational and intentional human subject, then how exactly shall we reevaluate the process in which "wiser" actions are first devised and then, ultimately, mobilized within the framework of distributed agency? I do not think we can assume that even a broad acceptance of distributed agency as a concept will *automatically* lead to more ecologically aware individual citizens living in a society that successfully interacts more wisely with the nonhuman environment.

I am not suggesting, to be clear, that Bennett's work is somehow uncritically anthropocentric. Quite to the contrary, it is the acute effectiveness of new materialist critiques of humanist conceptions of anthropocentrism, such as those brought forth by Bennett, that reveal these new questions regarding the relation between disanthropocentric subjectivity and political agency.[5] Within the context of distributed agency, even if we assume a given subject's newfound sense of interdependence with the more-than-human world will lead to more eco-friendly thinking and intentions, there is no guarantee these new intentions will lead directly to intentional acts with preordained and knowable results. In fact, distributed agency muddies exactly this construction of causality. Consequently, in regard to political subjectivity and activism, distributed notions of knowledge and agency raise a set of unique, and hopefully productive, challenges to traditional theories and practices of social movement organizing (which remain, to this point, predominantly based upon an intentional human activist-subject). As Bennett suggests, "If human intentionality can be agentic only if accompanied by a vast entourage of nonhumans," then the necessary task ahead is to "devise new procedures, technologies, and regimes of perception that enable us to consult nonhumans more closely, or to listen and respond more carefully" (2012, 108). It will be imperative, therefore, to reconfigure knowledge formation practices, and their relation to political subjectivity and agency, in ways that better recognize "human culture is inextricably enmeshed with nonhuman agencies" (2012, 108).

Environmental scholarship is only just beginning to interrogate the assumption that an ethics based in distributed, or postanthropocentric, subjectivity will, as a matter of consequence, lead to more ecological subjects and environmentally sustainable societies. Stacy Alaimo's hugely influential concept of transcorporeality, via its emphasis on humans' intimate and material interconnection to each other and the nonhuman world, is one immensely helpful step toward a new ecological ethics and environmental stance.[6] I share Alaimo's sense that the Western liberal subject, as we know it, is no longer a tenable figure, and that there is an embryonic and profound political potential embedded within distributed subjectivity and agency (2016, 4–5). While the scholarship of the nonhuman turn is, of course, generally committed to a progressive and justice-based environmental movement, much of its focus has maintained an ontological framework that allows for only relatively vague gestures toward its implications for environmental politics itself. In this context, *Material Insurgency* critically engages with the possibility that sociopolitical movements may soon discover they are operating within a redefined framework: one in which (because of an increasing recognition of distributed agency) the relationship between political actions and human-intentioned futurity is significantly less definitive. From this standpoint, I suggest we are now tasked with fundamentally reimagining political activism and social movements in a fashion that no longer assumes the autonomy, rationality, and intentionality of the traditional humanist subject. The political subject and the political act in a *distributed* world simply will not look at all like the politics of liberal humanism.

Taking distributed agency seriously, in summary, will mean grappling with the limitations it places upon human mastery over the environment, even in arenas where we might prefer to still claim it. In other words, we must resist at all costs the temptation to assume that we can at once disrupt the deepest assumptions of humanist concepts of subjectivity and agency while, at the same time, maintaining a familiar political subject-activist who, through generally recognizable modes of social movement organizing, successfully influences and shapes a given human society to promote more responsible interaction with the more-than-human world. Once we have unsettled the human intentional subject, as posthumanism and new materialist theory have undoubtedly accomplished in recent years, it becomes simply impossible to depend upon familiar models of liberal democratic political activism. It is not written in stone that the decentered human subject will automatically live as a more ecological citizen, and it is certainly not clear that this distributed subject will wield an effective and justice-oriented politics. Scholars will need to recognize that even those of us deeply committed to a critique of humanism, one that we hope might build a more just and equal posthuman model for our social, economic, and political institutions, might not find each and every impact of this radical postanthropocentrism to our immediate liking.

New materialists' expectations for the political impact that might follow from these reworked ontologies, furthermore, generally tend toward an at times problematic conception of contemporary structures of power: that is, the complex relation between the state, transnational capital, and the citizen-subject. We cannot afford to assume that a change of consciousness in, for instance, a majority of the U.S. population will equate to political change at the necessary scale and pace; that is, not without a sustained and deeply critical engagement with the dynamics of power in the era of late capitalism. To be sure, a small but significant set of voices has been theorizing the relation between posthumanism (and the new materialisms) and political theory. Of this set, Bennett's work on the politics of "agentic assemblages," Donna Haraway's engagement with feminist and posthuman successor sciences, and Timothy Mitchell's writing on distributed agency and historical change are of particular relevance to this project. Building upon Bennett's work, political theorist Stefanie Fishel explores the ways a growing body of knowledge on "microbial communities give[s] a bodily and material example in which multiple perspectives and objects—beyond human-created institutions and subjects—can be seen as vital and necessary to politics and human survival" (2017, 5). Beginning from the microbrial, Fishel's work makes clear the extent to which new materialist theories might potentially disrupt both our sense of the individuated political subject and the political systems and institutions in which she operates.

In her fascinating book of new materialist political theory *The Microbial State*, Fishel contends, "If humans take a decentralized view of the world and the "stuff" or material of politics seriously, this puts the very categories of politics into question" (2017, 42). Working from a perspective steeped in theories of the state and international relations, Fishel argues that if we recognize "the human is a hybrid forum of nested sets of complex permeable bodies, this leads to a new conception of 'bodies politic' . . . [as] a set of evolving and interlocking organic systems within systems" (43). This is potentially transformational, she contends, exactly because it "challenges a basic assumption about modernity, especially those surrounding the role of human agency, subject creation based on this agency, and what this subject's relation with nature and culture entail" (43). It is imperative, therefore, that eco-theorists recognize the limitations inherent to an overemphasis upon change at the level of individual consciousness, and instead dedicate more attention to the myriad ways in which the broader contours of liberal democracy are also fundamentally challenged by postanthropocentric thinking. As Fishel points out: "Our ideas of the state—and the body politic—are limited because of the way we understand bodies as autonomous sovereign actors in rationalist theories, ergo our politics are limited" (43). Theorizing the state as a distributed entity, rather than a fully self-contained and independent institution, opens up promising avenues for theories of political power and activism, but also raises many questions that remain as yet less explored. Fishel's work, importantly for our purposes here, helps to move us beyond the assumption that a distributed subjectivity leads automatically to an ecological transformation of society, and instead compels us to look at the complexities inherent in rethinking entire cultural and political formations.

Another essential strand of the current conversation in theories of the state focuses upon the category of the *citizen* itself, elucidating the myriad challenges social movements will face in the quest of transforming theories of posthuman subjectivity into an effectual environmental politics. Expanding and contemporizing Foucault's concept of biopolitics in her recent book *Neocitizenship*, Eva Cherniavsky explains the particular importance of distinguishing between *governmentality*, as a process of regulating a given population, and *discipline*, as the hegemonic "norming" of individuals in order to "bind" them to a particular social order (2017, 16). Cherniavsky argues the State, within and under neoliberalism, is more and more focused on the former while becoming increasingly less concerned with manufacturing consent through discipline. Suggesting that this process is redefining the very idea of the citizen as we know it, she coins the term *neocitizenship* as she explores the transitional "forms and contexts" of "political participation" available to the "neoliberal subject" (32); a subject whom we should now understand as "dominated but undisciplined" (36). In other words, the state is increasingly less interested in creating a hegemonic view (a shared assumption of what is "real" or the "correct" way to view contemporary structures of society); instead, it manages its citizen-subjects through their data-based visibility (153). Adroitly tracing these changes, Cherniavsky examines the move from "normative culture," in which the State "interpolates" the citizen-subject's interiority, to a "serial culture," where citizens are released into "a minutely regulated environment" (37). The citizen becomes more and more visible to the State (often reified as an "identity" or group "affiliation"), but the state is increasingly "opaque and elusive to her" (37). Therefore, if the "state no longer 'frees' the individual but operationalizes her," Cherniavsky suggests, freedom is thus transformed into mere "functionality" (58–59).

It follows from the above that if the state does not need the consent of the governed, or is no longer invested in creating a commonly shared view of its own legitimacy, then traditional academic "ideology critique" approaches become rather less impactful (2017, 60–61). In this context, new materialist and posthuman scholars can defamiliarize and reimagine cultural assumptions concerning the relation between human and nonhuman communities as thoroughly as we like, without necessarily impacting the state's ability to control the population. That is, if Cherniavsky is correct that the state no longer "norms" its population through hegemonic processes (or is at least less and less dependent upon doing so), then a sociocethical shift in the population is less disruptive to State power. This is because "[t]he interests of ruling elements are served by decomposing the social body and permitting us to dwell in whatever (un)realities of our own devising" (154). The immensity of this challenge for scholars of new materialisms dedicated to their work's implications for a more effectual environmental politics, and a more socially and environmentally justice-oriented society, cannot be understated. In darker moments, we might imagine the posthuman subject, and her distributed environmental politics, becomes simply another "label" and "affiliation," respectively, or an identity the state can manage as just another "unreal" cultural perspective (154). In a more hopeful light, new materialist and posthuman theory—such as Fishel's work on the microbial sciences pointing toward a new vision of the state and body politic as complex assemblages—might be seen as the first steps in a vast reorientation of theory, practice, and politics in a posthuman and postnatural world. It would, by necessity, need to be a step toward thinking political power beyond individual consciousness change and community-wide socioethical transformations.[7]

All of this should be taken as a further explanation as to why I find it useful to turn to literary nonfiction and fictional narratives with these challenges in mind: working upon these shifting and decomposing foundations means that we must first admit how much we currently do not know empirically, recognizing the limits of our own experience. The imaginative worlds of these environmental writings, along with the creative edges of environmental organizing strategies, I suggest, can provide a productive space within which to start rethinking our politics from the bottom up, where we find an unsteady foundation now understood as a complex set of shifting, agentic, nature-culture assemblages. This is also why the book's title, *Material Insurgency*, operates on two unique but related registers.[8] First, the new materialisms and posthuman critical theory have become simultaneously productive and disruptive forces, and it is this theoretical insurgency that animates this project's approach to environmental literature and politics. And, second, these postanthropocentric theories compel us to think in new ways about an environmental politics capable of effective social movement organizing, while operating within the context of material and distributed, rather than exclusively human-centered, agency. This twofold concept of material insurgency is then understood as a problematic to be explored throughout the book, rather than a prescriptive theory, in part because it implies that the posthuman subject is not automatically a more ecological one; and, even more so, because distributed agency itself resists certainty and closure. While many approaches to this problem will be necessary, this project turns predominantly, though not exclusively, to the speculative narratives of various genres of environmental literature with clear but hopeful eyes.

The opening chapter, intending to track the ways dominant and emerging trends in the climate change movement currently script political subjectivity and agency, focuses upon contemporary environmental political theory and a recent prominent environmental campaign, the movement to halt the construction of the Keystone XL Pipeline. Examining the relation between the U.S State and the fossil fuel industry through the lens of political theorist Timothy Mitchell's concept "Carbon Democracy," this chapter explores the existing power dynamics between the State and climate activists. Rather than offer an exhaustive review, I use this first chapter to introduce and press questions (that are then explored further in the literary texts in later chapters) regarding how comprehending agency as distributed across the human and nonhuman might (productively) complicate environmental activists' sense of their campaign's strategy and goals. Intriguingly, it becomes clear many environmental organizations are reluctant to admit to the limitations of human-directed action to mitigate climate change, and I argue this reticence is based upon a fear of creating a public resigned to environmental catastrophe (rather than motivated to "act" to stop it). This concern over fatalism, I contend, brings into sharp relief the challenge posed by thinking environmental politics as "distributed" in a postnatural and posthuman age. Therefore, we are left with a question that is taken up, in different ways and to different ends, in each of the following chapters: that is, What might it mean to *know*, to *care*, and to *act* in environmentally responsible ways within a world where humans are no longer understood to be the sole or privileged agents of historical change?

Chapter 2 focuses upon Henry David Thoreau, the icon of U.S. environmental literature and thought, to suggest Thoreau's work may offer insights into contemporary debates within environmental theory, specifically regarding knowledge formation practices and agency. Turning predominantly to a few key scenes in *Walden*, I examine the complexities of his approach to relational knowledge formation processes, hybrid-objects, and liminal spaces. Building upon the groundbreaking Thoreau scholarship of Laura Dassow Walls, I suggest that her explication of Thoreau's knowledge formation process, one more attentive to embodiment and positionality than traditional empiricism, might serve as an integral building block in the development of a distributed environmental politics. Thoreau's approach to "relational knowing," as Walls categorizes it, begins a through line in this book in which his theories of knowledge formation practices and agency intersect with contemporary posthumanist concerns of materiality and distributed agency. One goal of this book is to explore the resonance between Thoreau's sense of agency and knowledge formation and more contemporary posthuman (and new materialist) theories of subjectivity and ways of knowing, and therefore the readings in this second chapter echo through the following chapters in what I hope are increasingly evocative ways.

Chapters 3 and 4 both draw our attention to texts of environmental justice fiction in order to more fully explore the relationship between postanthropocentric agency, social movement organizing, and nonlinear conceptions of temporality. The chapters together explore whether Karen Tei Yamashita's and Leslie Marmon Silko's representations of distributed agency and radical social movement organizing—in which the traditional human political act is reconfigured as contingent, limited, co-produced, or is even altogether absent—might offer eco-critical scholars an evaluative measure for rethinking political efficacy. My readings of *Through the Arc of the Rainforest* and *Almanac of the Dead* bring into relief a similar preoccupation in each novel; that is, how to represent an effective political resistance to transnational global capitalism within the context of a world unfolding through distributed agency. In chapter 3 specifically, I explore how *Through the Arc*'s narrative is driven by distributed agency to fascinating affect, however, my reading suggests that the novel's problematic grasping for narrative closure foregrounds the difficulty of imagining political change without a traditional human activist-subject. By drawing attention to the novel's ambivalence regarding the decentralization of the human subject, my analysis raises important questions that scholars and activists will have to address to better formulate distributed agency's potential for a positive impact upon contemporary sociopolitical organizing. Next, chapter 4 explores *Almanac*'s integrated depiction of distributed agency and nonlinear temporality in order to narrate a revolutionary politics of decolonization and environmental justice, via an overlapping set of *material temporalities*. The novel effectively evades the strictures of narrative closure altogether and, as a result, expands our awareness of distributed agency's deep impacts upon progressive politics. Exactly because the question of revolutionary transformation in Silko's novel is left at once incomplete and open-ended, it lingers as an inchoate yet ever-present possibility in the reader's mind. A spatial and nonlinear approach to temporality in this novel depicts the revolutionary moment as, though possibly not quite here, also somehow ever-present, ultimately advocating for a patience that is not passive and a progressive politics that is not Progress.

Chapter 5 advances critical readings of two recent and popular novels which fall within the new genre of climate change fiction: Nathaniel Rich's *Odds Against Tomorrow* and Chang-Rae Lee's *On Such a Full Sea*.

Both novels present intriguing and complex representations of what I choose to term *disintentional politics*, from the perspective of two very different subjectivities. My reading of *Odds Against Tomorrow* interrogates its depiction of the newly decentered human subject and how they might react to the sudden realization that while human agency is partly (and consequentially) responsible for climate change, it is also limited in its ability to control or manage the resulting weather-related events and their socioeconomic impact. That is, after Mitchell Zukor, a privileged yet troubled math "quant" on Wall Street, has his assumptions of human exceptionalism disrupted by the flooding of New York City, he does not easily transition into an ideal environmentally conscious member of a broader ecological system. Instead, Mitchell is deeply disturbed and unsettled through his discovery of the myriad inadequacies contained within humanist promises of the rational and autonomous self, and this leads to a crisis of subjectivity with, at best, ambiguous results. The chapter then turns to a selective reading of Lee's *On Such a Full Sea* with an eye toward the narrative's construction of a (partial) political imaginary and its limitations. This is a politics of materiality that, I suggest, begins with the premise that each individual exists in physical relation to a larger ecology; an ecology that should be understood to include the social, institutional, and nonhuman environment. Neither text, in the midst of their extended representations of disanthropocentric political subjectivities, is quite able to produce a coherent version of futurity. And thus, my readings examine how the social, economic, and political disruptions of climate change call upon a type of political agency and efficacy that is difficult to imagine from our contemporary humanist viewpoint. Carving out a liminal space between the binary construction of intentional and unintentional acts, this chapter explores what it might mean to organize without a rational and intentional goal, to work within a type of disintentional politics.

The sixth, and final, chapter engages Kim Stanley Robinson's near-future science fictional depiction of climate change in his *Science in the Capital* trilogy. The examinations of contemporary political campaigns, environmental nonfiction and environmental justice, and climate fiction in earlier chapters set up this chapter's closing engagement with distributed agency and its political potential. As the character Frank Vanderwal, who works in the National Science Foundation (NSF) in Washington, D.C., develops what he terms a "passionate science," he draws from Thoreau in an attempt to transform the National Science Foundation's approach to climate change by promoting a situated, subjective, and materialist approach to the technological interventions necessary to address an abrupt climate change event. Thoreau's appearance in this work of speculative climate fiction might surprise many scholars steeped in postmodern skepticism of Thoreau as the poster child for American Romanticism; however, his deceptively complex approach to inhabiting and knowing the nonhuman world—as explored in chapter 1—provocatively informs this main plotline in Robinson's trilogy. This narrative ultimately conjures a near future that outstrips traditional humanist binaries in intriguing ways. As a result, this final chapter allows for a more complete examination of the interconnections between knowledge formation practices, distributed agency, and nonlinear temporality that previous chapters have only partially, but hopefully provocatively, explored. My reading of Robinson's speculative fiction posits that, as sociopolitical strategy takes the decentered human subject and embodied forms of knowledge formation more fundamentally into account, scholars and activists committed to justice-oriented social movement organizing will be tasked with learning to critically inhabit a present moment—to some degree always an *unknowable now*—that anticipates an uncertain, rather than promissory, future.

1

Climate Change Environmentalism and Distributed Politics

> If you could do it nonstop, it would take you six days to walk from Henry David Thoreau's Walden Pond to President Barack Obama's White House. For the Sierra Club, that journey has taken much longer. For 120 years, we have remained committed to using every "lawful means" to achieve our objectives. Now, for the first time in our history, we are prepared to go further . . . the Sierra Club will officially participate in an act of peaceful civil resistance. We'll be following in the hallowed footsteps of Thoreau, who first articulated the principles of civil disobedience 44 years before John Muir founded the Sierra Club.
>
> —Michael Brune, Executive Director, Sierra Club

On February 13, 2013, the Sierra Club's then-president Allison Chin and chief executive officer Michael Brune, along with forty-six other environmental leaders and celebrities of various degree, sat down on the sidewalk across from the White House. As this is, apparently, an illegal act, all were eventually arrested.[1] Just days beforehand, the Sierra Club had released an official announcement outlining why its leadership, for the first time in the organization's storied history, had agreed to fully endorse and participate in an act of civil disobedience. The intended target of the protest, which had motivated this venerable mainstream organization to endorse and participate in a nonviolent, illegal tactic for the very first time, was none other than then sitting Democratic president Barack Obama (whom the Club had staunchly supported in his 2008 presidential campaign and, though possibly with less unabashed enthusiasm, again in 2012). At the time, it was widely agreed that Obama had the power of final decision over the proposed Keystone XL Pipeline, a proposal TransCanada hoped would increase pipeline capacity for carrying their Tar Sands oil from Alberta, Canada, to ports on the U.S. Gulf Coast.[2]

This break with a 120-year tradition of advocacy by only lawful means is really quite momentous in the history of mainstream environmental activism. According to the official announcement, the Club was motivated by a deep frustration with continued political inaction on climate change, despite deepening scientific consensus that the majority of warming is human caused. In other words, the Sierra Club was growing tired of accepting a prominent mainstream assumption about climate change: we know but can't (or won't) act.[3] On her blog, Sierra Club president Allison Chin wrote, "We are watching a global crisis unfold before our eyes. To stand aside and let it happen—even though we know how to stop it—would be unconscionable. Enough is enough. Today at the White House, I am standing up and doing whatever it takes to fight the climate crisis and stop the Keystone XL pipeline" ("Today We Take Part"). This statement, notably, maintains a clear focus upon so-called political will. Chin explains, "It couldn't be simpler: either we leave at least two-thirds of the known fossil fuel reserves in the ground, or we destroy our planet as we know it. That's our choice, if you can call it that" ("Today We Take Part"). With this binary choice duly unveiled, she confidently concludes, "We have a clear understanding of the crisis. We have solutions. What we don't have is time. We cannot afford to wait, and neither can President Obama" ("Today We Take Part"). From the Club's perspective, we know and must act swiftly. This was in 2013.

While it was already, at the time, readily apparent that the impacts of global warming had arrived (and obviously even more so now), the above statement's murky treatment of the relation between stopping the Keystone XL, keeping two-thirds of known fossil fuel reserves in the ground, and "stopping" climate change is telling.[4] It is understandable, of course, that the Sierra Club might find it difficult to effectively trumpet this unprecedented decision to participate in civil disobedience without overhyping the stakes a bit. The Club clearly chose, and probably reasonably so, to highlight the Keystone XL Pipeline as a symbol for the broader goal of leaving two-thirds of known fossil fuel reserves in the ground (clearly a more immense challenge). For Chin to argue, however, that even the most ambitious of their proposed solutions would *stop* climate change is a purely political (and fanciful) statement. Rather than acting to "stop climate change," it may have been more accurate for Chin to have written something along these lines: "We are confident that actions taken now to halt the expansion of fossil fuel infrastructure will slow the pace of CO_2 emissions in the future, ultimately lessening the severity of the ongoing climate change emergency by significant measures of degree." But, I am willing to admit, this doesn't have quite the same ring to it.

Transitioning beyond a fossil fuel infrastructure, of course, is inarguably the right thing to do and an absolute necessity. My point here, and a fairly obvious one perhaps, is that the binary language of traditional political rhetoric is not subtle enough to capture the complexity of organizing a movement to address, mitigate, and prepare for (but not "stop," as Chin chooses to phrase it) a planetary scale shift in climate patterns already set into motion. And this gap in our language when describing climate activism is indicative of substantial theoretical challenges to traditional concepts of sociopolitical organizing, exposing the limits of humanist and positivist frameworks more broadly. It is worth considering for a moment, though, what other explanations might be fair to expect of Chin, as she describes the Club's motivations for civil disobedience. The options do seem limited and this narrowing of choices certainly contributes to her reliance upon a very familiar type of environmental rhetoric. This returns us yet again to one of the major frustrations so often iterated within mainstream circles of the global climate change environmental movement: the idea that we have the technical expertise to transition away from the worst CO_2-producing energy sources, but we have achieved very little movement in that direction due to complex cultural, economic, and political forces resisting systemic change.[5] As traditional concepts of humanist thought are substantially disrupted in the era of climate change, we are tasked with thinking, planning, and organizing upon, and from within, this unsteady, shifting, and transitional space. Rather than trying to identify the correct political strategy and provide a prescriptive program, this chapter will instead attempt to elucidate the challenges, limitations, and possibilities of thinking seriously about a distributed environmental politics in a posthuman and postnatural world. The very narrow engagement with climate change environmentalism in the final section will set up the move to literary depictions of political subjectivity, knowledge formation, and agency in the following chapters, by outlining the limits of traditional political activism and examining some of the challenges the movement faces if it hopes to further its field of possibility.

Environmentalism in a Carbon Democracy

Global environmental policy scholar Paul Wapner is one of several prominent political theorists who have made the case for some type of post-natural environmental politics for the Anthropocene. Arguing for what he terms a "post-nature environmental politics," he suggests we will need to move beyond the assumption of environmentalism as a protector of a pristine natural world. "We are not in the Holocene anymore," he warns, "environmental advocates can no longer try to protect nature from humans . . . [because] the human-nature divide has broken down" (50). This is standard fare now in eco-theory of all stripes, of course, as it builds from the argument, so persuasively articulated in William Cronon's seminal essay "The Trouble with Wilderness; or Getting Back to the Wrong Nature," that dominant social constructions of wilderness problematically separate nature from human society.[6] Wapner's continuation of this logic, however, leads us to the crux of the problem with thinking political agency through the lens of postanthropocentrism. "This calls for an environmentalism," he contends, "that does not lament human action but directs it in more sustainable, just, and ecologically healthy directions. Environmental politics, then, involves bringing power to bear in the service of a livable future" (50). The underlying reasoning here is an example of how environmental political theorists tend to recognize and favor the reconfiguration of the relation between human and nonhuman worlds, into a more flattened, less hierarchical one, without fully grappling with this transformation's impact on human agency. It is necessary, for instance, to decipher exactly what type of power climate change environmentalism actually wields and exactly how, and upon whom or what, it should be brought to bear. In Wapner's articulation, the binary between nature and culture has been disrupted, but human agency seems to remain fully intact. It is not plausible, however, to embrace a postanthropocentric and distributed sense of subjectivity, while simultaneously retaining the humanist construct of a rational and autonomous political agent. While we certainly can and should do what is possible to direct existing agentic assemblages toward a justice-oriented sustainability, we clearly have more thinking to do regarding exactly what it means to "direct"—study, plan, act, review, etc.—within a world comprised of distributed agency.

Stacy Alaimo extends her influential theory of transcorporeality in her recent book *Exposed: Environmental Politics and Pleasures in Posthuman Times*, to helpfully engage with the complex relation between the decentered subject and political activism. Transcorporeality, she reminds us, is her way of describing how "human bodies are not only imbricated with one another but also enmeshed with nonhuman creatures and landscapes" (67). While her book explores a myriad of activisms outside the mainstream environmental groups, she explores ways in which environmental politics can be forged through "connection, interrelation and intersubjectivity," as she suggests "[p]leasure spirals through these ethical ontologies that are unmistakably material rather than abstract" (26). Alaimo's critique of sustainability discourses effectively exposes the gaps in traditional political theory that I am exploring here. She argues:

> The dominant style of sustainability ... [assumes] a disembodied spectator outside an externalized and inert world. Sustainability proceeds with the presumption that human agency, technology and master plans will get things under control. But the crises of the Anthropocene render that stance absurd, as the unintentional effects of human activity, and its interactions with other forces, outpace even the best laid plans. (173)

Mainstream sustainability discourses, Alaimo correctly points out, are too easily incorporated into capitalist logics and often maintain an investment in liberal humanist concepts of holistic subjectivity and autonomous, intentional agency, wherein human rationality maintains the power and control to destroy, or save, the natural world entirely on its own terms. While this framework certainly "offers a comforting sense of scientific distancing and objectivity, trans-corporeal subjects are often forced to re-recognize that their own material selves are the very stuff of the agential world they seek to understand" (174). This is an excellent articulation of the challenge we face in rethinking political agency in which the human political subject is not discrete from, but instead enfolded within and dispersed across, a complex network of human and nonhuman communities and dense, intra-active agencies.[7]

Significant theoretical steps have already been taken, certainly, along this ambiguous yet promising path. Political theorist Timothy Mitchell, for instance, whose work focuses on theories of the state and international geopolitics, has long explored how attention to the complexity of human and nonhuman interrelationships helps us better assess historical change.[8] Mitchell's scholarly work in political theory, to my mind, is surprisingly underutilized in environmental humanities scholarship to date, and has particular relevance for new materialist theories.[9] While addressing environmental issues in an era of the corporate state has certainly seemed daunting already, Mitchell's theory of the state engages a set of problems that operate at a level even more foundational and unsettling. Rather than simply criticizing a too-cozy relation between capitalism and democratic process (which implies the link might be severed, leaving us with a liberal democratic state finally free of corporate influence), Mitchell suggests our contemporary democratic system and fossil fuel economy are interdependent to the point that it is not clear what either would look like—or, for that matter, would continue to exist—without the other. "The forms of democracy that emerged in leading industrialized countries by the middle decades of the twentieth century," he explains, "were enabled and shaped by the extraordinary concentrations of energy obtained from the world's limited stores of hydrocarbons, and by the socio-technological arrangements required for extracting and distributing the energy they contained" (252–53). This means we must consider the impacts of these two systems—Western liberal democracy and carbon-based capitalism—as having developed in tandem throughout the twentieth century. Mitchell calls this Carbon Democracy, and it has major implications for environmental politics.

Particularly when placed into conversation with Cherniavsky's work on neocitizenship outlined in the introduction, the implications of Carbon Democracy cut to the very foundation of contemporary Western liberalism. If in fact the contemporary state is inextricably fused with the fossil fuel economy, then in addition to creating the path toward a post-carbon economy, movements for social and environmental justice must also imagine a new era of democracy: a system capable of moving beyond the role of manager for the "world's limited stores of hydrocarbons," the technocratic focus upon facilitating fossil fuel extraction and distribution, and the institutional fortification of hierarchical class structures that benefit transnational corporate profit models. Therefore, it will be incumbent upon contemporary movements for environmental and social justice to reimagine both systems simultaneously. The democratic system as it currently exists, Mitchell suggests, may be incapable of operating outside or beyond a carbon-based economy. If socioecological movements only aim to "recapture" the liberal democratic state from corporate interests, then Mitchell's work suggests that—even if successful—they may not be satisfied with the democratic institutions they eventually wrestle from the capitalists. Or, in other words, they may find no there there. He explains, "A . . . limit that oil represents for democracy [itself] is that the political machinery [or the liberal democratic state] that emerged to govern the age of fossil fuels, partly as a product of those forms of energy, may be incapable of addressing the events that will end it [the carbon-based economy]" (7). This is an intriguing twist on the current leftist truism regarding the corporate state, wherein transnational corporations—with the fossil fuel industry high on the list—have stolen or, more accurately, bought democracy away from average citizens. In this latter framework, it is proposed that our society cannot address climate change until the democratic machinery is wrested back from transnational capital and its lobbyists. In Mitchell's account, however, democracy and the fossil fuel economy are not only co-dependent, but actually co-constitutive. And, in their current developmental stage, they are quite possibly inseparable.

All of this is to suggest there may be very good reasons why contemporary political mobilization is no longer functioning as we might expect; as we see traditional models of protest continually fall upon the increasingly deaf ears of the state. And to make the state listen again, activists and organizers may have to do more than simply restore liberal democracy by separating it from the interests of carbon capital. Freedom under Western liberal democracy in the carbon economy, Mitchell suggests, has really always been a limited bargain, wherein certain privileged subjects receive limited civil freedoms in exchange for accepting the monopoly of fossil fuel corporations. Self-determination is, then, an abstract idea that, in practical terms, means consent to imperial rule (70–71). This is reminiscent of Marx's claim regarding the limitations of political freedom under capitalism, an argument he makes, in part, by criticizing Bruno Bauer for confusing political emancipation with human emancipation. Political emancipation, as Marx writes in "On the Jewish Question," ultimately only provides "the liberty of man as an isolated nomad" (35). The politically "free" and "isolated" individual, without exercise of the fullest experience of human freedom, is only free enough to reapply, as it were, for a new sort of domination.

We must, then, while continuing to interrogate and reimagine the posthuman and distributed political subject, also be attentive to the existing structures of power (i.e., the state, national and transnational corporations, etc.) shaping the contemporary and near-future political, economic, and cultural terrain. Exploring the contemporary cultural norms within the collective unconscious of Western modernity, Stephanie Lemanager expertly articulates the ways in which this modernity is experienced as "living oil." Describing the United States as a "petrotopia," or an example of "petromodernity," Lemanager explains how the "modern fossil-fuel complex" extends beyond the political and the economic to saturate the cultural life of Western citizen-subjects (66–67, 74–75). As LeMenager accurately points out, mainstream environmentalism will not succeed without rethinking its "rhetorics of rights, consumption and sacrifice" because each of these "foreclose[s] structural critique" of the kind most necessary (24). Petitioning for participatory rights or advocating for a transformation in individual or public consciousness might have some limited impact; however, if LeManager, Mitchell, and Cherniavsky are correct, it will not necessarily initiate a substantive transformation of what Naomi Klein has called our "fossilized democracy" (362).

If the state is less and less responsive to citizen subjects and also less interested in maintaining a socioeconomic structure that maximizes the public good, then this obviously limits the options available to social movement organizers. The "structural critique" Lemenager rightly diagnoses as closed off by the liberal discourse of rights and responsibilities, is itself in need of reimagining if we are to better understand the power of the corporate state beyond hegemonic theories of power. When the state appears content to dominate—as opposed to discipline or norm—its citizenry, the traditional methods for transforming emerging concepts into effective movements (messaging through texts, phone banks, mass emails, supporting electoral campaigns, organizing rallies, attending marches, and even committing civil disobedience) seem inadequate to the moment. How many minds do you need to transform, or how many people need to march on D.C., to create change under a state that quite simply does not care about its citizens' interests? What is, we might ask, effective environmental activism for the *neocitizens* of a *petrotopia* governed by a posthegemonic *carbon democracy*?

It is important to note that this is far from a new condition. As Cherniavsky explains, the deconstruction of the citizen has been a central tenet of neoliberalism for the past four decades and, according to Mitchell, contemporary institutions of Western democracy have been indelibly linked to at least one dominant industry for much of the past century.

Therefore, if the state no longer requires the consent of its subjects in the manner we generally assume, then it would seem that "ideology critique" in the academy is clearly not as useful as theorists might like to think (Cherniavsky 2017, 60–61). On the streets, it goes to reason, the same goes for various strategies of consciousness raising. And many of those engaged in Left politics have not yet recognized this transition to a contemporary condition in which the idea of a "citizen" has morphed into a "de-democratized citizen" (137–39). Creating ecologically minded citizens is clearly a good thing, but it is also no longer a clear path toward political progress for social and environmental justice. We are then faced, I am suggesting, with a double-bind: both an increasingly unresponsive state apparatus on one side and a traditional set of political organizing concepts, on the other, that have lost their edge.

The history of this co-emergence of contemporary democracy and the fossil fuel economy, as tracked by Mitchell, also examines its inverse—that is, social movement organizing external to the state—which has, historically speaking, had its fair share of wins and losses in the fight for workers' economic and democratic rights. In the coal-based economy of the early stages of the Industrial Revolution, for instance, labor organizing forced political concessions and laid the path for the welfare state of industrial capitalism. Mitchell points out that the coal-based economy had particular infrastructure needs that left it vulnerable to democratic and economic claims by its workers. Huge quantities of coal were found in a relative few places making it easier for coal miners, for example, to disrupt flows of key fuel via strikes. They were able to disrupt the system effectively, predominantly through united work stoppages (19). The welfare state, as it formed during the European Industrial Revolution, according to Mitchell, should be seen as a concession to workers that still unfortunately, in the end, operated as a form of control and consolidation of corporate-state power (26). Carbon democracy, at its conceptual core, forces us to consider how recognizing the contemporary democratic Western nation-state and the fossil fuel economy as essentially inseparable alters our understanding of political power and historical change. Rather than two distinct power sources in varying degrees of interrelation, we must recognize their co-development throughout the Industrial Revolution as one complex story of inextricability.

The state and the fossil fuel industry, operating together as a carbon democracy, control the flows of carbon and capital in such a way as to perpetuate themselves and prove the principle of unlimited growth at all costs, as a mutually beneficent and exclusive system of joint profit with literally life-threatening results for vast majorities of human and nonhuman communities. One response to this condition, posited by Paul Wapner, suggests a post-nature politics of climate change environmentalism should focus on building its capacity (political, economic, and social) to prioritize unlimited *justice*, rather than unlimited *growth* for human and nonhuman communities alike. Quite clearly, and laudably, this is an attempt to turn the maxim of unlimited growth toward a justice-oriented, rather than an accumulation-oriented, project. Latour discusses something similar, as well, in his call for prioritizing "systems of engendering" over systems of "production" (*Down to Earth*, 88). If our political system is not designed or equipped to stop transnational capital, however, but instead to actually facilitate (and be facilitated by) it, then it is harder to imagine the type of social movement organizing that might feasibly succeed in breaking the systemic link between democratic and fossil fuel institutions, while also providing something in its stead. The pace and manner in which we come to recognize existing dominant power structures as distributed between inextricably linked political and economic systems will necessarily inform our social movement organizing strategies and actions. These movements will also need to be understood as part of a networked structure of power that is itself distributed, dispersed, and intricately interlinked across human and nonhuman communities, all of which find themselves in peril from contemporary carbon democracy.

Echoes of new critical materialism and distributed agency abound in Wapner's postnatural environmental politics. Expanding from Wapner, I will contend that a distributed environmental politics must be willing to engage with and learn to work from within distributed agency. This is such a different construction of political agency that we, as of yet, have only begun to imagine the possibilities and challenges it implies. Writing in the journal *Global Environmental Policy*, to an audience presumably comprised of predominantly environmental policy academics and professionals, Wapner argues:

> The end of nature does not simply erase the boundary between humans and nature, but fundamentally changes the identities of the two spheres as they co-constitute each other. . . . Put differently, the end of nature de-essentializes both nature and any other notion of a distinctive human essence as a response to climate change or other environmental dangers. (48)

The destabilization of the nature/culture binary and its consequences, particularly for new materialist scholars, is propelling eco-theorists toward an understanding of agency outside traditional humanist ideals of intention and rationality, with the emphasis instead upon what Barad has now famously termed "intra-action," the distributed agency that flows from the inextricable mixture of human and nonhuman actants.[10] A major benefit of framing the power wielded by a distributed environmental politics as intra-active is that it fully defamiliarizes mainstream assumptions about how power, historical change, and even temporality operate. While there are many challenges in this reorientation, which I engage more fully below and in the chapters to follow, there is also room for optimism: this defamiliarization of agency opens a window for reinventing activism in a moment where such inventive thinking seems entirely necessary. More than just Wapner's post-nature politics, which leaves the rational and intentional human subject to act in ways promoting justice over profits, environmental scholars and activists will need to develop a distributed environmental politics that understands its power as fully embedded within a complex mesh of nature-culture agentic assemblages. This, in part, explains why I feel compelled to focus significant attention, in the literary analyses in the following chapters, upon the fraught relation between social movement organizing and intentionality. It is entirely possible that we might be tasked with formulating a new political form of engagement while simultaneously admitting that we are not entirely certain our present *intent* can be sufficiently attached to a definable future *result*. Before turning to those literary depictions, the remainder of this chapter looks to a major campaign of mainstream climate change environmentalism in order to further highlight some of the challenges so far outlined and to raise several questions that will continue to animate my approach to the analyses developed in chapters 2 through 6.

Keystone XL and Pipeline Politics

The environmental nonprofit organization 350.org, originally founded by author and climate change activist Bill McKibben and six of his Middlebury College students in 2007, aims to "build the global grassroots climate movement that can hold our leaders accountable to science and justice" (350.org).[11] For more than a decade, the organization has remained focused on its goal to reduce greenhouse gases via a transition to a green energy economy. The number 350 is scientifically and symbolically important, as it is drawn from climate scientist James Hansen's calculation that 350 parts-per-million of CO_2 in the atmosphere is the upper limit at which human society has historically flourished.[12] As early as 2010, 350.org's campaign began to focus much of its attention on one specific North American fossil industry project: the Keystone XL Pipeline proposed by TransCanada Corporation (now renamed TC Energy).[13] The project was intended to be the fourth phase of an already existing pipeline network connecting tar sands oil from the Athabasca Oil Sands region of Alberta, Canada, with the Gulf Coast of Texas. Since the pipeline would cross the border between Canada and the United States, and due to some finer points of U.S. energy law, the final decision on the project would likely fall to then sitting Democratic president Barack Obama. This helped elevate Keystone XL from an obscure addition to existing carbon infrastructure into a signature environmental campaign and political flashpoint.

The Keystone XL has remained caught up in an epic frenzy of political maneuvering, federal agency reviews, lawsuits, and judicial decisions. An early environmental impact review, issued in 2012, came under intense scrutiny, for instance, after it became public knowledge that the State Department's selected, nongovernmental contractor was also involved in reviewing other proposed projects by TransCanada, the corporation hoping to build the pipeline.[14] After intense pushback, President Obama announced he would commission another, presumably more independent, review and make no decision until 2013. Tellingly, the contracted agency conducting this subsequent review was also criticized for having too many economic links to the fossil fuel industry. Energy experts were left to explain that it is difficult to find any environmental review contractors that are truly independent of, and do not also accept contracts from (i.e., work for), the very same fossil fuel companies under review.[15] In response to Obama's decision to slow the process and conduct another review, congressional Republicans, by adding a provision onto a separate bill in January 2012, forced the president to instead make up his mind within sixty days. This created an artificial, but binding, deadline, which Obama conveniently used as an excuse to deny TransCanada's application (though really this was a deferment, rather than a nixing of the project, as Obama made clear that TransCanada could reapply).[16] Conveniently, this would place any actually final decision well after what became his election to a second term that November. This absurd political football inspired by the Keystone XL decision laid bare, in excruciating ways, the

Kafkaesque challenge of asking a carbon democracy to regulate fossil fuel infrastructure projects. And the game was only at halftime.

The Obama administration's second State Department Environmental Impact Review, which also concluded that the pipeline would not add significantly to overall CO2 emissions in coming decades, was deeply disappointing for environmentalists. It was broadly assumed to be priming the pump, if you will, for a coming approval of the project.[17] However, in the final months of his eight-year presidency, and almost four years after the first State Department Review was released, Obama did ultimately reject the pipeline. His argument for doing so relied heavily on technicalities in the permitting process, however, and still left the door open for TransCanada to reapply. Then there was one more surprise. And this one environmentalists, and political pundits the world over, did not see coming: Donald Trump was elected the next President of the United States. And in January 2017, in one of his administration's very first official acts, he reversed Obama's decision, and the pipeline was back on the to-do list. Until it wasn't. Two consecutive judicial decisions from the same Montana Federal Court, the first handed down on November 9, 2018, in Montana and the second in April 2020, put the project, at least temporarily, on hold. The Trump administration appealed the decision, and environmentalists, even with the incoming Biden administration promising to nix the plan, would do well to remain vigilant. In other words, stay tuned; and expect more delays, legal battles, and unexpected turns.

This quick sketch of the Keystone XL project's history is relevant exactly because of the political morass of indeterminacy it reveals. As a rallying call and focal point for environmentalists, one would have to allow that the campaign to stop Keystone XL—in addition to the very central fact that to this point, ten years later, the pipeline is still not operational—has successfully captured public attention and raised awareness about how these infrastructure decisions impact long-term planetary health. There is a certain success, no doubt, in delay itself. The Keystone XL campaign, it should be noted, has also brought together alliances that span such stakeholders as Nebraska farm owners, green eco-activists, and Indigenous tribes. This type of coalition building is no small feat.[18] While there is a lot of merit to the strategy of targeting fossil fuel corporations and their infrastructure directly, it is also clear that the ongoing saga of the pipeline's progress through the regulatory process leaves us with more questions than answers regarding this strategy's efficacy. The intricate, weaving, and drama-filled story of this one proposed fossil fuel project is in itself a matter of interest; it is truly an epic story comprised of petty partisan politics, minutiae of environmental law, absurdities of carbon capitalism, and the complexities of posthuman politics. The campaign has been mostly dependent, in the end, on judicial rulings for its most recognizable successes, and it is safe to assume that the legal wins do not come to be without the initial and ongoing activism in the field. It seems likely that a strategy relying too heavily on the courts, however, will also eventually become vulnerable to the vagaries of carbon democracy. The recent Republican administration's almost singular focus on filling judicial seats with corporate-friendly judges should be cause for concern.[19] Also relevant, and at least equally worrisome, are the increasing number of anti-protest laws passed by state legislatures around the country, effectively criminalizing the most often used tactics of the Blockadia activists.[20] Both of these developments highlight the challenge of environmental organizing in a carbon democracy, as the state works to uphold the interests of the fossil fuel industry and weaken the rights of citizen protestors.

A fuller history of the Keystone XL and pipeline politics is necessary, and will undoubtedly be written, but this is not my intention here, nor is it possible in this chapter's remaining space. There are many other environmental campaigns as well that one might reasonably want to take up in order to critically engage emerging strategies and tactics across contemporary global climate change and climate justice environmentalisms. For instance, the Extinction Rebellion movement, which spent much of 2019 deploying Occupy-like encampments and civil disobedience tactics in England, or the Sunrise Movement, an inspiring youth-led campaign in the United States.[21] The selective analysis to come, however, predominantly focuses on the strategy and reasoning behind the decision to target Keystone XL and promote the "Keystone Principle" in mainstream climate environmentalism, as expressed by McKibben and a few other prominent leaders, in hopes of providing a better understanding of several key challenges social movement organizers face in the current climate that then animate my analysis of the literature in following chapters. While there have been some recent successes at the level of litigation, and these hard-won victories should be celebrated, what it means for the broader transition beyond a carbon economy remains to be seen. This pipeline activism still operates within a certain understanding of agency, wherein a citizen protest receives state recognition and subsequently leads to policy change (as it is assumed the sovereign subjectivity of the citizen is recognized by the state), and the intervention I propose below is to inquire as to whether this framework can be understood as sufficient to propel an adequate societal engagement with the ecological crisis we face. In other words, if this is the political economy we currently operate within, is it enough? To be clear, my goal here is not a critique of Left political practice at the level of day-to-day strategy; the dual approach of direct action and litigation against new carbon economy infrastructure has proven quite effective, and personally I support (and have participated in) such campaigns. I am not arguing there is another set of tools ready at hand that the proponents of the Blockadia movement are missing; quite to the contrary, I am suggesting our current construction of political agency contains certain hardwired limits, leaving us with few effective options. Consequently, the critical work of this project moves to another register, a theoretical intervention based in ecocritical, posthuman, and new materialist approaches, in search of the political possibilities of distributed agency.

More than merely a symbolic campaign, opposing Keystone XL was, from very early on, presented as a paradigm for a new environmental activism. Writing in the popular environmental news site *Grist* in 2013, KC Golden, a policy analyst with the nonprofit advocacy institution *Climate Solutions*, in Seattle, makes this point clear: "Keystone isn't simply a pipeline in the sand for the swelling national climate movement. It's a moral referendum on our willingness to do the simplest thing we must do to avert catastrophic climate disruption: stop making it worse" ("The Keystone Principle"). Golden's articulation of what he calls the "keystone principle" suggests a desire to cast the campaign as more than simply symbolic; it now becomes paradigmatic. "It's true that stopping a single pipeline . . . will not 'solve' climate disruption"; therefore, he continues, "[t]he question—for Keystone protestors as it was for Rosa Parks—is whether the action captures and communicates a principle powerful enough to inspire and sustain an irresistible movement for sweeping social change" ("Keystone"). The principle is simple and direct: no more investments in fossil fuel infrastructure. "No amount of clean energy investment," he explains, "will stave off disaster unless we stop feeding the fossil fuel beast with capital now" ("Keystone"). Halting the Keystone XL project was intended to exhibit that climate change environmentalism—through more direct intervention in fossil fuel infrastructure decisions—was ready to direct the public's attention to the foundational causes of greenhouse emissions: the carbon economy itself. While the transition to a green economy is full of "gray areas," he concedes, the Keystone Principle presents a choice that is "clear and binary: do it and we're toast. So don't" ("Keystone"). If this escalation of the strategy into a win-or-lose binary seems like an attempt to lay out a clear road map to victory for the entire movement, well, Golden is even more explicit in conclusion: "That's what Keystone is about. It's not just a pipeline. It's a principle" ("Keystone"). I am interested in investigating how political agency is scripted within this new principle and, furthermore, to explore how distributed agency complicates this script and opens up new, difficult but hopefully productive, questions for environmental organizing.

McKibben's own narration of 350.org's origins is an informative starting place for our analysis and, as he tells it in *Eaarth: Making a Life on a Tough New Planet*, it all began with a moment of self-assessment. After twenty years of writing about the perils of climate change, he came to a blunt realization: "Nothing concrete had come of my work or anyone else's; Washington had done absolutely nothing to slow down climate change" (206). Unsure of how to start, he only knew for sure that he "wanted to try and make something happen politically" (206).[22] After a few small events in Vermont, he explains, he came to feel that local and regional political work was somewhat limited in terms of its reach and ability to address such a global issue. He and his students began to wonder if they "could do something beyond funky Vermont" (207). The plan that McKibben and his students finally settled upon was to facilitate small, local actions in communities across the world, each disparate event unified via a common political message calling for 80 percent cuts in CO_2 emissions.

Each event was organized and coordinated through 350.org's central website, as McKibben learned to rely upon his students and "the kind of intuitive knowledge of the internet that comes with being twenty-two years old" (207).[23] When the day arrived, this initial organizing resulted in 1,400 organized events across the country and "one of the largest days of grassroots environmental protest since the original Earth Day" (208). He and his students felt successful, even "smug" he concedes, until "about six weeks later, when the Arctic began to melt, and it became clear that almost everyone had underestimated the speed and size of global warming now under way" (209). And that "led to our small group deciding to see if we could make our same tactic—distributed political action—work on a global basis" (210). McKibben's choice of the phrase "distributed political action" clearly invites a comparison to my focus upon distributed agency and political efficacy in this book. In fact, just slightly earlier, while describing the satisfaction he found in the work, he explains that it was "unbearably moving to watch the pictures come in—this was distributed political action, the way that a farmers' market is distributed food production or a solar panel is distributed power" (209). The phrase, in this context, is intended to emphasize the decentralized nature of their organizing strategy and to denote the day of action's simultaneously local and global impact and relevance. One might stretch the meaning of "distributed political action" here a bit further, as well, by noting that the actions are dispersed across global communities and facilitated by the internet, bringing humans together through technological networks in a manner that now seem obvious, but which was relatively new a decade ago as 350.org formed its strategy. In terms of agentic power distributed across human and nonhuman communities, as we will see below, McKibben is acutely aware of—and rightfully terrified by—the feedback loops that are contributing increasing CO_2 emissions around the globe, and how they challenge traditional concepts of environmental management. There is no indication, however, that McKibben is thinking beyond liberal humanist political subjectivity or agency when deploying this phrase.

While 350.org's early strategy centered upon raising public awareness about climate change and petitioning policy-makers to respond to the growing scientific consensus, the move to oppose Keystone XL Pipeline was the result of a shift in strategy.[24] While the search for a proper and effectual approach for climate change environmentalism continued, organizers were finding themselves facing increasingly nonresponsive economic and political institutions; they were discovering that political agency, as it has been commonly conceived for decades if not centuries, seemed less and less effectual. The campaign's new focus became an attempt to, as McKibben put it, take away the "social license" of the fossil fuel corporations and their leaders. The move indicates the organization's realization that climate change environmentalism needed to do more than simply educate the public and advocate for legislation. Bringing this message to the White House at the start of Obama's second term in January 2013 led to the Sierra Club's historic decision to participate in civil disobedience (described in the opening pages of this chapter). Michael Brune, executive director of the Sierra Club, was among those arrested. In a public statement, he declared:

> We need Barack Obama at his absolute, formidable best. We need the Barack Obama who was able to inspire millions to believe in the possibility of change and the power of hope. We need that leader to . . . show the American people that solving

the climate crisis is not a burden but an incredible opportunity. ("The Day We Move Forward")

Much as Sierra Club president Allison Chin argued in her announcement of the Club's decision to participate in civil disobedience, Brune's message emphasizes that this is indeed a political question, rather than a technical one, and, rather than a challenge to capitalist profitseeking, a fantastic "opportunity" for new economic growth.[25] The workings of carbon democracy, of course, problematize all of these approaches to engaging fossil fuel infrastructure projects. It is the original necessity of these exact types of infrastructure projects that Mitchell argues fostered today's (mutually dependent) democratic systems and carbon economy. Whatever type of democratic process and economic growth Brune sees as ready to flourish during the transition to a green economy, therefore, will necessarily look much less familiar than he seems to realize.

McKibben, for his part, saw his public exposure outside of environmental circles skyrocket in the summer of 2012 with the August 2 publication of his article "Global Warming's Terrifying New Math" in *Rolling Stone Magazine*. The article's lengthy subtitle clarifies McKibben's desire for his readers to brush up on their math skills: "Three Simple Numbers That Add Up to Global Catastrophe—and That Make Clear Who the Real Enemy Is." McKibben claims that these three numbers, which were first published in a financial analysis report in the UK, "upend most of the conventional political thinking about climate change. And it allows us to understand our precarious—our almost but not quite finally hopeless—position with three simple numbers" ("Terrifying Math"). The first numerical digit of significance is 2 (as in degrees Celsius), this is the target limit for temperature increase allowable under the Copenhagen Accord signed by 167 countries. The second number is 565, which McKibben explains is important because "scientists estimate that humans can put roughly 565 more gigatons of carbon dioxide into the atmosphere by mid-century and still have some reasonable hope of staying below two degrees" of temperature increase ("Terrifying Math"). And the third and final number is 2,795 (also gigatons), the "fossil fuel we're currently planning to burn. And the key point is that this new number—2,795—is higher than 565. Five times higher," he helpfully points out. This number, really more of an estimate, is derived from an analysis of "how much oil, gas, and coal the world's major energy companies hold in reserve" ("Terrifying Math"). While the *Rolling Stone* article purports to lay out the quantitative facts of the case, it is also simultaneously, of course, a call to action.

In a tone reflecting that of the Sierra Club's rationale for civil disobedience outlined at the beginning of this chapter, McKibben's article aims to simplify the political goals for climate change environmentalism by providing numerical certainty. The argument is that if we can transition to green energy sources in time to limit the globe's use of fossil fuel to that cap of 565 tons of carbon, then the effects of climate change will be more manageable.[25] For the purposes of building the movement, McKibben is cautious yet hopeful: "We know how much we can burn and we know who's planning to burn more . . . [and] the more carefully you do the math, the more thoroughly you realize that this is, at bottom, a moral issue; we have met the enemy and they is Shell" ("Terrifying Math"). McKibben is unwilling to linger too long upon the idea that, no matter what we do from here on out, climate instability to some degree is upon us and will increase. By echoing the famous Earth Day slogan and changing the proposed enemy from "it is us" to "they is Shell," he productively moves the environmental critique away from blaming individual citizens and, instead, readily naming and shaming those corporate entities responsible for the vast majority of CO_2 emissions to date (and whose stock values depend upon continued future emissions). The assumptions are still, however, deeply invested in traditional modes of political activism.

McKibben moves to quickly provide a political target and a socioeconomic solution: a campaign to force large institutions and governments to divest their holdings in fossil fuel companies. This is clearly intended to prevent the stark reality of the situation from leading to a sort of resignation, and instead foster and expand a "movement" of engaged individuals acting collectively. And it makes sense from just about any rhetorical or messaging perspective. In other words, he is not looking to depress any potential advocates for the environment; he is more interested in cultivating angry, hopeful, or otherwise fired-up activists. Therefore, McKibben is sure to conclude with a "call to arms" with detailed actions for his readers. The final paragraphs begin to outline a new 350.org initiative; to begin a divestment campaign, similar to the divestment campaign that targeted Apartheid South Africa, at the university, city, and state level, urging these organizations to pull their investments from the top two hundred companies most directly profiting from the carbon economy.[26]

In regard to catalyzing significant action on climate change policy, McKibben does himself admit to the ineffectuality of traditional political advocacy. After discounting individual action and consumer choices as well-meaning but hopelessly miniscule, McKibben offers a brief analysis of environmental politics. He writes, "A more efficient method, of course, would be to work through the political system, and environmentalists have tried that, too, with the same limited success. They've patiently lobbied leaders, trying to convince them of our peril assuming that politicians would heed the warnings" ("Terrifying Math"). And while he concedes that "sometimes it has seemed to work," he also points out that President Obama's most significant move to lower carbon emissions up to that point, the increase in fuel efficiency for automobiles, is the type of minimal reform that would have helped if "adopted a quarter-century ago" ("Terrifying Math"). Now, however, and "in light of the numbers . . . just described, it's obviously a very small start indeed" ("Terrifying Math"). McKibben goes on to suggest that climate change environmentalists need an overt enemy and "[g]iven this hard math, we need to view the fossil-fuel industry in a new light. It is Public Enemy Number One to the survival of our planetary civilization" ("Terrifying Math"). Building on this idea, he (almost in a tone of wondering aloud) concludes that, "If people come to understand the cold, mathematical truth—that the fossil-fuel industry is systematically undermining the planet's physical systems—it might weaken it enough to matter politically" ("Terrifying Math"). The progression from providing empirical evidence, to producing a significant cultural shift, and, finally, sparking measurable political action pretty well outlines a traditional sense of how social movement organizing can (by galvanizing public opinion and forcing elected officials to respond) succeed. What it means to make something *matter* politically, however, is an increasingly fraught question.

McKibben's concern regarding his readers' possible emotional responses to his dire message becomes clear relatively quickly: he is worried that a sense of fatalism will prevail. Additionally, if McKibben is less willing to dwell on the most complicated and dire aspects of climate change for too long in his more overtly political communication, I would suggest that this is exactly because we have yet to fully grapple with what distributed agency might mean for political agency. It seems a dangerous political position to maintain and, therefore, time and again the argument moves quickly to a solutions-based rhetoric, distancing himself from the question of our limited options and power in the face of climate change. McKibben had earlier expressed this concern in *Eaarth*, in which he worries whether admitting that the planet is now already fundamentally transformed (i.e., the Holocene is behind us, and we have entered and will remain in the Anthropocene) may lead his readers to apathy. In a reflective moment, he writes, "My only real fear is that the reality described in this book, and increasingly evident in the world around us, will be for some an excuse to give up. We need just the opposite—increased engagement" (McKibben 2010, xv). Dwelling on the limitations of our individual and collective human agency does seem "scary," as is thinking about the contingency of our actions, the (partial) lack of control we actually have over the manner in which the present will become the future, because of a sense of loss regarding the myth of human autonomy. This is part of the challenge for thinking political intervention in a postnatural and posthuman moment in the midst of a geologic-scale shift from the Holocene to the increasingly erratic earth systems of the Anthropocene. While environmental scholars have been focusing on articulating new paths to political solidarity and creative advocacy through interconnection, shared vulnerability, and indeterminacy, leaders of mainstream environmental organizations, as shown above in the cases of Chin, Brune, and McKibben, have been less likely to dwell for long on the question of limited human agency. They often understandably choose, instead, to favor more traditional rhetoric about stopping climate change and saving the world through human ingenuity and perseverance. And, as a bonus, spurring economic growth while we do it!

Across all these campaigns, a notable and persistent feeling of uncertainty exists, a shifting in the foundations of both strategy and potential targets. It is also fair to say this uncertainty emanates, to some degree, from an (at least) partial recognition of the challenges raised by material, vibrant, nonhuman agency; this is particularly evident within references to the oft-discussed "feedback loops" and already "baked-in" temperature rise—from previous CO_2 emissions—set to unfold in coming decades (2010, 20–21). It is also evident that a significant portion of this uncertainty in the mainstream environmental movement—whether this is consciously recognized or not (and it is mostly not)—stems from the predicament of a decentered political subject and the disrupted notion of the political *act*. This decentered, posthuman subject, who must now operate from within the breakdown of the nature/culture binary, also poses challenges to liberal humanist conceptions of political change. If we too quickly turn to solutions, we may be missing an opportunity to better understand our current predicament in meaningful ways. McKibben himself, as we noted earlier, utilizes the term *distributed political action*. The question is what it would mean to consider this political agency as not only distributed across human communities but also as interspersed with the nonhuman. That is, not only to foster a network of distributed human organizations but also to think of these human political movements as decentralized themselves; as integral and influential, yet only a part of the co-production of what is to come.

Possibly without necessarily realizing it, McKibben is beginning to examine the path for environmental politics in the midst of the transition from a humanist subject to a decentered, posthuman subject (charged with operating in an increasingly unknowable global climate). In the early chapters of *Eaarth*, McKibben warns his fellow environmentalists that "first we really do need to come to terms with where we are. We need to dampen our intuitive sense that the future will resemble the past, and our standard-issue optimism that the future will be ever easier" (McKibben 2010, 85). Climate change, he contends, has transformed our world into "an uphill planet . . . where gravity exerts a stronger pull than we're used to. There's more friction than we're used to. You have to work harder to get where you're going" (85–86). The transition beyond the fossil fuel economy will need to consist of a transformation of energy sources in the midst of a fundamental change in the planet itself, which is already well under way. And, thus, a fundamental change within human society and its relation to the nonhuman is, weirdly, both necessary and already occurring. Both the necessary changes to human society and the already occurring changes to the planet raise significant questions about human agency, from slightly different angles. If the Anthropocene is here and is in significant part a human creation—or a result of Western-constructed imperial, colonial, and capitalist systems, to be more specific—what is the human subject's role and agentic capacity in this transformed and transforming world? How to organize a movement within a wildly shifting set of conditions becomes the question.

Distributed Potentialities

There are obvious ways in which climate change highlights the limits of human power: increased intensity of major storms, a decrease in predictability of weather, social and economic disruptions, and so on. However, more subtly, McKibben seems interested in the distributed nature of climate change itself. He is fascinated, not to mention appalled, by the greenhouse gas emission feedback loops that he calls "booby traps." He writes,

So far we've been the cause for the sudden surge in greenhouse gases and hence global temperatures, but that's starting to change, as the heat we've caused has started to trigger a series of ominous feedback effects. Some are fairly easy to see: melt Arctic sea ice, and you replace a shiny white mirror that reflects most of the incoming rays of the sun back out to space with a dull blue ocean that absorbs those rays. Others are less obvious, and much larger: booby traps, hidden around the world, waiting for the atmosphere to heat. (McKibben 2010, 20)

One of those "booby traps" is described in terms that further exemplify the distributed nature of climate change. He explains that, for instance, "temperatures over eastern Siberia had increased by almost ten degrees in the last decade. That's melting permafrost on the land, and hence more relatively warm water is flowing down the region's rivers into the ocean, where it may in turn be melting the icy seal over the underwater methane" (21). His interest in feedback loops allows the complex interrelations between human and nonhuman agency to take center stage, for a moment, in his story. Distributed agencies that may normally occur below the level of consciousness, or outside the purview of the political, are suddenly essential agents in propelling our present moment into an uncertain and largely unpredictable future. And, he tells us, "That's scary . . . because we're not directly releasing that methane. We burned the coal and gas and oil, and released the first dose of carbon, and that raised the temperature enough to start the process in motion. We're responsible for it, but we can't shut it off. *It's taken on a life of its own*" (21–22; my emphasis). This realization of our instigating, but not controlling, role in the changing climate is admittedly terrifying.[27] But we must be careful how we respond to that fear, McKibben suggests, and he openly worries that his readers will be overwhelmed into resignation and complacency.

In what ways does the overwhelming size of this crisis change our conception of the political act, if at all? Are there ways in which a realization of human limitations can become something other than scary, demoralizing, or demotivating? The proposals tendered in the later chapters of *Eaarth* actually offer an important cautionary tale. Attempting to find the way forward by conjuring the local and dispersed socioeconomic networks of a sustainable localism, McKibben offers five adjectives that, he suggests, "may help us think usefully about the future" (102). These five supposedly helpful adjectives are "Durable, Sturdy, Stable, Hardy, Robust" (102). He chooses these terms because he understands them—deploying a few more adjectives—as "squat, solid [and] stout" (103). For McKibben, this selection helps "conjure a world where we no longer grow by leaps and bounds, but where we hunker down, where we dig in" (103). The choice of descriptive terms for this local-oriented future does seem, for one thing, rather problematically gendered. In fact, the author implicitly admits as much by using the following metaphor to describe these words as ones "we associate with maturity, not youth; with steadiness, not flash. They aren't exciting, but they are comforting—think husband, not boyfriend" (103). The assumption of a certain traditionally defined masculinity inherent in sustainable futures is worrisome inasmuch as it draws upon the more regressive aspects of localism. It also ignores and erases much of the work of environmental justice activism, which is so often led by women, and particularly women of color in underrepresented urban communities. In a more productive vein, while attempting to find the agentic capacity within shared vulnerability and indeterminacy, Alaimo has argued that "a sense of precarious . . . openness to the material world can be an environmental stance," wherein embracing precarity, vulnerability, and even a sense of experimental fun allows her theory of transcorporeality to open paths toward new and deeper ecological ethics (Alaimo 2016, 11). I share this sense of the potential of a distributed subjectivity and agency and find the definitive move beyond McKibben's "stout" localism encouraging; however, exactly what sorts of political activism(s) will emerge without the traditional dependency upon the sovereign independent subject remains unclear.

Bruno Latour has recently suggested we direct our attention away from the *Local* to what he calls *Terra*, or the *Terrestrial* (Latour 2018, 40–42). This operates as a helpful reorientation of McKibben's localist future, and provides a lens for thinking localism without essentialism and homogeneity. For instance, McKibben asks his readers to reorient their sense of the future as such: "The project we're now undertaking—maintenance, graceful decline, hunkering down, holding on against the storm—requires a different scale. Instead of continents and vast nations, we need to think about states, about towns, about neighborhoods, about blocks" (McKibben 2010, 124). A traditional global versus local binary permeates McKibben's thinking here and the limitations are quite clear. "'Big was dynamic' when the project was growth, we could stand the side effects. But now the side effects of that size—climate change, for instance—are sapping us. We need to scale back, to go to ground" (124). The strictures of the local/global binary constructed here limit the potential of McKibben's attempts to look forward. Aiming for a new polestar such as *Terra*, as Latour contends, will redefine Progress as something other than globalism and economic growth while helping us engage with the particularity and materiality of life itself.[28]

A politics of *Terra* would reject the more regressive elements of localism (which have been effectively outlined by scholars such as Ursula Heise, particularly in her proposal for an eco-cosmopolitanism that resists the lure of localism).[29] Latour wants his localism, in other words, without the conservatism. "Whereas the Local," according to Latour, "is designed to differentiate itself by closing itself off, the Terrestrial is designed to differentiate itself by opening itself up" (Latour 2018, 54). The challenge here is one between theory and practice, while Latour lauds the theoretical potential of a "local and open" *Terra* politics, McKibben is probably rightfully concerned that an open stance, a vulnerable one, is in practice more than a little unnerving. This sense of the risk is exactly what McKibben worries will compel his readers to ignore the problem and capitulate to human society's current path of self-destruction. But if one must be realistic about our current situation, the engagement with these challenges might be best if it recognizes the reality—or materiality—of assemblages, interdependency, and distributed agency in the era of climate change. A geopolitics, Latour suggests, in which the "'geo' designates an agent that participates fully in public life," rather than simply a "framework in which political action occurs" (41).

Despite McKibben's desire to define for his readers "what a movement looks like," what I find more intriguing in his writing is the level of experimentation he admits is necessary (McKibben 2010, 124). In actuality, it appears that McKibben is fairly well aware that there is no existing formula for success. It even seems unclear, for that matter, exactly how to recognize political victories in the traditional sense of goal-oriented campaigns. His decision to title the book *Eaarth*, with the extra 'a,' in itself is suggestive of this uncertainty; this significantly altered planet we now inhabit will also necessarily play a role in the transformation of human society and therefore our understanding of political subjectivity and social movement organizing. The logic behind 350.org's focus on the Keystone XL Pipeline and their eventual turn to target the fossil fuel industry at large displays their desire to create a new paradigm of environmental political action. The frustratingly slow progress, I have suggested, can in large part be accounted for in two ways. First, the campaigns do not fully appreciate the complex nexus between Western liberal democratic institutions and the fossil fuel industry (or Mitchell's Carbon Democracy), making it hard for them to decipher their targets as they shift from Obama to Shell to Trump (never quite sure where the differences lie and the similarities begin). Second, the campaigns have not yet comprehended that the tactical tools of traditional social movement organizing are also being complicated by the shifting grounds of subjectivity and agency, as they continue to rely upon a notion of autonomous and rational agency that is increasingly unrealistic in the posthuman and postnatural Anthropocene.

A distributed environmental politics for the Anthropocene will need to embrace a new set of assumptions and cultivate new tools of assessment for determining the effective political "act." This will at first appear, as McKibben admits, quite scary. No doubt in part because it seems impossible, or irresponsible even, to imagine political struggle and social movement organization outside of a human-centered, strategic, purposeful, and goal-oriented action.[30] If we are not "acting" upon a strategy toward a measurable and specific goal, then we must be complacent or apathetic, right? What other option exists? We are left with another question, though, as well: How does the Left organize and fight for a postcarbon society—one that would emphasize low- or no-growth economies, racial justice, Indigenous rights, gender equality, and a newfound humility and respect for the complexity of nonhuman nature—up against a distributed structure of power, a carbon democracy that is designed to limit democratic activity and promote unlimited carbon capitalism? Environmental scholars and activists must carefully consider the web of fundamental dependencies between the state and, rather than just capitalism generally, a global, carbon-based, extractive capitalism specifically. Carbon democracy's essential unresponsiveness must be seen for what it is—a new normal that disempowers most forms of traditional activism—and thus serve to invigorate a search for alternative methods of social movement organizing.[31] Environmental writers and activists should resist the impulse to rush past these questions surrounding the limits of human agency, as they do when they quickly formulate traditional goal-oriented campaigns based upon the unmitigated agentic power of the intentional political actor, due to the concern it will promote fatalism. It may be the case that the space of uncertainty, created by the realization of distributed agency and its disruption of rational and intentional agency, is the place in which we need to be willing to dwell a bit longer.

If McKibben's localist future proves disappointingly conservative, despite his progressive intentions, one can thankfully look to other examples of scholarship and activism, many of which share the central tenets of the Keystone Principle, which strive for more radically open and justice-oriented models. Naomi Klein has coined the term *Blockadia*, to aptly capture the Keystone Principle's focus on direct action that targets fossil fuel infrastructure projects (disrupting construction through civil disobedience and amplifying the message that we must "leave it in the ground"). Additionally, echoing Mitchell's concept of "Carbon Democracy," Klein notes that Blockadia is a grassroots pro-democracy movement aiming to replace existing "fossilized democracies" (362).

One of the most inspiring and well-known actions was the Indigenous-led fight to stop the construction of the Dakota Access Pipeline at Standing Rock Reservation in 2016. The #NoDAPL campaign was extraordinary in many ways. In the first chapter of *Imagining the Future of Climate Change*, Shelley Streeby looks to the events at Standing Rock as a model for effective place-based direct action campaigns. The protests against fossil fuel infrastructure within and near Indigenous land, she explains, display a "revitalized politics of place," as well as "reveal how place-based struggles can connect people who are widely separated geographically but bound together in confronting common antagonists and sharing common goals" (Streeby 2018, 44). This is a different model for local, place-based politics that Glen Coulthard, a political theorist and member of the Dene First Nation, has termed, when based upon an Indigenous perspective as it was at Standing Rock, "grounded normativity" (Coulthard 2014, 13). Grounded Normativity emanates from a "place-based foundation of Indigenous decolonial thought and practice," and builds upon "Indigenous land-connected practices and longstanding experiential knowledge that inform and structure . . . ethical engagements with the world" (13). The long-standing and deep engagement with the complex relation between human and nonhuman communities within Indigenous thought and culture, and as exhibited in the generative practice of "grounded normativity," provides a politics-of-place with potential to avoid regressive localism and remain open to disanthropocentric subjectivity and distributed agency.

One of the most enlightening accounts of the #NoDAPL campaign is provided by Nick Estes, as both a scholar and firsthand participant, in his excellent book *Our History Is the Future*. Estes, a member of the Lower Brule Nation, points out (as is also well chronicled in an abundance of reporting on the pipeline's original fast-tracked approval process) that the

Dakota Access had originally been planned to cross the Missouri River above the city of Bismarck, which is "90% white," before being revised to instead cross the river "just upstream from an 84 percent Native residential area" (Estes 2019, 10). Astoundingly, Estes points out, this move was first suggested by the Army Corps of Engineers, not Energy Transfer Partners, the company behind the Dakota Access (11). Initiated by the Oceti Sakowin (the Sioux Nation), the camps at the "confluence of the Cannonball and Missouri Rivers, north of Standing Rock Indian Reservation" were joined by other Indigenous peoples and activists from all over the country, and held their ground from April 2016 to the early months of 2017 (1). "The #NoDAPL camps didn't just imagine a future without settler colonialism and the oppressive institution of the state, but created that future in the here and now" (253). While Estes makes clear we must look closely at "all its faults," he ultimately argues that "the values of the new community: that Indigenous peoples not merely survive, but thrive" is the "brief vision" of what the #NoDAPL and camp life brought to the fore: "a future premised on Indigenous justice" (252). And this justice-oriented future manifested at Standing Rock: "Free food, free education, free health care, free legal aid, a strong sense of community . . . and security were all guaranteed. Most reservations in the United States don't have access to these services, nor do most poor people. Yet, in the absence of empire, people came together to help each other . . . the camps were designed according to need, not profit" (252).[32] The story of Standing Rock, unfortunately, also provides another example of the state-sanctioned violence used to suppress protest and protect the carbon economy.[33] In all, 832 protestors were arrested by the time "the last Water Protector was led off the land in handcuffs" and many, many more were injured (64). According to Estes, four members of the community face future court dates, with the potential of years in prison on the line (64).

The #NoDAPL campaign is also another tortured tale of corporate power, political maneuvering, and back-and-forth judicial decisions, compelling both sides to declare victory prematurely at various points. After a seeming victory for the Standing Rock protesters in early 2017, when the Army Corps of Engineers suggested it would explore alternate routes, the Dakota Access Pipeline ultimately was approved and became fully operational in the summer of 2017. A contributor to *Forbes* magazine was gleefully wishing it a happy first birthday the next summer, while also predicting: "With no letup in sight, the U.S. is also positioned to remain the world's largest producer of oil and gas, and with a century of experience, pipelines will continue to be required" (McGown 2018). As of this writing, however, the pipeline's existence is suddenly and unexpectedly again in limbo, as a recent judicial decision has determined the flow of oil must halt during another, more extensive, review by the Army Corps of Engineers.[34] For our purposes, the recent energy generated by the Keystone Principle, the idea of a Blockadia strategy generally, and specific campaigns such as #NoDAPL, displays the value in the twin strategies of direct action and litigation for the environmental movement, and provides a place to assess the myriad potentialities and challenges these fights for climate justice and Indigenous autonomy engender.[35]

As my reading of Keystone XL above implies, this balance of direct action and litigation, while proving to be a valuable approach, remains challenged by the broader critical frameworks of carbon democracy and distributed agency. As this chapter comes to a close, we turn to a question Estes raises near the end of his own book: "How can settler society, which possesses no fundamental ethical relationship to the land or its original people, imagine a future premised on justice? There is no simple answer. But whatever the answer may be, Indigenous peoples must lead the way" (Estes 2019, 256). Drawing upon the "capaciousness" inherent to the Indigenous approach to "kinship," Estes goes on to suggest, "Perhaps the answers lie within the kinship relations between Indigenous and non-Indigenous and the lands we both inhabit" (256). The sense of distributed networks of connection across human and nonhuman communities in this approach is striking and essential. The long history of Indigenous resistance to colonialism and the disanthropocentric tenets central to many Indigenous cultural, spiritual, and scientific knowledges provide a historical and theoretical depth to Indigenous scholarship and activism that Estes chronicles in detail in his book. What I find equally compelling about Estes's question, however, is its speculative nature and the radical openness to new coalitions, formations, and agencies it implies. The goal of this chapter has not been to judge the effectiveness of pipeline politics at the scale of tactics, but rather to engage this influential strategy of global climate change environmentalism as a jumping-off point for contemplating distributed environmental politics. While writing about the Occupy Wall Street (OWS) movement of a decade ago, Cherniavsky has recently suggested that to "champion" the movement or to "chart its deficiencies" is to miss the point, because it assumes "we have a calculus for assessing left political strategies" ready to hand (Cherniavsky 2017, 175). Instead, she suggests we are better to recognize from the start that our existing "measures of political efficacy are themselves in crisis" (175). I could not agree more on this point: we need to very carefully consider, in this moment of disruptive transition, whether we really have the evaluative tools we need.

What Cherniavsky did find compelling about OWS was the participants' inchoate recognition that there is "no existing subject" with a clear path to appeal to the state and, therefore, they aimed to "simulate another plane" altogether (176). The value for political theory is in the register of this new simulation, not in the short-term column of wins and losses. And from this perspective, "[T]he interesting question about OWS is not so much what it gets right or wrong, but how it struggles to imagine the form and scale of politics itself" (176). Returning to Estes's speculative thinking about the future of the climate justice movement, and the centrality of Indigenous scholarship and activism, his approach suggests there is an opportunity for reimagining environmental politics, as Cherniavsky argues more generally is necessary for the Left, already embedded in the construction of, and resistance to, carbon economy infrastructure. He writes:

> New pipelines are creeping across the continent like a spiderweb, with frightening speed, but in the process, they are also connecting and inciting to action disparate communities of the exploited and dispossessed. Each pipeline exists in relation to other pipelines, and while DAPL technically only extends from North Dakota to Illinois, it is fundamentally a transnational project, interlining with other pipelines and infrastructure to ship oil to a global market, crossing the boundaries of settler states and trespassing through Indigenous territory. (Estes 2019, 253–54)

The "spiderweb" of existent and proposed pipelines might lend itself to a response infused with new kinships across disparate communities and new ways of thinking about interdependency (the "mesh," as Timothy Morton has called it, of our existence within place and time) as an agentic force, rather than a passive and too easily exploited fragility.

While Timothy Mitchell has shown that resistance to the vagaries of the carbon economy became more difficult for the labor movement during the transition from coal to oil in Europe more than a century ago (because oil's infrastructure of pipelines was more diffuse and less labor intensive than coal's more centralized infrastructure of mines and train systems), the immense scope and breadth of contemporary pipeline infrastructure might now help connect the impacted "communities of the exploited and dispossessed."[36] For his part, Estes sees such an example emanating from the #NoDAPL campaign, as the "Water Protectors personify water and enact kinship to the water, the river, enforcing a legal order of their own. If the water, a relative, is not protected, then then the river is not free, and neither are its people" (256). Through the creation and practical commitment to a "legal order of their own" that is based in an Indigenous sense of expansive kinship with the more-than-human, the Water Protectors offer an example of disanthropocentric activism that posits its own new form of politics.[37] This activism based in grounded normativity posits a political subject that outstrips the existing frameworks of the dominant settler-colonial political apparatus. Providing an example of a speculative move beyond the hardwired limits of perceived contemporary political possibility, the Water Protectors of the #NoDAPL campaign, and of the broader campaigns for Indigenous autonomy in the Americas, suggest the prospect of another political plane altogether. These important and productive instantiations of a political subject charting new paths of resistance act as radical gestures toward the possibility of an effective distributed environmental politics, a movement for environmental and social justice that might create its own "form and scale."

2

H. D. Thoreau and the Practice of Distributed Knowledges

> Most of us are still related to our native fields as a navigator to undiscovered islands in the sea. We can any afternoon discover a new fruit there, which will surprise us by its beauty and sweetness. So long as I saw in my walk one or two kinds of berries whose names I did not know, the proportion of the unknown seemed indefinitely, if not infinitely, great.
>
> —H. D. Thoreau, *Wild Fruits*

While reading broadly across contemporary climate fiction during the early stages of writing this book, I found myself surprised by a provocative juxtaposition: namely, Kim Stanley Robinson's critical-utopian climate fiction and Henry David Thoreau's nineteenth-century eco-philosophical writing. Robinson's *Science in the Capital* trilogy, specifically, incorporates transcendentalist philosophy into its exploration of the possible scientific, economic, and cultural responses to abrupt climate change, as Ralph Waldo Emerson and, especially, Thoreau play a significant role in the evolution of a main character, Frank Vanderwal. As I will discuss in the closing chapter, Frank, a scientist at the National Science Foundation (NSF), undergoes a professional and personal transformation that challenges his original objective and deeply empiricist worldview. While becoming increasingly convinced of the need to infuse scientific practice with justice-oriented cultural and political commitments, he begins to relinquish his long-held, empiricist approach to knowledge making and problem solving. The NSF, as a result, becomes an experimental laboratory for a new system of knowledge formation practices and climate policy approaches striving to muster sufficient and effective responses to ever-increasing climate disruptions. Despite my initial plan to examine the relation between posthuman theories of knowledge formation, postanthropocentric agency, and environmental politics through predominantly contemporary fiction, I kept coming back to this relatively prominent role of nineteenth-century Romantic thinkers in a science fiction narrative about the crisis of climate change in the early twenty-first century. It highlighted for me not only the continued influence of Thoreau in contemporary American environmental thought, but also the way certain challenges to thinking the human place in nature span across these time periods in evocative ways. It became increasingly clear, as well, that the preoccupations of my project's privileged texts were not entirely, or only, a function of their historical time period.

Robinson's *Science in the Capital* trilogy builds a narrative that insists that the crisis of climate change must, at least in part, be addressed by what Frank comes to call "passionate science." This is an approach to scientific practice that I argue in chapter 6 is, in good part, indebted to Haraway's concept of Situated Knowledges and which, in the course of this chapter, I will trace back to Thoreau's own relational approaches to knowledge formation. In Robinson's novels, Frank's personal and professional transformation serves as a symbol of what is depicted as a necessary shift from empirical to embodied, subjective, passionate science. Of particular note, he becomes a habitual reader of a website called emersonfortheday.net, which features a daily quote from Emerson or Thoreau. For the scholar of environment and literature, Robinson's choice of these transcendentalist figures as a motivating force in his character's transformation may at first seem an unlikely one. In this opening chapter, therefore, I begin by examining Thoreau with an eye to the role he plays in Robinson's trilogy. That is, the nonconformist of Concord becomes a source of motivation for Frank's quest for a social, scientific, and political approach that might outstrip the limitations of purely humanist and empirical approaches to global climate change. So, what is it exactly about Thoreau's nineteenth-century writings that might catalyze the destabilization of contemporary scientific practice and climate change mitigation practices in the twenty-first century? Is there a Thoreau for the Anthropocene? And, possibly, a Thoreau for distributed environmental politics?

After happening upon the "Emerson for the Day" website, Frank finds himself especially compelled by the posted quotes attributed to H. D. Thoreau. In fact, "the great philosopher of the forest at the edge of the town" was "extremely useful to Frank—often more so, dare he say it, than the old man [Emerson] himself" (Robinson 2007, 15). Thoreau's literal and perceptual inhabitation of the borders, and a philosophy focused upon unsettling simple binaries, ignites Frank's exploration of alternative ways of knowing and inhabiting the world. In his trilogy, Robinson draws upon the aspects of Thoreau's work that examine the border zones and hybrid-objects that occupy the nexus points of science, culture, and nature. The Thoreau that destabilizes these binaries—between mind and body, culture and nature, science and poetry—compels Frank to reexamine the assumptions and operative binaries that motivate his disciplinary expectations. Frank is searching for what he hopes will be a more flexible way of interacting and interpreting the quickly changing world he encounters daily: an emergent "way of seeing" that may help society adapt and find new methods of inhabiting a changing climate, an unpredictable present, an unimaginable future.

Frank's desire to remain open to the world, to notice his surroundings anew, resembles the practice, or state of being, that Thoreau terms "Useful Ignorance" in his famous posthumous essay "Walking." Frank realizes that Thoreau had, as he puts it, "lived the day, and paid ferocious attention to it, as a very respectable early scientist" (15). Frank credits Thoreau for helping him develop a new motivation, a commitment to "slip out the door in a frame of mind to see the world and act in it" (15). Seeing the world and acting in the moment, while privileging an attentiveness to detail and an open eye to hybrid phenomena operating outside conventional frameworks, as it did for Thoreau, fires Frank's imagination. Early in the third and final novel, a quote from Thoreau's journal, challenging the fundamental tenet of Cartesian dualism, has a sudden and deep impact on his thinking. Frank reads the following from Thoreau: "They are fatally mistaken who think, while they strive with their minds, that they may suffer their bodies to stagnate in luxury or sloth. A man thinks as well through his legs and arms as his brain. We exaggerate the importance and exclusiveness of the headquarters" (15). The assumption of objectivity and the privileging of the uniquely human rational mind, those foundations of empirical scientific method, are fundamental tenets for Frank prior to his transformational process. His reading of Thoreau, however, coincides with his own increasingly experimental behavior in both his private and professional life.

The connection between Robinson's trilogy and Thoreau's work is embedded, in significant part, in the difficulty of thinking knowledge formation and agency outside of liberal humanist constructs. This connection is most evident in the ever-present tensions, contradictions, and incomplete logic of Thoreau's philosophy and Robinson's depictions of a near-contemporary society struggling to find a viable path for dealing with climate change, even as it continually disrupts assumptions of human exceptionalism, autonomy, and agency. The uncertain and contradictory elements of Thoreau's critique of anthropocentrism display the difficulty of thinking outside the fundamentally dualist constructs of liberal humanism. His attempts to do so, however incomplete, offer a productive starting place for an investigation of Western environmental theory's varied attempts to mount trenchant critiques of, and alternative models to, the liberal human subject, empirical objectivity, and autonomous agency.

It is important to consider, at this point, the rationale for turning to a figure such as Thoreau as inspiration for a climate change environmental politics that should and must prioritize a justice-oriented approach to addressing climate change. One might rightly wonder whether it is necessary, or even appropriate, to return to the writings of a nineteenth-century white, male author when the work of contemporary environmentalism is, as it should be, focused on building momentum for a sociopolitical and economic transition that foregrounds racial justice and radically repositions underrepresented voices to the center of the movement. If this is the intention, if this is the necessity, as I certainly understand it to be, then possibly it is unwise to return to the likes of Thoreau at all. There is no doubting that many of the existent systemic inequalities in today's settler-colonial society are the direct result of the capitalist and racist foundations of Euro-American colonialism. I do, obviously, ultimately decide to foreground Thoreau in this chapter, but it does not mean that he should receive a pass for the colonialist, racist, and misogynist views he held, which are too often evident in his published writing and private journal. There is, however, a complexity to Thoreau that, while certainly missed in popular culture (where he is either—and only either—an environmentalist hermit/saint or a hypocritical blowhard), often goes unrecognized in U.S. literary and cultural studies. I do not purport to offer a character defense, but it does seem essential to briefly outline the recent work in Thoreau studies that paints a more complex picture of Thoreau's ideas on gender, race, the institution of slavery, and the dispossession and genocide of Native Americans.

Laura Dassow Walls dedicates a substantial amount of attention, in her recent and definitive biography *Thoreau: A Life*, to the exploration of his engagement with antislavery thinking and activism. His retreat to nature was never an escape, she persuasively explains, but a path toward engaging the world from a new and more justice-oriented perspective. Until reading Walls's biography, in fact, I myself had never realized that Thoreau's "Slavery in Massachusetts" essay, based on a speech he delivered on July 4, 1854, at an abolitionist rally that included the likes of William Lloyd Garrison and Sojourner Truth, made such an impact upon its publication. Published in the *Liberator*, *New-York Daily Tribune*, and the *National Anti-Slavery Standard* within the month, it quickly "propelled him into the most militant ranks of radical abolitionists" (Walls 2017, 348). Ever the anti-institutionalist, Thoreau never officially joined the Abolitionist movement, a fact that is often attributed to his lack of interest in societal affairs at best or a complacent (and complicit) racism at worst, but the details of his biography offer a glimpse into a more nuanced reality. Though records are sparse, Walls lays out the clear evidence recognizing the "Thoreau household . . . [as] a trusted station on the Underground Railroad" (318), and the family regularly, for decades, helped escaped slaves continue north (most often to Canada).[1] One of the most significant accomplishments of Walls's biography (and there are many), is to remind us that the Thoreau who wrote *Walden* and "Walking" is the very same philosopher we meet in "Resistance to Civil Government" and "The Plea for John Brown." She draws lines through and across his philosophical development that bridge the poet and the scientist, the hermit and the gadfly, the casual misogynist and the Suffragist supporter. While many "begged Thoreau to be silent," for example, he gave his speech in support of John Brown anyway, when literally no one else was ready to yet do so (451). On the evening of his speech, while Brown's trial was still ongoing in Virginia, according to Walls, "not one person in the nation had stood up in public to defend John Brown . . . and everywhere the newspaper headlines pitched hysteria against him" (451). Thoreau did, of course, deliver the speech, though as a "minority of one in an explosive atmosphere" (451).

While addressing these issues of privilege inherent to Thoreau's worldview and writing, Lance Newman's excellent, recently published *The Literary Heritage of the Environmental Justice Movement: Landscapes of*

Revolution in Transatlantic Romanticism is a helpful resource, as it convincingly makes the (somewhat surprising) case for the importance of Romantic writing and thought for today's Environmental Justice campaigns. The broader argument for the continuing relevance of key Romantic figures is fascinating and worth reading, but in the case of Thoreau specifically, Newman writes: "When he awoke from the liberal dream of Transcendentalism into the material light of morning at Walden Pond, he saw clearly that his life of the embodied mind in nature occurred within a socio-environmental context that was fundamentally unjust. The pressing issue of his day, of course, was slavery" (Newman 2019, 211). Walls's and Newman's explorations into Thoreau's engagement with the key moral issue of his time do not claim to exculpate him for his thinking and writing when it falls prey to misogyny, racism, and savagism. Their careful scholarship does, however, add a complexity to our historical understanding of his current place in environmental and social justice literature. Based on his research, Newman comes to the following conclusion:

> The reality is that Thoreau's thinking evolved over time. In particular, his understanding of the human community evolved in parallel with his insight into nonhuman nature. . . . The exploitation of labor (both wage and slave) and the appropriation of nature were thus twin features of an intensely destructive modernity. He also acknowledged the need not just for individual self-reform but also for collective action in pursuit of wholesale social change. (203)

This seems a key point: the cultural image of Thoreau as the self-involved Romantic hermit is just not historically accurate. As scholars look closer at the reality of Thoreau's written legacy and the historical context in which he lived and wrote, they are increasingly discovering a Thoreau that outstrips any one categorization. However, it does seem increasingly clear that within this problematic and complex legacy, there is much more to Thoreau's commitments to antislavery work than is often recognized.

As early as his first book, *A Week on the Concord and Merrimack*, Thoreau is searching for new methods of engagement with the major social and ethical issues of the period. "He was experimenting wildly with form, dangerously in thought" even at this early stage, as he attempted "to offer a new moral framework strong enough to bear the weight of modern science, eloquent enough to assert that preacher and poet were one, and sharp enough to address the ethical challenges of slavery, industrialization, and wars of conquest" (Walls 2017, 272). Regarding Thoreau's developing, though ultimately incomplete, work to critically engage with his prejudices about Indigenous peoples, Walls summarizes her assessment as such:

> So while it's true that, like his cohort, he inherited the savagism of his day, Thoreau also made a point of seeking out living Indians and asking them about their lives. Eventually it dawned on him—and, in his understanding, he is virtually unique among white writers of the nineteenth century—that Indians were not vanishing savages but a living and vital people struggling against tremendous obstacles, with some real success, to adapt and make a future for themselves in modern America. (Walls 2015, 9)

Accordant with Walls's thoughts on the matter, literary scholar John Kucich offers a detailed and nuanced account of Thoreau's three visits to Maine and how they profoundly impacted his perceptions of the Penobscot people and their culture. His return trips to Maine, Kucich explains, were expressly planned so that he could meet and learn about the Penobscot more than any other goal (certainly more than moose hunting; he was sure he wouldn't like the inevitable end result of the hunt and, when that moment came, his assumption was correct).[2]

During one of his travels north, one of three trips he would chronicle in *The Maine Woods*, Thoreau met Joe Aitteon of the Penobscot, who acted as his guide for a multiday hunting and camping trip. In his writing about these trips, Thoreau's views sway back and forth between imperialist ideologies of savagism and receptive open-mindedness. And the Penobscot, Kucich explains, were also careful to limit how much they shared with Thoreau, understandably careful to explain their culture in broader terms while also selecting carefully what and how much to share ("Lost," 33).[3] One night, Thoreau was invited to an evening of eating, storytelling, and, eventually, sleeping around the fire with Joe and several other Penobscot. Thoreau mostly listened as the men talked and told stories, switching back and forth between English and their shared native language. "That was a pivotal night in Thoreau's life," Walls contends, "Until that night, 'the Indian' had been a figure casually encountered on the margins of his own world, or a remote and vanishing legend from books of history and romance. After that night, they were for Thoreau, far more—just what, he spent his last years trying to understand" (338). And, Walls continues, "The reckoning begun here would force Thoreau to rethink everything he knew" (339). It is essential to avoid uncritically foregrounding canonical voices without a careful consideration of gender and racial privilege, and I do not choose to focus on Thoreau here without such considerations. This brief overview only scratches the surface of the solid critical work that is ongoing in contemporary Thoreau Studies scholarship to sift through both the problematic and the productive elements of this long-debated thinker.

I hope it will also become clear that Thoreau has left us with essential sketches to new "ways of seeing" that might benefit environmental thought and activism in the twenty-first century. Thoreau's interest in the complexity and agentic capacity of nonhuman natural processes, for instance, is extremely relevant to contemporary conversations in eco-theory. As Jedediah Purdy has suggested: "What an Anthropocene reading of Thoreau shows . . . is just how long and actively Americans have been dealing with, interpreting, and learning from a transformed world," and that "much in the old canon remains useful, even illuminating and exciting, in an Anthropocene time" (125). Accordingly, this chapter trains its focus upon the question of agency (human, nonhuman, and distributed) and whether or not the more practical and complex approach to nonhuman agency evident in Thoreau's work offers an opportunity to rethink the ways we currently imagine the relation between knowledge formation and agency. In regards to materiality, Rochelle Johnson has previously suggested that Thoreau, in a precursor to contemporary theories of New Materialism, understood "matter as activity" (Johnson 2014, 608). She persuasively argues that Thoreau's sincere and sustained engagement with nonhuman matter, his "participation" with it even going so far as to impact his "formation" of subjective identity (608), "informed" and "constituted" his being (624). Consistent with Johnson, it is also my contention that Thoreau attends to the interdependency of the human and nonhuman in a more complicated, vexed, and contradictory manner than has often been allowed. The complications inherent in Thoreau's desire to reconceptualize the relationship between the human and the nonhuman are indicative of the difficulty of thinking outside humanist assumptions that are foundational to empiricism, subjectivity, and agency.[4] It is these elements of Thoreau's work that help his ideas find their way into twenty-first-century climate fiction and continue to inspire scholars, building from Thoreau's inchoate explorations, to reconsider our relation to, and ways of knowing, nonhuman nature.

Situated Knowledges and a Passionate Scientist

H. D. Thoreau is consistently turned to, for vastly different reasons, by scholars from multiple disciplines in order to depict the bard of Concord as a monumental thinker or early example of some later theoretical trend. And this chapter does look backward to focus upon Thoreau with an awareness of his status in the biocentric imaginary within environmental humanities scholarship. My goal here is not to recover Thoreau for any one particular methodology or approach, but rather to examine the problematics in his work that speak to continuing, unresolved issues in environmental thought in our own immensely challenging times.[5] A more sustained look at Thoreau's depictions of human subjectivity and the nature/culture binary, for instance, opens up an opportunity to unpack traditional assumptions about his work. The eminent Lawrence Buell has made the point that *Walden*'s "'failures' enhance its representativeness both as a document of the environmental imagination and as a microcosm of Thoreau's achievement, for he was never able to get beyond an inchoate, fragmentary sketch of his grand effort to comprehend the Concord environment in its multidimensional totality" (126). I agree with Buell regarding the productive potential of Thoreau's "failures," and also want to suggest that certain aspects of these inconsistencies continue to bedevil environmental thought as it has attempted to articulate critiques of anthropocentrism, empiricism, and, more generally, to redefine the nature/culture binary in ways that more consistently emphasize the interconnectedness of the human and nonhuman worlds. Thoreau's insistent attention to border spaces, fluidity, and hybridity are related to the ongoing challenges we face in effectively confronting the problematic essentialism and hierarchies of anthropocentrism, while remapping and re-envisioning complex nature-culture assemblages in terms of distributed subjectivities and agencies.[6]

This chapter also traces a genealogy of distributed knowledges that begins with Thoreau's *Useful Ignorance*, productively theorized as *Relational Knowing* by Thoreau scholar and biographer Laura Walls. Walls's work is indebted to feminist, science, and materiality studies scholar Donna Haraway's concept of *Situated Knowledges* and, from there, we are led to sci-fi writer Kim Stanley Robinson's more recent narrativizing of *Passionate Science*. Thoreau's attention to materiality, hybridity, and the complex linkages and relations across subjects, objects, actions, and ideas suggests a speculative path forward for distributed politics (the political subject and her agency after humanism). But also the never-quite-complete nature of his work—the so-called failures and contradictions in his writing—is indicative of several vexing and continuing challenges for contemporary eco-theory: most importantly, it should remind us that there is no essential ecological self calmly waiting behind the humanist, capitalist, and anthropocentric layers, which eco-theorists are attempting, in our various ways, to peel away. The transition to a more ecological society, if we are to remain on the path of discovery down which materiality beckons, will be fraught with challenges as we undo the simple binaries and racialized hierarchies endemic to dominant ideologies of humanism, scientific objectivity, and late capitalism.

Walls's seminal book *Seeing New Worlds: Henry David Thoreau and 19th Century Natural Science* develops a new, and now widely accepted, perspective on Thoreau's work from the 1850s through to his premature death in 1861. Thoreau's intention in turning more fully to natural history and science in the 1850s, Walls establishes, is to tell a "history of man and nature together" as an "interconnected act" (Walls 1995, 10). During these years, Thoreau labors, through close attention to particular processes of the natural world in and around Concord, to combine transcendentalism with empiricism, poetry with science, the mythical with the material. According to Walls, while Thoreau might conceive of Nature as "one great whole," in a break from Emerson (and Coleridge and Kant before him), he becomes intensely interested in an emergent alternative to what she terms their "romantic rational holism (94)." Through his study of the natural world's "constituent and individual parts," Thoreau begins to see nature, consequently, as a series of *facts* rather than as only a universalized *symbol* (94). I will argue later that this change of emphasis is one that displays a distinctly different understanding of human and material agency as well.

The division between World and Idea, or Nature and Thought, so prominent in Emerson's philosophical writings, leads to a paradox in which the philosopher can only discover true existence through a purposeful extraction of oneself from the world of objects. This, in turn, leads to the "subordination of material nature as no more than a passive vehicle for the currents and energies of a life force that is . . . only in the human soul" (69). This dualism, as Walls points out so cogently, aids and abets the growing institutional rifts between the natural sciences and the humanities. When understood through the lens of this binary framework, Thoreau's move to the natural sciences was for a long time explained as a retreat from his poetic aspirations. However, Walls, and much of the ensuing revival in Thoreau Studies since *Seeing New Worlds*, uncovers the potential of examining his final decade of work as an attempt to occupy the boundary between these two polarized opposites. He ultimately denies the division between poetry and science altogether. While the "popular image" of Thoreau as an aloof lover of "untainted nature" relies upon and "reasserts the tragic and sterile dualisms between subject and object . . . [and] the human and the natural," these are the very dualisms that "he fought to disrupt and disown in the name of creating a future that might succeed the 'evil days' ushered in by romantic alienation in a commodified society" (13–14). Thoreau's struggle to disrupt these "sterile dualisms" is the point from which we will begin to explore the ensuing destabilization of the nature/culture binary in his work and how it limns an early recognition of distributed agency.

Radical openness, rather than closed systems, motivates Thoreau's relational approach to knowledge formation. Buell describes much of Thoreau's writing as an attempt to discover Concord's "multidimensional totality," but I find this particular phrasing somewhat problematic. I cannot help but wonder if Buell, who tends to privilege an ecocentric reading of Thoreau, is not attempting to tidy up the complex tensions within Thoreau's work a bit too quickly. To my mind, this phrasing actually operates as an attempt to repackage Thoreau's contradictions into a new sort of holism. This re-totalizing approach seems to make the problem a little less complex, less unwieldy, and quite likely less productive. That is, by reinscribing a totality that encompasses (should I say limits?) the multidimensionality of Thoreau's work, Buell attempts to emphasize a holistic and ecocentric alternative at work in Thoreau's writing, a reassuring commensurability with conventional frameworks for thinking the nature/culture binary.[7] Instead, I hope to read Thoreau's failures, contradictions, and inconsistencies in a less comforting fashion and, in so doing, begin an exploration into what the nature-culture relation might look like in a *postnatural* environment inhabited by *posthuman* humans.

Walls describes Thoreau's approach to science by drawing a connection between his practice and feminist science studies scholar Donna Haraway's concept of Situated Knowledges. Walls, channeling Haraway, uncovers "the redemptive value of 'sitedness'—of knowledge that has the enabling properties of being sited, in discipline, place, history, gender, personality" as a helpful frame for rethinking Thoreau's later science-oriented essays (Walls 1995, 10). Although certainly incomplete or inchoate, Thoreau's determination to attend to the subjective experience of knowledge formation and his skepticism of pure objectivity do seem to anticipate Haraway's concept of situated knowledges. Walls draws a line from Thoreau's binary-busting writing to "Haraway's quest for a 'feminist objectivity' which defies the transcendent God-vision of the unmarked gaze by insisting on the 'embodied nature of all vision' through eyes which are 'active perceptual systems'" (10). The critique of "God-vision," the myth of disembodied objectivity, which Walls identifies within Thoreau's turn to particularity and subjective positionality (and away from the rationalist and universalist approach we find in his mentor Emerson), connects in provocative ways to the questions raised in Kim Stanley Robinson's *Science in the Capital* trilogy. That work, as explained above, suggests that the climate change crisis can only be addressed by a 'passionate science,' a practice that, I will later argue, draws upon the lineage of Haraway's concept of *situated knowledges* and Thoreau's *useful ignorance*.[8]

Thoreau is searching for ways of seeing the world, and his relation to it, that might enable a clearer understanding of his own experiences and help him to act more responsibly and ethically as a result. The traditional notions underlying this whole process—from evaluative and rational thought, to the intentional act, and through to its knowable and predictable results—are currently under scrutiny (via numerous theoretical approaches in the new materialisms). Thoreau's exploration of relational knowing exhibits his awareness and desire to reimagine the complex relationship between human and nonhuman agency.[9] From his journals, it is evident that Thoreau read Alexander Von Humboldt almost directly after his time by Walden Pond and "began to visualize a way to banish the tragic dualisms that set man apart from nature" (Walls 1995, 93). And during this time he begins to focus more squarely upon the "reciprocity" between humanity and the natural world and hopes to interact with Nature without "becoming masterful" (124).[10] This approach leads to an understanding of knowledge production, and knowledge itself, as both scientific and poetic. "In this way, countering the tyranny of 'system or arrangement,' does community become the basis for Thoreau's theory of knowledge" (143). Walls points, in particular, to a series of journal entries in the early 1850s, in which Thoreau ponders the interdependent relationship between humans and nonhuman nature leading to the decentering of the human subject.[11] She proposes that, for Thoreau,

> true knowledge is generated and maintained by the community of knowers, a "round robin" in which the center rotates,

which includes all as subjects and all as objects. In this way Thoreau breaks down the dualism embedded in the foundation of "rational" holism, which assumes that knowing can take place within the isolated, rational mind. (Walls 1995, 143–44)

This is a case for relational ways of knowing that embed the scientist in the world as a member and participant within the field of study; as the "center rotates," the scientist also becomes a contributor to, and object of, the knowledge production system (rather than a unique, outside observer).[12] Subject/object binaries dissolve as their ever-shifting relational interdependence is foregrounded, and a radical alternative to the detachment of Western scientific practice emerges in Thoreau's approach to relational ways of knowing.

The critique of liberal humanist conceptions of human control over nature, the newly professionalizing sciences, and rational approaches to knowledge making become increasingly evident. In regard to Thoreau's later work, Walls argues, influenced by Humboldtian science, it evolves into something she terms "empirical holism," which she portrays as precursor to an ecological science.[13] Walls is predominantly interested in displaying this approach as one that debunks many assumed disciplinary differences, such as science and poetry or empirical and qualitative inquiry. Thoreau's attention to particularity and the details of the varied seasons in his Concord woods brings about his revelation that the immensity of variability within the natural cycles challenges any closed system of predictable order. Additionally, "Thoreau's participation in science maps a range of conflicts and potentials in environmental thought" that eventually lead him to a "radical view of nature as a self-generating, creative agent by incorporating Humboldtian proto-ecological science into traditional and romantic forms of natural theology" (Walls 2000, 17). Thoreau's oblique relation to objectivity gestures toward the value of subjective and emplaced experience and its ability to inform our close scrutiny of the natural world's processes.

The art of sauntering, as Thoreau describes it in the essay "Walking," is of course an attempt to better understand the self and the nonhuman world, but it is also an investigation into the relationship *between* the so-called natural world and the human society of Concord. Categorizing his own sustained and persistent daily walks in the woods "occasional and transient" forays into nature implies both the vastness and complexity of the natural world and humans' limited knowledge of it. Thoreau explains, "For my part, I feel that with regard to Nature I live a sort of border life, on the confines of a world into which I make occasional and transient forays only" (Thoreau 1982, 625). When probably one of the most committed observers of natural phenomena to ever go for a walk laments his inability to spend enough time in nature to even approach an understanding of it, I guess we should probably take note of our own limitations as well.

The movement away from Knowledge, when represented as something akin to the search for universal Truth, is embedded in Thoreau's concept of Useful Ignorance. He argues for the benefit, instead, of "Sympathy with Intelligence," and we should recognize the resonance this phrasing contains with the concept of situated knowledges (623). Both share a foundational valuation of the practice (simultaneously personal, relational, and experiential) of limited, embedded, and experiential knowledge making. That is, knowledge as contingent and deriving from a material place and a particular viewpoint. For Thoreau, to catalogue and finalize your impression is forever forestalled by a new revelation, transition, etc., and this was a challenge he found exciting, rather than entirely frustrating.[14] Hence, a skepticism and awareness of one's limited perspective becomes a powerful benefit. In rethinking Thoreau's depiction of the nature/culture binary through the lens of distributed types of knowing and acting, I hope to display that the so-called original environmentalist's commitment to the practice of situated knowledges offers a productive opportunity to investigate the complex interaction between human and nonhuman agency.

In turning to *Walden* in the next section, I am interested in evaluating the relationship between Thoreau's intentional engagement with border spaces and hybridity, and how these foci become components of a broader commitment to situated (embodied and emplaced) knowledge. What follows will then also examine the ways in which Thoreau's reconsideration of empiricism relates to his treatment of agency as a force distributed across the human and nonhuman worlds. Within this reading of just a few well-known passages from *Walden*, I hope to highlight that there is at least as much attention to chaotic border spaces between nature and culture, materiality and the transcendental, etc. as there is to the process of reorganizing a holistic system out of these parts. While many materialist readings of Thoreau rightfully turn to his later journals and the excellent posthumously published texts *Wild Fruits* and *Seeds*, edited by Bradley Dean, I remain mostly focused on *Walden* in this short treatment of Thoreau's attention to hybridity. As Purdy, while critically engaging with the environmental movement's more romantic canonization of Thoreau, asks: "What if we instead read *Walden* as a work engaged with Anthropocene themes? How might Thoreau look as part of a different chosen inheritance, one oriented to a different environmental imagination?" (Purdy 2015, 147). There is still, in a nod to its complex layers, much to uncover in *Walden*.

Hybridity's Alternative Maps

An exploration of Thoreau's nontraditional depiction of agency in *Walden* would do well to begin with "The Pond in Winter" chapter, in which ice cutters arrive to cut, stack, and store Walden's winter ice in preparation for its eventual sale. In this brief narrative, Thoreau depicts the natural, economic, and philosophical systems that confront each other at the level of the local (the pond) and the global (economic markets). For more than two weeks Thoreau watches from his "window a hundred men at work like busy husbandmen, with teams and horses and apparently all the implements of farming" (Thoreau 1982, 538). Thoreau's description of the event is reliably rife with disdain and even a sense of violation at the removal of what he deems "the only coat, ay, the skin itself, of Walden Pond in the midst of a hard winter" (535). The commodification of the pond does, as one might surmise, elicit what can be deemed a Romanticist critique of modernity's valuation of economic success at the cost of the aesthetic appreciation of nature. All this commotion, he complains, solely for a "gentleman farmer" to "cover each of his dollars with another" (535). However, in addition to this predictable lament over the commodification of the pond's ice, there are also more complex and possibly unexpected impulses at work in this story.

As a result of his self-aware construction of an authorial liminality at the intersection of the so-called natural and the cultural, these passages depict a nuanced representation of the relationship between his supposed pastoral escape to Walden and the ongoing industrialization of New England (including its role within an increasingly global marketplace). As such, this passage provides an opportunity to examine the ways in which materiality and situated knowledge, distributed agency, and critiques of linear history each operate in Thoreau's narrative. The ice of Walden itself will play its own role in this tale as well, as it, rather than the author himself, becomes the nodal point for thinking an agency that is distributed across the human and nonhuman. Importantly, the ice becomes a site for the practice of situated knowledge making and an example of a *hybrid product* that is at once natural and cultural, as I will explain shortly. Thoreau depicts the ice cutters as adroit at their business, technologically savvy, and generally succeeding with their enterprise, but he also enthusiastically points to the instances in which "the frozen soil took a piece of steel out of a ploughshare or a plough got set in the furrow and had to be cut out" (536). Or, as he recounts, the bit of joy he felt when a laborer "slipped through a crack" in the ice. Though Thoreau does mention he was quick to offer the man "refuge in [his] house" to warm up safely, he seems to relish in depicting a noncompliant nature as he imagines the frozen pond and soil engaging in a type of nonhuman, unintentional monkeywrenching of the project (can nonhuman agency become ecotage?). Even if these more obvious examples do seem to emphasize a distinct nonhuman agency, they set the table for more in-depth explorations of materiality and agentic assemblages to come.

The relationship between the economic goals of the project and the actual results, as described, highlights the interaction of human plans (economic, technological) and nonhuman agency. The precise accounting of the capitalist marketplace is thrown off, one might suggest, by its insufficient accounting for distributed agency. Thoreau writes of the ice:

> However, a still greater part of this heap had a different destiny from what was intended; for, either because the ice was found not to keep so well as was expected . . . or for some other reason, it never got to market. This heap, made in the winter of '46–'47 and estimated to contain ten thousand tons, was finally covered with hay and boards; and though it was unroofed the following July, and part of it carried off, the rest remaining exposed to the sun, it stood over that summer and the next winter, and was not quite melted till September, 1848. Thus the pond recovered the greater part. (537)

The vagaries of the marketplace, in this case, leave the ice to melt and return to the pond once again in its liquid form. The melted ice rejoins the unpredictable cycles of Walden Pond and its surrounding ecosystem; the cycles are never quite the same as the season before, as each season is never, and can never be, a simple replica of the last. The forces of environmental and human agency (by Thaw and Thor as he calls them in the Spring chapter) are simultaneously organic and constructed by and integrated with the cultural.

Even the pond itself, de-clothed of its icy outer layer, is not presented as necessarily right or wrong (a pristine or ruined ecosystem), as Thoreau seems to intimate that there is no one *correct* or *proper* existence for this pond (as certain more Romantic constructions of the natural world might like to suggest). Instead, Thoreau's scientific and philosophical approaches are trying to get at exactly how these varied seasonal and annual existences come to be, how they change, and, finally, in what way the forces are knowable to the implicated human observer. This is indicative of the uncertainty that underlies Thoreau's more straightforward critique of the ice cutters, the capitalist project employing these laborers, and his general happiness to see the water "return to the pond" (as the plan unfolds in ways that the "gentleman farmer" had not foreseen). It is not, at least only, that this imagined scene seems so *unnatural*—it is more accurate to say that he realizes that nothing is unnatural in the end. This becomes overtly clear when we read this scene in tandem with the thawing bank of the spring chapter where Thoreau famously concludes that "there is nothing inorganic" (549).

After the ice has been removed, Thoreau reflects upon the strange possibility of Walden Pond being ice-free drastically earlier than he has ever witnessed previously. Walden Pond, temporarily removed of its icy winter shell, becomes a condition of possibility firmly based in distributed agency. Here we see Walden Pond as an ecosystem constructed by both human and nonhuman forces that together lead to Thoreau's narrative, at the heart of which are musings I contend are grappling with the effects of an agency distributed beyond the human subject in significant ways. While in some ways the human and nonhuman forces do continue to appear distinct from one another, there is also an increasing understanding of their overlap and interaction. What one might want to read as a romantic vision of man's inability to impede the natural processes of the pond, despite his best efforts, becomes something else entirely. After describing the mechanics of the removal and the details of the story, Thoreau wonders whether, in as short as thirty more days, he might "hear a solitary loon laugh as he dives and plumes himself, or shall see a lonely fisher in his boat, like a floating leaf, beholding his form reflected in the windows, where lately a hundred men securely labored" (538). These musings upon the loon and fisherman descending upon Walden become infinitely more interesting when we consider that Thoreau imagines both of them as arriving in just thirty days' time *because* he is conjecturing that the ice cutters will leave behind a pond with, well, less ice. And with its seasonal process of ice formation significantly disrupted, the pond will open up to loons and fisherman earlier that coming spring. In this manner, Thoreau seems to be thinking through the interaction between a human economic system, which turns Walden's ice into a commodity, and the natural processes of the pond and surrounding ecosystem.

Thoreau's engagement with the distributed agency that is the mixed community of Walden pond's ecosystem raises a set of provocative questions: In what unpredictable ways do these nonhuman systems simultaneously facilitate, alter, and even forestall human planning and action (economic or otherwise)? How will the removal of the ice, a human alteration of the ecosystem, alter those nonhuman forces? And, finally, what new stimuli, options, and/or impediments emanating from these amalgamations will co-produce the upcoming spring season for both the human and nonhuman communities? As he waits for the thawing of the pond, Thoreau's thoughts are brought back to this question of environmental agency and human knowledge, or, more accurately, the question of a human's ability to empirically know and therefore control natural processes. In a detailed description of the thawing process of the pond (less well remembered than his attention a few short pages later to the thawing sandbank), Thoreau's attention to detailed accuracy is remarkable. First, in order to explain why Walden "never breaks up so soon as the others," we are informed that it is "on account both of its greater depth and its having no stream passing through it to melt or wear away the ice" (539). In case the reader is not content with these broader explanations, Thoreau provides a detailed quantitative comparison of temperatures between Walden and Flints Pond. "A thermometer thrust into the middle of Walden on the 6th of March, 1847, stood at 32 degrees, or freezing point; near the shore at 33 degrees; in the middle of Flints Pond, the same day, at 32.5 degrees; [and] at a dozen rods from the shore . . . 36 degrees" (540). The specificity of these observations is indicative of the influence of Humboldt's scientific practice upon Thoreau's relationship to nature.[15] We learn about Walden by first comparing it to nearby Flint and then attempt to better understand the processes of the spring thaw, through the general observation that Walden is perennially the last local pond to lose its ice and via specific observations regarding pond depth, the thickness of ice, and water temperature. Through this process, Thoreau offers this final explanation: "This difference of three and a half degrees between the temperature of the deep water and the shallow in the latter [Flints] pond, and the fact that a great proportion of it is comparatively shallow, show why it should break up so much sooner than Walden" (540). The observed quantitative data are here used to draw together a conclusive statement of fact.

Thoreau also pauses to draw attention to the parts of this process that, even as he closely observes and describes it, function to some degree outside his ability understand or "see" what is occurring. Of particular note to Thoreau are the great, thundering cracking sounds the ice emits at random intervals during the spring thaw. "The cracking and booming of the ice indicate a change of temperature," he reminds us (541). And, "In the right stage of the weather a pond fires its evening gun with great regularity. But in the middle of the day, being full of cracks, and the air also being less elastic, it had completely lost its resonance" (541–42). It is from these initial observations that Thoreau feels comfortable moving from localized observations to a grander, more sweeping generalization of these *rules* of spring. This leads him to one of the book's more famous statements—more often seen as important for its metaphorical and allegorical meaning. "The phenomena of the year take place every day in a pond on a small scale. . . . The day is an epitome of the year. The night is the winter, the morning and evening are the spring and fall, and the noon is summer" (541). These famous lines comparing the cycle of a day to the seasons of the year exhibit Thoreau in his most poetic, universalist, and confident tone. When read in the context of the surrounding scientific and observational approach to the pond's natural systems, however, the passage takes on another resonance altogether. Significantly, Thoreau moves quickly away from these rules pertaining to the thawing pond's cracking sounds, and the greater order of the universe to which they portend, to consider the randomness of this material agency. He admits, "The pond does not thunder every evening, and I cannot tell surely when to expect its thundering; but though I may perceive no difference in the weather, it does. Who would have suspected so large and cold and thick-skinned a thing to be so sensitive?" (542). The sensitivity of the pond that Thoreau himself is unable to predict leads him to surmise: "The earth is all alive and covered with papillae. The largest pond is as sensitive to atmospheric changes as the globule of mercury in its tube" (542).

Thoreau's attentiveness to the sensitive, chaotic, and nonstatic quality of the nonhuman ecosystem encompassing Walden Pond seems to temper any remaining tendency to look for universal and static laws of nature.

Entering into more complex terrain than a mundane critique of the spoiling of a picturesque natural landscape, the ice cutters scene opens up a series of at least three interesting problems: first, the importance of materiality, particularity, and situated knowledge in Thoreau's work; second, the complex functions of agency as distributed across the human and nonhuman; and third, the ways in which these first two problems lead to a crisis of perception regarding linear temporality. Thoreau explores a variety of complex intra-actions, to borrow Barad's term, between the ice cutters' ability to change the pond's winter cycles so dramatically and the unpredictability of nature's responses to their profit-driven actions. The concept of intra-action, however, implies something more than just human action followed by environmental response, or vice versa. Instead, the narrative depends upon the—at times disquieting—inextricability of the two types of agency, so that, in actuality, we need to resist the impulse to assume the separation in the first place. It is important to note, however, that Thoreau is only a precursor here to Barad's theories of intra-action: while he depicts the complex interaction between the human and nonhuman, productively disrupting the dualism, Barad's theory of intra-action denies the original binary construct itself.[16] My point, for now, is that Thoreau's telling of the removal of Walden's ice in the winter of '46–'47, and his reaction to it, struggles with the question of an agency that is co-produced by the human and nonhuman; grappling with the relationship between a decentered human and a complex, active nonhuman world. He is looking for other ways of telling the story of industrialism and the Industrial Revolution's impact on the human/nonhuman relationship, and in this exploration offers us possibilities for understanding postanthropocentric agency and subjectivity in the age of climate change.

The narrative of the ice removal quietly displays the importance of localized, personal, and flexible models of observation, comparison, and hypothesis based upon his year-in, year-out experience in the area. The story depicts an interplay of human and environmental agency leading to what Thoreau imagines will be the open waters of Walden Pond in some "thirty days or more" after the ice cutters complete their work. The poetic and the scientific work together here as Thoreau's passionate science—founded upon the distributed ways of knowing embedded in Useful

Ignorance and Relational Knowing—allows him to see his world in new ways. It is not until the next and final chapter, "Spring," that we receive a quick explanation of what actually occurs after the removal of the ice from Walden pond. As we have seen in the previous chapter, Thoreau explains how he imagines the loon and fisherman coming early to the pond that he assumes will not fully refreeze. "The opening of the large tracts by the ice-cutters commonly causes a pond to break up earlier; for the water, agitated by the wind, even in cold weather, wears away the surrounding ice. But such was not the effect on Walden that year, for she had soon got a thick new garment to take the place of the old" (539). At first, he simply wonders what will happen, but then suggests that he knows what *should* happen: the pond, he predicts, will open up earlier than usual. Yet, in the end, he must admit to being surprised that the opposite occurs—the pond fully refreezes and remains frozen till well into spring that year.

The "Pond in Winter," however, concludes with another investigation of the capitalist marketplace, and its ability to connect regions of the world, as Thoreau imagines the "sweltering inhabitants of Charleston and New Orleans" purchasing the ice and therefore, Thoreau muses, having "a drink at [his] well" (538). Beyond these imagined connections brought on by the commodification of Walden's ice, the "unnatural" situation of the ice-free pond reminds Thoreau of the connection between global economic systems (demand and technological innovation, etc.) and local/regional ecosystems. In furthering this imagined trip of the Walden ice to reach as far as "Bombay and Calcutta," Thoreau expands the market of global commerce to include a philosophical and intellectual exchange that he sees as having more potential (and certainly interests him more) than the former form of globalization. He imagines it this way:

> The pure Walden water is mingled with the sacred water of the Ganges. With favoring winds it is wafted past the site of the fabulous islands of Atlantis and Hesperides . . . floating by the Ternate and Tidore and the mouth of the Persian Gulf, melts in the tropic gales of the Indian seas, and is landed in ports of which Alexander only heard the names. (538)

For Thoreau, in this scene, the chopped, stacked ice of Walden Pond becomes a hybrid product, containing within it both contamination and possibility. It becomes inextricably natural and cultural: a hybrid product with material, economic, and philosophical potential.[17]

After this particular attempt to commodify the ice fails, as it slowly melts back into the pond without ever reaching the marketplace, Thoreau imagines his own version of Walden's water's entry into the global economy. In this rendering, the ice, having melted back into the pond after its aborted trip to market, rejoins the pond in liquid form. The water then becomes a vehicle for imagining the philosophical and spiritual exchange of ideas in a different type of global marketplace. At the pond, Thoreau imagines that he might "meet [Bramin's] servant come to draw water for his master, and [their] buckets as it were grate together in the same well" (539). Walden and the Ganges River, and its "sacred water," are "mingled." Here we have yet another hybrid entity reminiscent of the famous railroad bank to which we shall soon turn our attention. In this case, however, it is important to remind ourselves that Thoreau examines the potentiality of the ice of Walden Pond, as hybrid-object, in a search for a moment, a space, of interdependency between human and nonhuman systems.[18] The value of nature in this case is defined not through a privileging of "pristine" or "untouched" landscapes or "natural" objects, nor do these passages solely operate to lament all human interaction with nature as destructive. Instead, for Thoreau, there is both contamination and possibility in these interactions taking place in each material moment.

This narrative is, of course, also purely speculative. We might say, in fact, that it becomes a counterfactual story highlighting alternative mappings of the world in which the water of Walden and the Ganges River are impossibly blended together (and therefore the commodified and the spiritual aspects of each are intermixed as well). This mapping therefore, besides ignoring geographical factors, also refuses conventional political, economic, and cultural categories.[19] In a moment, we will return to this concept of alternative, and also oppositional, maps in regard to Thoreau's cartographical representation of Walden Pond itself. In first moving to the famous sandbank scene of the Spring chapter, we will confront another hybrid-object of nature-culture in the bank of the railroad itself. And, finally, we will discover that both these hybrid-objects of Thoreau's study, the ice of Walden pond and the sandbank of the railroad line, serve as two parts of a triangle of hybridity that is sketched, both in literary and cartographic terms, in the final scenes of *Walden*.

Arguably the most famous and discussed passage in *Walden* is Thoreau's description of a thawing sandbank in "Spring." This sandbank, he explains, is in the "sides of a deep cut on the railroad" that he passes on his "way to the village," and gives him "delight" to behold (544). In reading this scene in tandem with "The Pond in Winter," I am interested in thinking about the Spring chapter in slightly less commonplace ways. That is, I want to hold onto the uncertainty evident in Thoreau's disorientation caused by the iceless pond in winter (and more specifically the complex interactions between economics, technology, natural cycles, human and nonhuman inhabitants) while examining Thoreau's attention to the complex integrations occurring in the thawing bank. It is my impression that this scene, while more recently read for its important attentiveness to materiality, its intriguing openness to extended engagement with the grotesque, and its blurring of nature/culture boundaries, is still too fully understood through the lens of readings that prioritize the optimistic depiction of Spring as rebirth and reawakening.

The hybridity of the scene is first and most obviously present in Thoreau's description of the bank's thawing process. For instance, over the course of one rather dense and metaphor-laden paragraph, Thoreau describes the bank as indicative of how "blood vessels are formed," as reminiscent of "the sources of rivers," and finally as an exemplary model to raise the now famous question: "What is man but a mass of thawing clay?" Thoreau leads us in this moment from the inner biology of the (human) animal body to the natural cycles and geographic realities of a river system, all in order to finally draw a parallel between the human body and the clay of the earth. It is important to note, as is now customary, that this bank is cut along the railroad line and therefore is from the start a mix of technological innovation and natural cycles as well. As Thoreau admits, though this phenomenon might still be a relatively rare occurrence, "the number of freshly exposed banks of the right material must have been greatly multiplied since railroads were invented" (545). This "hybrid product," like Walden's ice before it, is multiplicity and amalgam.

As Thoreau describes it, the sandbank becomes a hybrid product that follows the laws of both liquid and solid mass simultaneously. He explains, as the sandbank thaws, "Innumerable little streams overlap and interlace one with another, exhibiting a sort of hybrid product, which obeys half way the law of currents, and half way that of vegetation" (545). Inspired by the boundary-blurring imagery he reads into the railroad cut, Thoreau leans into an extended meditation upon the materiality of human existence. Reminiscent of his treatment of the commodified ice of the pond, the careful attention to the materiality of the bank breaks down supposed borders between the animate and inanimate, the human and the nonhuman, as streams of inanimate melting clay become animal blood vessels. Thoreau explains, "[I]t is somewhat excrementitious in its character, and there is no end to the heaps of liver, lights, and bowels, as if the globe were turned wrong side outward; but this suggests at least that Nature has some bowels, and there again is mother of humanity" (549). Thoreau values, and even lauds, this sandbank for its "excrementitious character"—it is good to be inside-out! This destabilization of perception, the inside-out quality of nothing less than a new creation story (as the "bowels" of the bank signify nature as humanity's "mother") serves as a stark and riveting, albeit also somewhat revolting, depiction of the embodied species-being. Again, Barad is instructive here, as she explores this disruptive concept in her work on distributed agency: "As boundaries are reconfigured," she writes, "'interior' and 'exterior' are reworked. That is, through the enfolding of phenomena, as part of the dynamics of iterative intra-activity, the domains of 'interior' and 'exterior' lose their previous designations" (Barad 2007, 181). As a consequence, she continues, we are confronted with a "spatiality [that] is intra-actively produced. It is an ongoing process of the material (re)configuring of boundaries" (181). In Thoreau's description of the melting sandbank, accepted and expected borders are transgressed and the reader is also confronted with their own corporeality (and even their mortality), through close examination of the "blood vessels" of the sand (of the material earth). The human body then becomes, not individual and impermeable, but rather almost as "excrementitious," as pervious and oozing, as the sandbank itself.

The melting ice of Walden and the railroad-cut sandbank each seems to ignite Thoreau's interest in the permeable and dynamic borders between animate nature, material objects, and the human body. It is intriguing that the thawing bank fosters an optimism and hope in Thoreau, and it is important to note that this is far from an idealized wilderness scene, or even a pastoral garden. The bank as a hybrid-object becomes a wounded and even bloody borderland. It is also, ultimately, the unintentional result of an assemblage of forces combined in the technological (the engineering equipment and industrial tools) and the natural (seasonal cycles, physics, etc.). The melting bank is unpredictable, unmanageable, and temporary. From Thoreau's vantage point, it appears not fully practical and refuses simple instrumentalization; it destabilizes the intended transformation of this particular slab of earth into mechanized purposiveness and a mere conduit of capital (as the ice of Walden Pond did for its own process of commodification). Seeing the bank's "bowels" confronts the viewer with the lack of clear and consistent borders between that which the humanist might prefer to see as separated and stable entities. Yet, Thoreau does also contend that if we can only decipher this inner message, we can "turn over a new leaf at last," via a sustained attention to the minutia of the thawing, inside-out earth and the scientific-poetic processes it inspires in the participatory scientist-artist. Hybrid-objects elicit compound ideas; dualisms dissolve and multiplicities abound.

For certain, the hybrid, disorienting, and unbounded qualities of the sandbank thoroughly astound Thoreau. Writing of this same scene, Jedediah Purdy reflects, "This vital, filthy, gorgeous unity persuades him that the earth is alive at every point, and only beginning its passage into future forms" (Purdy 2015, 149). "Vital, filthy and gorgeous" all at once, for sure. I am less certain about unity, however. There is, of course, unity in amalgamation. But we should also be sure to linger long enough upon the dissolving, the melting, and the oozing, and not try to reorganize it too quickly into a unitary and bounded singularity. If some sort of unity will indeed reconstitute itself, it certainly must be a different kind of union than previously known. Thoreau's hybrid-objects suggest a more relational and open system than a holistic, bounded, and singular unit, wherein the interdependency of the parts disrupts the boundedness of the whole. Purdy is probably more onto this when he writes: "For Thoreau, insight into nature seems to arise from, even require, rupture and profanation" (151). To fully comprehend Thoreau's relevancy to environmental theory in the Anthropocene, we cannot be afraid to dwell in the rupture, occupy the profane, think and act from within that which is undone.

Parabolic Walks

Patrick Chura, in his excellent study of the relationship between Thoreau's literary life and his work as a surveyor, adds another intriguing layer to the sandbank scene and the question of unity. While describing the process Thoreau undertook to make his famous map of Walden Pond, Chura highlights a further (and clearly intentional) connection between the human, the nonhuman and the sociotechnological in Thoreau's thought. He points out, "By sighting his cabin from the center of the pond and the railroad embankment, Thoreau created a three-sided figure that brought key locations into a form of contact with each other" (Chura 2010, 31). In examining early field notes of Thoreau's survey of the pond, Chura is able to determine that "Thoreau recorded a numerical bearing between these points and used that bearing to create his sketch" (31). Chura is quite right then when he suggests the "idea that the surveyor determined the position of each location using the other two—that each location was a vertex of a planned triangle—is thought provoking" (32). This seems another way of thinking about the unity of a place: interdependent parts in relational kinship, a togetherness dependent upon each part that remains elastic, possibly even transitory. Thus, the perceived larger whole, as quickly as it appears, turns our attention back to its relational parts.

Walden's remapping ultimately subverts the reader's expectations in at least two specific ways. First of all, as Chura explains, the pond is presented upside-down, in that the north end of the pond is at the bottom of the sketch. Secondly, property and town lines that Thoreau well knew crossed close by Walden's shores are nowhere to be seen. Instead, the three highlighted features of the landscape are Thoreau's cabin, the railroad line, and a carefully surveyed Walden Pond complete with length, breadth, and depth. As a result, "To simply say that Thoreau's priorities differ from professional norms seems inadequate," Chura suggests, "In turning his map upside down and eliminating property lines, he gave his reader a cartograph that was the inverse of utilitarianism, rejecting key tenets of both mapmaking and land surveying as accepted cultural norms" (40). The reader's attention is drawn instead to the cabin, the pond, and the railroad in turn. And, further, if one lingers long enough on any one of the three, its connection to the other two becomes clear, as each forms a corner of an almost perfect isosceles triangle. Could this triangulation suggest a particular reorientation of the human-in-place as well? As Purdy notices in his own study of this scene: "Walden takes place, quite self-consciously, in a landscape transformed by long and intensive habitation. Thoreau tells us the woods around the pond has been cleared, that boats have sunk to its bottom, that it is regularly harvested for its ice" (151). This noninstrumental mapping also models a type of agency that is complexly distributed across the landscape, the human presence, and particular cultural and technological systems. Again, relationality is the key. "There is nothing pristine in this place," Purdy reminds us, "no basis for a fantasy of original and permanent nature. There is only a choice among relationships with and attitudes toward ever-changed places" (151).

We have already explored the sandbank's depiction as a hybrid product: a simultaneously natural and cultural cut in the earth onto which Thoreau invests one of his most famous odes to the excess, dynamism, and beauty of nature. Thoreau's surveying process, and its literary resonation, now draws the railroad bank even deeper into the relational space that Thoreau envisioned for Walden Pond and its surrounding woods. Thoreau's attention to hybridity, border spaces, and alternative mapping strategies, with an emphasis on a process of relational knowing, might offer something slightly new for contemporary environmental theory. As Branka Arsic has argued, "Thoreau's treatment of the world in terms of relations" operates to "incessantly remake it" (Arsic 2016, 314). But what do these relations make? What is emerging within and through these coalitions? We need to press on just a little farther to get a better sense of the environmental politics that might emerge from the confluence, as described above, of relational knowledges and hybrid agencies, and how exactly this is relevant for social movement organizing in the posthuman and postnatural context of the Anthropocene.

In his analysis of Thoreau's posthumously published essay "Walking," Chura is particularly struck by Thoreau's hesitancy to embrace closure as he examines the following passage from the essay: "The outline which would bound my walks would be, not a circle, but a parabola, or rather like one of those cometary orbits which have been thought to be non-returning curves, in this case opening westward, in which my hours occupies the place of the sun" ("Walking"). Thoreau's insistence on a parabola takes on a particular significance to Chura, as he points out this is distinctly not the "straight line or closed circle" that a professional surveyor would be compelled to walk (Chura 2010, 167). In fact, "Proposing the parabola as an alternative life course means that Thoreau is positioning himself in an unvaryingly mediary space with his 'house' as the focus . . . it also reintroduces open-endedness as a means of counteracting the implacably delimited profiles surveyors usually create" (168). Thoreau's remapping of Walden Pond is one that constructs a relation between human and nonhuman communities that refuses closure, instead privileging contingency, rupture, and impermanence. "Through his adoption of the parabola as his sauntering objective," Chura concludes, "Thoreau metaphorically refuses to close his survey" (169). Hybridity forestalls closure and categorization over and over again. This remapping of Walden Pond as a place of relational parts that remains open, unfinished, and as yet incomplete, which can as well be seen as a symbolic limning of the possible for hybrid, nature-culture futures, displays a unity founded upon—rather than delimitation—an open-ended limitlessness.

Thoreau's parabola as an alternative path for being, acting, and thinking in the myriad hybrid nature-culture assemblages in which we live, provides a promising new shape for distributed environmental theory and politics for the Anthropocene. It is not necessarily for answers that we should turn to Thoreau, however, nor should we attempt to define and label his work for one corner of ecocritical theory or another. Instead, this chapter has turned to Thoreau in an attempt to retrieve and renew the focus upon the contradictions and inconsistencies regarding the nature/culture binary that he failed to necessarily resolve. A focus upon the vexed border between form and chaos leads Thoreau to strive toward a practice of Relational Knowing and motivates his engagement with the intersections of human and nonhuman agency. Useful Ignorance also implies that you can inhabit a sort of border space between the two apparently contradictory aims if only the positioned subject is willing/able to practice the humility of learning to learn differently. Inhabiting two contradictory ideas, that is, really only becomes a contradiction if one thinks their thinking, if you will, is complete. It is within Thoreau's willingness to dwell in spaces of contradiction that I find potential in returning and learning from his intense engagement with the nature-culture of Concord's woods. The open-endedness of Thoreau's survey, the refusal of material and philosophical closure, is in good part what makes his writing relevant to contemporary environmental theory generally and this project specifically.

Thoreau's discussion of the swamp in "Walking" delivers sustained attention to the "muck" of the earth, and the "swamps" of the landscape continue at key moments in the essay. Though some moments in this passage might be read as a type of instrumentalism, for instance, when he muses: "A man's health requires as many acres of meadow to his prospect as his farm does loads of muck. These are the strong meats on which he feeds" (Thoreau 1982, 613), it is also clearly possible, and I think quite productive, to read these passages and Thoreau's broader argument for "sauntering" as more than merely a romantic exaltation of nature. Instead, reading the swamp as another hybrid-place in the Concord woods raises a more fundamental challenge to the privileged position of the empirical (and disembodied) observer through their detailed mediation upon hybridity and fragmentation. Thoreau sees this possibility for interaction as the attuned human Saunterer does "sometimes find himself" in this other-than-human place; this is the possibility for inhabiting and studying the border spaces that motivates Thoreau's ruminations throughout the essay. He seems to be searching for a way of seeing that allows for the decentered human and this denatured nature to interact, to learn about each other through the conjoined inhabitation of liminality. This sustained engagement with the intersection of hybrid-places, hybrid-objects, and hybrid-agencies is a search for new ways of *being, seeing, and knowing* that might emanate from the muck, rather than from thin air.

Relational Knowing facilitates an important conceptual move away from the holistic nature of much ecocentric and/or deep green philosophy. Attending to this "mixture," the porous and permeable borders, rather than the supposedly distinctive qualities of the human, the nonhuman animal and the material world, operates on multiple levels. Thoreau's concept of Useful Ignorance and insistence upon inhabiting the densest and most complex of intersecting relations, which I see as a predecessor to Haraway's recent call for "staying with the trouble" in the era of climate change (or, as she prefers, the Chtulecene), is a productive manner of engaging with the posthuman world's entangled agencies and hybrid subjectivities.[20] While I agree that deconstructing the nature/culture dualism that reifies human agency brings human mastery into question, it is also increasingly apparent one must be very careful not to assume that this layer-peeling will offer a new, singular, and stable environmental ethic, either. I fear we pretend to know too much when we assert the postanthropocentric, decentered subject is definitionally a more ecological one. In the next chapters, I will further explore the potential, and the serious challenges, such a commitment to openness, permeability, hybridity, and a decentered human subject raises for environmental humanities scholarly practice and the sociopolitical movements that aim to refashion our world into a more just and ecological society. Before doing so, rather than attempting to reconfigure this monumental thinker into simply a monument for yet another environmental theory, I instead want to credit Thoreau with an intensely worthwhile engagement with a set of problematics that, as they bedeviled his own writing, continue to trouble environmental scholarship and activism today.

3

Bacterial Insurgency in Karen Tei Yamashita's *Through the Arc of the Rainforest*

> Modern humanists are reductionist because they seek to attribute action to a small number of powers, leaving the rest of the world with nothing but simple mute forces. It is true that by redistributing the action among all these mediators, we lose the reduced form of humanity, but we gain another form, which has to be called irreducible. The human is in the delegation itself, in the pass, in the sending, in the continuous exchange of forms. Of course it is not a thing, but things are not things either.
>
> —Bruno Latour, *We Have Never Been Modern*

Karen Tei Yamashita's *Through the Arc of the Rainforest* depicts the rise and fall of a socioeconomic infrastructure dependent upon the extraction, production, and hyper-consumption of a newly discovered, all-purpose resource in the Brazilian rainforest. The eventual collapse of this system, near the end of the novel, is an event produced by a complex mixture of the human (cultural and economic flows of products, consumers, and information) and the nonhuman (a deadly Typhus virus and a mysterious "devouring bacteria" that feed upon the new material). Yamashita's narrative, in its attentiveness to mixture and interconnection, brings together a myriad of environmental, social, economic, and political forces that destabilize a series of conventionally accepted binaries: including the human and nonhuman, the local and global, and empirical and traditional ecological knowledge. As these binaries are explored and disrupted, the novel places agency into question in a manner that, ultimately, destabilizes traditional humanist conceptions of political subjectivity and efficacy.

Through the Arc presents the commodification of resources in the Brazilian rainforest as a threat to both the local human and nonhuman communities, and the social and environmental costs of intense resource extraction practices and global capitalism are also prominently foregrounded in the novel. The plastic-like resource, named Matacao, draws the interest of the GGG Corporation and the company moves its entire headquarters to the Brazilian rainforest, focusing its plentiful resources into the extraction and commodification of the material. The Matacao, which is extracted from the rainforest floor, is easily and miraculously transformed into everything from construction material that is sturdier than metal to hamburgers that prove tastier than the nonsynthetic original. Practically overnight, the GGG Corporation's investments transform the area of its discovery into an industrial site, a tourist destination, and a place of spiritual and religious importance. As the Matacao-based economy seems to be at its peak, however, the human community is suddenly ravaged with disease in the form of a typhus epidemic. The bacteria, traveling via bird feathers, spread quickly across the continent and beyond due to two global trends that develop alongside the discovery and development of the Matacao: Mane Pena's "featherology" and Batista and Thania Djapan's carrier pigeon communication network. Additionally, the nonhuman community is irrevocably damaged by, first, the wholesale spraying of DDT (to halt the typhus epidemic) and, second, another bacterium that literally devours the built environment. This social and economic collapse at the end of the novel is driven by a complex distributed agency comprised of intersecting human (social, economic, and political) and nonhuman (ecological and bacterial) phenomena.

This chapter highlights and places two central elements of the novel into conversation with each other (and with contemporary environmental scholarship more broadly): first, the novel's attentiveness to the issue of environmental (in)justice, and, second, how this attention to the complex interdependency of human and nonhuman communities leads to a destabilization of humanist conceptions of political agency in the culminating scenes of the novel. The narrative is driven by distributed agency to fascinating affect; however, the novel's problematic grasping for narrative closure foregrounds the difficulty of imagining political change without a traditional human activist-subject. The novel's ambivalence regarding the decentralization of the human subject, furthermore, raises important questions that scholars and activists will have to address if we hope to decipher distributed agency's potential impacts upon contemporary sociopolitical organizing. This literary reimagining of the relationship between the distributed nature of agency and sociopolitical organizing might well have significant implications for environmental justice (EJ) scholarship and activism. That is, while the EJ movement focuses necessary attention upon the complex relation between questions of social inequality and environmental degradation, it must also find effective organizing strategies that remain cognizant of the limitations of human knowledge and the rational and intentional human actor.

I highlight the significance for EJ theory and activism in particular because its core tenets are deeply invested in the disruption of the nature/culture binary, particularly within its attempt to bring attention to the socioeconomic structures that result in highly uneven exposure (based in race, class, and gender) to pollution across communities. Therefore, EJ theory is both already a fertile intellectual space for considering materialist theory's disruption of anthropocentrism and should demand a significant role in ongoing considerations of postanthropocentric subjectivities. In addition, particularly robust and trenchant scholarship in Indigenous Studies in recent years has pointed out that models for subjectivity and agency that operate outside Western ideologies already exist, and have existed for millennia, within native cultures, spiritualities, and sciences. This chapter, and the next, explore two quite different novels of environmental justice fiction in order to more fully interrogate the relationship between postanthropocentric agency, social movement organizing, and nonlinear conceptions of temporality. These readings of *Through the Arc of the Rainforest* and Silko's *Almanac of the Dead* bring into relief a similar preoccupation in each novel; that is, how to represent an effective political resistance to transnational global capitalism in a way that moves beyond what have proven to be the demonstrably ineffective models based in the existing forms afforded by Western liberal democracy.

Insurgent Bacteria

While examining the intimate relationship between environmental degradation and social injustice, EJ scholar Giovanna Di Chiro has argued that the concept of social reproduction is a particularly helpful tool. By developing an understanding of the environment as the varied spaces in which humans "live, work, and play," Di Chiro illuminates the importance of social reproduction theory as a theoretical tool that can help to more effectively integrate the environmental and social justice movements. "Most environmental justice activists' discussions of nature," she explains, "are balanced with an analysis of the impossibility of separating it from 'life,' from cultural histories, and from socially and ecologically destructive colonial and neocolonial experiences" (Di Chiro 1995, 317). It is important to note that social reproduction entails more than simple physical health, in that it also draws attention to the close relation between environmental sustainability and cultural practice. Understanding environmental and social justice issues and movements in a more integrated fashion brings to light the importance of rethinking the relationship between human and nonhuman communities as well. In this manner, "environmental struggles are about fighting for and ensuring *social reproduction* . . . it is the women (and men) activists fighting for environmental justice who have most convincingly foregrounded the everyday life (and death) stakes at the root of their environmental politics" (285). A threat to a community's health and its cultural futurity, as described here, is a challenge to the environmental and cultural foundations necessary for the functioning of a given community. Borrowing from EJ scholars Anne Whitt and Jennifer Slack, Di Chiro elaborates upon the concept of "mixed-communities" in order to emphasize the deep and too often unrecognized mutual dependencies between the human and nonhuman environments, and attempts to destabilize the persistent binary between the two (318).[1] When one considers mixed-communities, suddenly the relational and interdependent coexistence of the human, nonhuman animals, and nonhuman environment is brought to the fore, widening the scope of who and what counts as a community member and changes the calculations for community evaluations of what is good, and what is not, for its members.

Echoing Di Chiro, Eric Schlosberg and David Carruthers define socioenvironmental injustice as any impediment to the infrastructure of a particular mixed-community.[2] Building upon Amartya Sen's capabilities-theory of justice, Schlosberg and Carruthers further clarify the concept of social reproduction as key to the environmental justice movement. According to the authors, "Indigenous leaders . . . articulate environmental injustice as a set of conditions that remove or restrict the ability of individuals and communities to function fully—conditions that undermine their health, destroy economic and cultural livelihoods, or present general environmental threats" (Schlosberg and Carruthers 2010, 18). Foregrounding the stories of thirteen Indigenous American Tribes fighting to preserve sacred lands in the San Francisco Peaks of Arizona and the struggle of Chile's indigenous Mapuche against industrial development in their ancestral lands, Schlosberg and Carruthers describe the threat to these Indigenous peoples' land as necessarily environmental and cultural at once, and therefore it is most accurately understood as a battle for social reproduction (17–18). Attention to these types of activist approaches will help environmental justice scholars reimagine our understanding of, and approach to, issues of injustice that jointly effect human and nonhuman communities. Additionally, the roles mixed-community and social reproduction play in *Through the Arc*'s depiction of environmental justice compel readers to recognize that these complex nature-culture entanglements ultimately destabilize humanist conceptions of subjectivity and agency. That is, if the humans are not fully separable from the materiality of their own environment, then how do we understand their individual and collective ability to act from within this materially embedded position?

Political theorist Timothy Mitchell's writings on historical progress consistently complicate contemporary political assumptions as he critically engages with foundational concepts of modernity, such as the economy, progress, and democracy. I return to Mitchell's work here because of his persistent and in-depth engagement with the complicated relationship between historical progress and agency, which dominant approaches to political theory often overlook. In so doing, I also hope to put Mitchell's work on agency in political theory into conversation with new materialist and posthuman theories of agency. In his book *Rule of Experts*, Mitchell produces a revisionist history of World War II–era colonial Egypt in which he deconstructs the simple binary understanding of war as an unnatural, man-made phenomenon and disease as a natural, or other-than-human, event. Mitchell implores scholars of political history to not engage with any issue having "already decided who counts as an agent" (Mitchell 2002, 29). The chapter "Can the Mosquito Speak?" chronicles three major developments that combined to bring a nonnative, malaria-infected mosquito into a newly transformed, epidemic-conducive environment. First, he cites changes to the local and regional environment created by the construction of the Aswan dam. Second, local food shortages, partly because key fertilizers had been redirected toward military weapons facilities, left workers undernourished. And, third, infrastructure instabilities and safety concerns created by the war led to a change from sea-based to land-based shipping routes. This "chain of events in Egypt seem to create a triangle, formed by the interconnection of war, disease, and agriculture. . . . But there are no accounts that take seriously how these elements interact. . . . They shape one another, yet their heterogeneity offers a resistance to explanation" (27). This resistance, Mitchell argues, emanates from modernity's imagining of the "movement of history . . . [as] the power of reason to expand the scope of human freedom" (1). Consequently, the dynamic and intensely intertwined relationship between technology, agriculture, war, and bacterial disease (which, he argues, leads to the unnecessary death of thousands of laborers) is ignored and the stories remain separate: war and technology on one side of the narrative and disease and famine on the other.

Mitchell posits that a fuller recognition of what he terms "hybrid-agency," in which nonhuman communities are understood to have more than a simply passive role in an unfolding history created entirely by human-centered, rational agency, would radically alter our understanding of events such as the malaria epidemic among the Aswan Dam workers. He also clarifies, however, that these postanthropocentric accounts of agency simply do not fit comfortably into modernism's conceptual understanding of human reason and unchallenged agency. In fact, Mitchell's work highlights the sharp contrast between theories of distributed agency and traditional historical narratives. The dominant traditional narrative, he argues, operates to naturalize imperial practices via interpreting developments of domination as the undeniable progress of human reason and an increasingly unfettered agency over the nonhuman world. As a result, he argues for rethinking agency as dispersed between the human and nonhuman world in order to better account for the complexity of historical change. This would entail

> making this issue of power and agency a question, instead of an answer known in advance. . . . It requires acknowledging that human agency, like capital, is a technical body, is something made. Instead of invoking the force and logic of reason, self-interest, science, or capital and attributing what happens in the world to the working of these enchanted powers and processes, we can open up the question . . . of what kinds of hybrid agencies, connections, interactions and forms of violence are able to portray their actions as history, as human expertise overcoming nature, as the progress of reason and modernity,

or as the expansion and development of capitalism. (Mitchell 2002, 53)

Mitchell's call for critical attentiveness to questions of historical narrative and how we understand the creation of environmental and social injustices draws attention to a fundamental connection between the concepts of social reproduction and distributed agency. That is, when we move beyond the assumption that environmental degradation, or ecosystem restoration, for that matter, is a solely human-caused process of despoliation (or preservation) of a passive nonhuman nature, then we can begin to more seriously consider which cultural and political practices of "social reproduction" are most effective within the context of a radically altered human/nonhuman relationship.

While Mitchell utilizes the term *hybrid-agency* to denote a postanthropocentric concept of agency (as outlined above), throughout this book I have chosen to phrase it as *distributed agency*. I have been and continue to use *distributed* in lieu of *hybrid* to better draw attention to my particular understanding of the implications of a posthuman conception of agency (closely aligned with and indebted to Karen Barad's concepts of intra-action and agential realism). That is, the phrase *hybrid-agency*, as Mitchell uses it, lends itself to a conceptualization of agency in which multiple agents (human and nonhuman) convene to create historical change. On the other hand, and more attuned to the radical import of this concept, *distributed agency* highlights the always already interconnected, overlapping, and dispersed elements of agency. More than just multiple *actants* (to borrow from Jane Bennett borrowing from Bruno Latour) operating discreetly upon each other, it is more precisely that agency is mixture from the start. Moreover, Mitchell argues persuasively that hybrid-agency, when more fully considered, will prove (productively) disruptive to dominant views of history; however, he does not engage with the implications for political activism and social movement practice. If taken seriously, a more nuanced understanding of the complex relationship between human and nonhuman agency will fundamentally alter our understanding of historical change and, in turn, political agency. By definition, then, distributed agency (in line with the broader theories of disanthropocentric subjectivities) disrupts the humanist model for the rational, autonomous, intentional human actor. As suggested earlier, intentionality as a discrete property of the human individual is no longer a safe assumption.[3]

Yamashita's novel conjures a set of more-than-human agents of change, in fact, which we might term *insurgent bacteria,* in order to represent the only effective resistance to global capital's incursion into the Brazilian rainforest. This chapter, in turn, explores the importance of distributed agency in the novel's plot in order to determine the ways in which attentiveness to environmental agency decenters the human actor and breaks down dominant perceptions of the nature/culture binary. While the concept of distributed agency does not, of course, leave us with an entirely passive human (political) subject, it does raise "questions about the way the modern world is divided—into objects and ideas, nature and culture, reality and its representation, the nonhuman and the human" (Mitchell 2002, 10). The novel presents the impacts of (and resistance to) socioenvironmental exploitation in the Brazilian rainforest in a manner that, ultimately, destabilizes traditional humanist views of intentional agency. The exploitative practices of the GGG Corporation in the novel, indicative of the logics of transnational capitalism, also present a threat to the region's fundamental processes of social reproduction. As a result, the climactic moments of the novel are predicated upon an understanding of historical change based upon distributed, rather than human-centered, agency. Furthermore, the novel's culmination, more than merely indicative of Mitchell's or Barad's theories, actually complicates the theory of distributed agency further by raising the following question: Once the human actor is decentered from the narrative of historical change, what becomes of political agency itself? My reading of the novel that follows will attempt to grapple with the fact that the newly decentered human subject cannot suddenly be reconstituted as the sole agent of history when circumstances make it politically convenient. So, what forms, we should ask, might a distributed political agency take? It is with this new, irrevocably decentered human subject in mind that we now turn to Yamashita's fictional depiction of the environmental and social costs of resource extraction and transnational capitalism in the Brazilian rainforest.

The casual reader might conceivably ask whether or not the novel is merely an imaginative but fairly routine depiction of "nature striking back" against an extractive capitalism that is destroying a seemingly "pristine" environment. However, sustained attention to the representations of social reproduction and distributed agency in *Through the Arc* will clarify how the novel forestalls a reading based upon such simple binaries. Early in the novel, as the GGG Corporation grows its business in the Matacao, capitalism's ability to co-opt the natural resources, human spirituality, sociocultural interests, and traditional local knowledge of the Matacao region into its market logics appears to be endless. The entire natural and social world of the Brazilian rainforest is reconfigured: Indigenous knowledge of the healing powers of Brazilian bird feathers is transformed into a world-wide consumer craze, a couple's hobby and passion for messenger pigeons is turned into a highly profitable info-service, and Matacao plastic becomes the most fantastical and versatile commodity imaginable.

Despite the shock to the scientific world upon discovery of the Matacao, local inhabitant Mane Pena has long been well aware of this strange substance comprising the surrounding rainforest floor. As the government, international corporations, the media, and tourists from all over the world begin to descend upon the Matacao, we are told that Pena always knew that "the primeval forest was not primeval" (Yamashita 1990, 16). Pena's knowledge is confirmed when it is discovered that the Matacao plastic is the literal detritus of the industrial revolution and the global imperialist projects it spawned. In fact, the Matacao was formed when "[e]normous landfills of non-biodegradable material buried under virtually every populated part of the Earth had undergone tremendous pressure . . . liquid deposits of the molten mass had been squeezed through underground veins to virgin areas of the Earth. The Amazon Forest, being one of the last virgin areas on Earth, got plenty" (202). Interestingly, the trope of a *pristine nature* is simultaneously deployed and delegitimized in the telling of the Matacao's creation and discovery. As Ursula Heise astutely notes in her reading of the novel's disruption of the simple binary between the local and global, "A landscape where digging into the soil leads not to rock or roots but polymer makes implausible any return to nature via the immersion into the local" (Heise 2008, 102). The rainforest is presented as an amalgam of the human and the nonhuman, or a mixed community. And the Matacao itself, reminiscent of Thoreau's depictions of his surroundings at Walden Pond, is a hybrid-object. Literary scholar Molly Wallace has also suggested the Matacao substance operates as a *quasi-object*; at once a natural and cultural artifact. She quite correctly points out "the novel doesn't eliminate hybrids back to nature" but rather "makes them recognizable" (Wallace 2000, 151). Wallace then goes on to persuasively argue for a postmodern ecology that moves beyond the conceptual framework of modernism.[4]

Building from Wallace's reading of the novel, I will suggest that when quasi or hybrid-objects, such as the Matacao, are foregrounded in this way, these examples of what Wallace terms "denatured nature" present serious questions about the nature of agency itself. Similarly to Wallace, I also find it productive to approach *Through the Arc* as a theoretical model in its own right. However, it is a theoretical model that I hope to show remains (productively) incomplete. That is, if we understand the novel to be calling traditionally defined human-produced political agency into question, the conclusion becomes much more than a simple warning for readers to heed regarding the vagaries of extractive capitalism or the fragility of nature. When we more fully accept the disruptive capabilities of distributed subjectivities and hybrid-objects, we also leave space open for the immense potentiality of these transformative entities. We might, as Braidotti suggests, "explore the possibility that these 'hybrid' social identities and the new modes of multiple belonging they enact may . . . pave the way for an ethical regrounding of social participation and community building" (Braidotti 2010, 204).[5] Wallace closes her reading of *Through the Arc* by suggesting that increased attention to what "goes on in the middle" of these assemblages will lead to knowledge capable of helping humans "be more careful" (Wallace 2000, 151). While I am sympathetic to Wallace's hopes and find Braidotti's critical optimism inspiring, it is important to note that when we suggest humans be "careful," we reassert a rational and privileged human agency that is capable of practicing restraint as much as it is capable of carelessness. And here arises the crux of the problem: when *act* does not equal *result*, the modernist construct of agency begins to unravel to a point where we can no longer assume that knowledge alone is *power*. According to Barad, since "we are not outside observers of the world," and, additionally, are "a part of the world" and always "located [in] particular places," then "knowing is a matter of intra-acting" as well (Barad 2007, 184, 149). To be sure, the distributed ways of seeing and knowing the world that Barad outlines, and that are also expressed in Haraway's situated knowledges and Thoreau's relational knowing, are then intimately connected to distributed agency; together, these embedded and material practices of being, learning, and acting in the world inevitably reorient our sense of the limitations for, and potential of, societal-scale intervention into environmental systems (within which we now understand ourselves to be fully embedded).

Once fully operational, as one might expect, the GGG Corporation is at first fantastically successful in extracting, producing, and marketing this hybrid-object as a fantastically versatile commodity. These are the bread and butter practices of extractive capitalism, after all. Kazumasa Ishimaru, who due to a mostly unexplained childhood accident has a tiny satellite-like ball constantly hovering six inches from his head, quickly becomes central to GGG's new expansion plans.[6] This close relationship between Kazumasa, a transplant to Brazil from Japan, and his mysterious satellite-ball companion, which somehow also doubles as the novel's narrator, presents yet another layer of hybridity in the novel. The satellite-narrator explains early on: "It might be said that we [the satellite and Kazumasa] were friends, but although we were much closer, we were never referred to as such" (Yamashita 1990, 3). The reference to a more intimate relationship between the object and its human host than the narrator quite knows how to explain, suggests a heterogeneous and dispersed posthuman embodiment that encompasses Kazumasa, the satellite-ball, and the Matacao itself. As it turns out, the satellite, sharing some deep connection to the Matacao, has the ability to sense the location of undiscovered Matacao from seemingly any distance. This creates a complex relational entanglement eclipsing easy subject and object differentiation: Where does Kazumasa, as subject, end and where does the satellite begin? How do the shared and overlapping qualities of the satellite ball and the Matacao impact Kazumasa's sense of self, as his dispersed embodiment spreads out across the Brazilian rainforest and the transnational infrastructure of GGG's global supply chains for the Matacao?

GGG's president, J. B. Tweep, soon learns of Kazumasa's satellite and its mysterious ability to detect new deposits of Matacao and instantly jumps at the financial opportunity. Tweep concedes that GGG, "could start to chip away at one obscure end of the thing [the main deposit of Matacao rubber], but this place is crawling with scientists and environmentalists, with tourists to boot. Someone's bound to notice, and when we get going, we are going to need a lot of Matacao" (113). As Kazumasa is shuttled around the continent in search of new deposits, the satellite-narrator informs us of the breadth of the ongoing resource extraction.

> JB was ruthless in his expectations, weaving and tossing GGG's net farther and farther, oblivious to any obstacles . . . acres of flooded forest . . . hundreds of species of plant and animal life bulldozed under, rotting and stinking for miles in every direction; Indian homelands, their populations decimated by influenza. (Yamashita 1990, 144)

The destructive process of imperialist resource extraction has drastic and disruptive impacts, to say the least, upon the local mixed-community's social reproduction. The GGG Corporation, whose mobile headquarters is literally moved from New York to the edge of the Matacao piece by piece, constitutes a transnational corporation without any real investment in U.S. nationalist aspirations or any significant regard for national boundaries and interests. The company operates within the novel, instead, as an example of global capital's unregulated corporate profit seeking and orchestrates what is essentially a second enclosure of the commons.

The discovery of the Matacao material is paralleled by the discovery of Mane Pena's extensive knowledge concerning the healing powers of particular bird feathers. This knowledge is presented as a type of traditional ecological knowledge and through this healing practice, which comes to be known as "featherology," Yamashita investigates the collision of empirical science and local knowledge. The GGG Corporation's instant success in commodifying both these resources first displaces Pena from his local village and then co-opts him into the feather business in a dual role of company spokesman and scientific expert. As featherology catches on around the globe, J.B. Tweep and his corporation capture the market on all styles of healing feathers. He explains, "We've anticipated everything. Cases, accessories, post-yuppie tastes . . . that is top of the line, for the more affluent customer . . . But we've got a sort of Bic line, less expensive and by the pack . . . we're also looking into a line of disposable stuff using dyed chicken feathers" (106). This commodification of bird feathers offers a glimpse into the intersections between corporate profit-motive on a global scale and the way in which alternative local cultural trends are quickly commodified and assimilated into the structures of global capital. Even more importantly, we should note that capital here is only one element, albeit a powerful one, of a complex and distributed set of systems, logics and agencies that lead to the ultimate destruction of these very birds, whole communities of humans, and the ecological health of the Matacao region.

Ultimately, even more quickly than it was constructed, the economic empire of GGG is quite suddenly undone by two distinct catastrophic events that are linked only by the fact that the main perpetrator in each case is a microscopic nonhuman bacterium. The first causes a deadly outbreak of typhus, and the second bacterium mysteriously devours the Matacao plastic itself (destroying the built environment and economic structure based upon this all-purpose resource). The deadly typhus epidemic, spread by the popular consumer product (Brazilian bird feathers) and the throwback global communication system (messenger pigeons), moves quickly to nearby regions. The bacteria's biological behavior is represented as highly conducive to the newly configured human and nonhuman landscapes of the Brazilian rainforest. "Rickettsia were microorganisms that traveled via a minute species of lice, which in turn traveled via feathers, which, of course, traveled via birds and, of late, humans" (198). In fact, the very networks of exchange created by the imperialist practices of the GGG Corporation, originally meant to transport people, products, and information around the globe, now transport the small bacteria, Rickettsia, and facilitate the uncontrollably fast outbreak of disease.

While neither a conventionally defined human nor nonhuman agency is solely responsible for the severity and speed with which the typhus spreads, the mixed-community of the rainforest is nonetheless devastated by the result. The outbreak results in the death of thousands of Brazilians, including Mane Pena himself, as well as the destruction of huge swaths of the Amazon habitat. Tragically, in order to manage or limit the scope of the outbreak, the government responds by ordering a mass dispersal of DDT to eradicate the bird population of the forest. Government officials determine that, "Banning feathers was not enough.... It would be necessary to go to the source ... no birds could be spared if the disease were to be eradicated" (199). This devastating outbreak of typhus attests to the novel's attention to the confluence of human and nonhuman networks of exchange and the way in which these complex interactions create historical change. The resistance to explanation via simple binaries propels the reader toward an engagement with the everyday interactions between humans, human technology, nonhuman animals, microscopic organisms, and other actants that together comprise distributed agency.

Not long after the typhus outbreak, Kazumasa's satellite-ball suddenly begins to disintegrate due to what is described only as a "devouring bacteria" (206). It is quickly discovered that this second bacteria is having the same effect upon the entire "plastic world" created by GGG. In fact, "The tiny munching sounds that became so familiar to Kazumasa while he kept a vigil for his dying ball were now a deafening unison" (206). And as the all-purpose Matacao erodes, "People who stepped out in the most elegant finery made of Matacao plastic were horrified to find themselves naked at cocktail parties, undressed at presidential receptions. Cars crumbled at stoplights. Computer monitors sagged ... [t]he credit card industry went into a panic" (206–207). The "plastic-age," which has completely redefined the core infrastructure of the human-built environment in the region, is suddenly in complete ruins due to these previously unknown bacteria. The bacteria manifest at a moment in which transnational corporate capitalism, with its global market structure and profit-motive models, has transformed the built environment and set the table for mass (rather than possibly somewhat more partial) destruction. This is a multilayered, distributed agency at work here in that these bacteria target and feed upon the Matacao plastic, which is itself originally the product of an intricate combination of human and nonhuman agencies. These two narratives do not present agency as singular, but rather as a multiplicity of combined phenomena. Nor does agency belong to either the human or the nonhuman realm, but manifests as an inextricable mixture. The complex interaction between these supposedly impermeable borders refuses explanation based upon currently dominant conceptions of human agency. In this context, it is fair to say the phenomena that bring about the climactic moments of the novel, coalescing in the form of bacterial insurgents, exemplify a form of distributed agency.

Decentered Humans

Yamashita's novel insightfully challenges the neoliberal narrative of globalization in which market rationality and technological expertise exert total control over an inert and passive nonhuman environment. Furthermore, the presentation of a complexly integrated relationship between human and nonhuman agency throughout the novel productively opens up new avenues of inquiry for understanding the causes, and effects, of environmental and social injustice. In this way, the novel reminds us that it is important to locate and problematize any historical account that mobilizes a singular, overarching narrative of agency. However, I also suggest that *Through the Arc* presents us with an even more complicated effect of understanding historical change through the lens of distributed agency. That is, the novel does more than simply disrupt the dominant narrative of transnational predatory capitalism; it also envisions this disruption as an event without a conventionally defined, intentional political subject or activist. This productive destabilization, or decentering, of the liberal human subject, occurs in concert with an intensive exploration of hybridity across human and nonhuman entities.

While the rise and fall of the GGG Corporation's economic empire is certainly based upon particular deployments of economic policy, scientific methodologies, and cultural practices, which create the conditions for this massive threat to social reproduction, the catalyst for this destruction is also a distinctly other-than-human, material agency that operates outside of traditionally defined political subjectivity. There is no environmental organization or other traditional political activism depicted as moving to combat GGG's socially and environmentally destructive practices. Instead, the resistance emanates from unintentional, other-than-human organisms: the typhus-causing Rickettsia and the Matacao-devouring bacteria. Their unintentional, nonhuman agency, however, is also not clearly distinguishable from the human. Rather, the impact of the insurgent bacteria is presented as a complex assemblage of agencies, intimately interwoven with human socioeconomic and political systems that are always already hybridized entities of mixed-community themselves. This is all suggestive of a new construction of corporate power and modes of resistance that propel us into a complex, and at times indistinguishable, mesh of intra-activity and entangled actants.

If Mitchell's goal, in drawing our attention to distributed agency, is to articulate a different logic of history in order to disrupt dominant narratives of historical change that privilege certain singular and human agents of history, my reading of *Through the Arc* is more concerned with the implications of this move toward distributed agency for environmental justice and social movement practice generally. In the end, Yamashita's depiction of distributed agency is not conducive to traditional forms of political activism and organizing. The Rickettsia and "devouring bacteria" appear indicative of a postanthropocentric type of agency (as they create the only form of resistance that the GGG Corporation is unable to subsume into its business model), but this is clearly not a deliberative, conscious agency as typically envisioned. This raises some important questions for scholars and activists committed to thinking through the best practices of resistance to dominant systems of power and maximizing the political efficacy of movements working for environmental and social justice. Distributed agency's productive decentering of the human subject, its emphasis upon humility in the face of socioenvironmental complexity, and its compatibility with important environmental justice concepts such as social reproduction and mixed-community, make it an important conceptual building block in environmental scholarship (and beyond). However, the destabilizing effects of distributed agency, particularly its tendency to complicate the concepts of intentionality and futurity, raise serious questions regarding political agency itself. Consequently, the culmination of *Through the Arc* presses these questions: What is agency without an intentional subject and what exactly are we to make of these insurgent bacteria? And, finally, what type of oppositional political imaginaries can coexist with an increasingly decentered human subject living in a postnatural environment?

To a certain degree, *Through the Arc* suggests that, since there was no traditionally conscious or intentional plan for resistance, the exploitative system will continue as usual. The crumbling Matacao, and the end of GGG's system of profit, is a disruption but not a deviation from the path of neoliberal capitalism. Readers are unfortunately assured that even as the plastic world disintegrates, destruction of the rainforest continues relentlessly in surrounding regions. Near the end of the novel, for instance, as a procession of local people carries their recently deceased religious leader, Chico Paco, from the now disintegrating Matacao to his birthplace on the coast they come across "mining projects tirelessly exhausting treasures of iron, manganese and bauxite" (209). The mourners even pass an ongoing "gold rush" and lose "a third of the procession to the greedy furor" (209). The destruction of the rainforest for capitalist economic expansion continues despite the collapse of the GGG Corporation, productively forestalling a reading that might desire to privilege an oversimplified narrative in which the environment "strikes back" to free itself of human incursion and exploitation forever. Consequently, when one considers the lack of alternative or oppositional political imaginaries, the DDT-laden sections of the rainforest, and the continued destructive resource extraction practices, it becomes difficult for the reader to feel anything akin to hopefulness.

Ultimately, the novel struggles to produce the narrative closure that is expected of the novel form without falling back upon the binary modes of humanist systems of thought. As the narrative winds down, there is a rather surprising and problematic conjuring of the "lost perfection" of a prehuman nature. The narrator discloses that at some point in a not-so-near future, "[t]he old forest has returned once again, secreting its digestive juices, slowly breaking everything into edible absorbent components, pursuing the *lost perfection* of an organism in which digestion and excretion were once one and the same" (212; my emphasis). This conclusion surprisingly reifies the idea of a natural balance within an edenic nature prior to human interference that depends upon an outdated static, rather than dynamic, ecological model. Reinforcing the preservationist trope of a pristine ecological balance that supposedly existed prior to human intervention, the narrator also informs us that, despite its return, this forest can actually "never . . . be the same again" (212). The "lost perfection" of the past is apparently irretrievable.

Within the realm of the human community, a similar binary is also fully reinstated. Kazumasa and his partner Lourdes, with her two children, retreat into the jungle to live the pastoral cliché of farmers hidden away from the vagaries of society. Our final image of these two characters, in fact, is that of a recovered heteronormative family structure reaffirming itself through a connection to their, presumably private, plantation land: "Lourdes put her baskets down on the rich red soil of their land and embraced Kazumasa, who now stood casually with a rather newly formed posture, the sort to accompany, quite naturally, the tropical tilt of his head" (211). After such a provocative portrayal of the interaction between the human and nonhuman in the novel, it is difficult to come to terms with these two rather unsatisfactory final scenes in which Yamashita relies upon several myths (namely those of an edenic nature, the pastoral retreat, and possessive individualism) that are based upon the assumed nature/culture binary that she has so effectively destabilized up to this point.

Environment and literature scholar Ursula Heise, whose analysis of the novel predominantly focuses on the relationship between the local and global in order to trace the contours of what she terms *eco-cosmopolitanism*, also finds Kazumasa's retreat to the pastoral landscape troubling. Heise rightly wonders "how this image of bucolic bliss, of successful reconnection with the rural soil might be compatible not only with the idea of the Matacao as a symbol of the impossibility of such a reconnection but also with the environmental devastation of the Brazilian landscape Yamashita had so eloquently mourned only a page or so earlier" (Heise 2008, 104). I have to agree with Heise when she concludes that "this moment of closure does not quite fit the complexities of the plot" (105). Additionally, it becomes clear that the problem Yamashita faces in concluding *Through the Arc* is one that is endemic to the question of distributed agency itself. As it turns out, what is so interesting about the novel's (partial) resolution of global capital's exploitative practices is also exactly what turns out to be unresolvable, at least within the terms of traditional narrative structures. The weirdly nostalgic, humanist, and heteronormative conclusion, I want to suggest, is a result of the tension between the operations of distributed agency and the liberal humanist desire for linearity and narrative closure. This could be deemed a simple failure of the novel; however, it is more accurate to recognize this rather unfitting ending as indicative of the difficulty that distributed agency presents for our understanding of futurity and the traditionally humanist models of organization meant to produce it. Therefore, what if we were to look a bit closer and try to see the bacterial insurgency as meaningful despite its fundamentally unconscious elements? Might these unique radicals, these insurgent bacteria, help us grapple with the contingent nature of the future as well as the complex process that will bring it about?

It is important, first of all, to note the positive emotional response that the fantastically complete disintegration of the exploitative GGG Corporation's empire is likely to elicit from a justice-oriented reader. After absorbing GGG's relentless quest for profit, the destruction of the human and nonhuman communities surrounding the Matacao field, and capital's seemingly endless ability to co-opt any and all emergent alternative movements into its own profit model, witnessing the unraveling of this system is actually a quite pleasurable experience. The suddenly naked citizens, the crumbling buildings, and disintegrating credit cards finally offer a reprieve from the relentless success of GGG's schemes. There is a type of distinctive pleasure in imagining a form of opposition to predatory capitalism of which *we* are not the subject, even as this very scenario seems to call our own agency to create and sustain our world into radical question. That is, while the reader might revel in it momentarily, she must also take into account that this great unraveling is not a function of a human political subject or traditionally organized social movement in any way. While ultimately left unresolved in the novel, Yamashita invites the reader to confront these concerns via her representation of the insurgent bacteria; capable of undoing GGG's exploitative systems without traditionally defined intention while also remaining resistant to, and much more complicated than, the "nature strikes back" trope.

The central paradox of *Through the Arc* emanates, therefore, from the fact that its strength also appears to be a weakness. That is, the novel's attentiveness to distributed agency productively challenges the reader's assumptions regarding the relationship between human and nonhuman communities, helpfully destabilizing a presumed central position for humanity. It also forces us to consider the importance of mixed-community and social reproduction by highlighting the ways in which humans are never fully in control of, nor separable from, the nonhuman or human-built environment. Yet, these apparent strengths simultaneously result in a problematic conclusion that falls back upon the very dualism the novel otherwise operates to disrupt. In the end, the fall of GGG could not happen *without* human action, but it also certainly did not occur *because of* human action. This seeming contradiction speaks to distributed agency's resistance to explanation via dominant models of human subjectivity, agency, and progressive temporality. Distributed agency, as presented in the novel, does not seem amenable to projects for social change and political organization as we currently understand them. It would be, of course, outright impossible for the insurgent bacteria to offer us a kind of "vision" or political platform. And, as we have seen, Yamashita herself seems unable to imagine an ending based in distributed agency and, rather, falls back upon several tropes dependent upon dualistic models of liberal humanism.

Yamashita's bacterial insurgents are an example of distributed agency, phenomena emanating from a complex mixture of human and nonhuman assemblages, which should in fact make us question the traditional insistence upon the initial divide, or binary, between the human and nonhuman. These bacteria are not presented as an unintentional nature "striking back" against intentional human exploiters of nature, nor are they, however, intentional political agents themselves. Instead, they are a unique manifestation of a complex and inseparable mixed-community of, using Barad's terminology, agential forces. The novel itself does not, in the end, know quite what to do with its own creation either, ultimately falling back on a more simple binary relation between the human and nonhuman communities that allows for a more traditional sense of narrative closure. This desire for narrative closure strikes me as similar to the traditional progressive political desire for a purposive plan toward an attainable goal, a linear endpoint to be achieved through human-centered intentionality.

Engaging with distributed agency requires the practice of Relational Knowing and, also in the tradition of Thoreau, a commitment to a radical openness that inherently resists the expected closure of linear storytelling. But it is this very radical openness, the indeterminacy of distributed agency, that raises questions regarding exactly how we might imagine a distributed environmental politics. Yamashita tidies up the ending of her novel in ways that diminish distributed agency's radical potential. Similar to twentieth-century literary scholars who insisted on separating Thoreau's poetic philosophy from his natural science writing, the novel fails to fully embrace an approach of Relational Knowing, distributed agency, and the decentered subject. The hybridization of the human subject (no longer autonomous and bounded) and its knowledge formation practices (no longer removed and objective) is a trouble worth staying with, to echo Haraway's recent call to arms. We clearly do not yet have a fully theorized political organizing model into which we can comfortably insert Yamashita's insurgent bacteria, and my goal here is not to definitively define a posthumanist version of political agency without intentionality. Rather, I hope to display that my reading of the novel continues the already ongoing destabilization of our current, still deeply humanist, conceptions of agency and intention. Additionally, the new materialist turn in environmental scholarship, that is currently reshaping our understanding of postanthropocentric conceptions of agency, raises important questions regarding the subsequent impact of this reframing upon our ability to organize and act in ways that effectively promote social and environmental justice.

The bacterial insurgency in *Through the Arc* places the reader upon relatively unfamiliar ground when compared to traditional concepts of environmentalism as a social movement, and it also points to a critical issue within current theoretical models of material ecocriticism and environmental justice scholarship. This is of particular relevance and importance to EJ scholars and activists because of the field's foundational interest in exploring the interactions of human and nonhuman actors within mixed-communities. As environmental scholars and activists more fully appreciate that our uncertain future will not be solely the result of a rational and intentional humanist subject, then we are also tasked with the challenge of constructing strategies for social movement organizing that can be effective within the contours of distributed agency. In so doing, it remains imperative to recognize that our ability to theorize these models (not to mention the political organizing work itself) is partial, unwieldy, and irrevocably imbricated with agencies outside our awareness and control.

Through the Arc of the Rainforest depicts a global capitalism that successfully incorporates all forms of traditionally defined sociopolitical resistance, leaving us to wonder if there is something to be learned from the distributed agency that animates the insurgent bacteria of the novel's climax. This should compel us to ponder the role of the human in a political movement that unfolds within the framework of distributed agency and posthuman subjectivity. If we recognize that Yamashita's sustained attentiveness to distributed agency raises the distinct challenge of creating the expected narrative closure for a novel, then Leslie Silko's *Almanac of the Dead*, to which we turn in the next chapter, is an intriguing disruption of linearity altogether. Building from the challenges explored here, in the next chapter I will argue, by expanding our investigation of alternative and radical political subjectivities in environmental justice fiction, that *Almanac* displays both the immense potential and possible complications of constructing activism within the nonlinear temporalities that distributed agency, in part, helps to make viable. Silko utilizes a nonlinear and spatial narrative structure in order to effectively evade the strictures of narrative closure. Thus, the question of revolutionary transformation in the novel is left at once incomplete and open-ended; and, therefore, an inchoate yet ever-present possibility.

4

The Material Temporalities of Leslie Silko's *Almanac of the Dead*

> We don't believe in boundaries. Borders. Nothing like that. We are here thousands of years before the first whites. We are here before maps or quit claims. We know where we belong on this earth. We have always moved freely. North-south. East-west. We pay no attention to what isn't real. Imaginary lines. Imaginary minutes and hours. Written law. We recognize none of that. And we carry many things back and forth. We don't see any border. We have been here and this has continued for thousands of years. We don't stop. No one stops us.
>
> —Calabazas, *Almanac of the Dead*

Consistent with the novel's fundamentally nonlinear structure, the most influential catalyst for the narrative in Leslie Marmon Silko's *Almanac of the Dead* does not appear until approximately one-third of the way through the novel. In the chapter "The Journey of the Ancient Almanac," readers learn of four children, "the very last of their tribe," who centuries ago carried a book northward from their people's home in present-day Mexico (Silko 1991, 246). As the story is told to the twin sisters Lecha and Zeta by their Yaqui grandmother, Yoeme, "The pages were divided four ways [among the children because] . . . the people know if even part of their almanac survived, they as a people would return one day" (246). On their journey, the four children eventually come across an abandoned village where only one old woman has remained behind, alone and starving in her small home. The old woman hosts the children for a few days but it becomes clear that only the unique and powerful qualities of the almanac, combined with the attentive and decisive decisions of the eldest, a twelve-year-old girl, can save the children from being killed and eaten by the hungry and deranged woman (250–51). Drawing upon a philosophy of patience and vigilance her elders had advised, the eldest child eventually recognizes the danger and devises a plan to extricate the traveling children. Though only three of the four ultimately survive, the remaining members of the group are able to continue north with all four sections of the almanac (252).

This short tale echoes through the rest of the novel, as its emphasis on the tension between patience and action, as well as the spiritual and material, becomes a central element of the narrative's various justice-oriented sociopolitical movements. Yeome explains to her granddaughters: "The children [in the story] . . . had been reminded. A human being was born into the days she or he must live with until eventually the days themselves would travel on. All anyone could do was recognize the traits, the spirits of the days, and take precautions" (251). The Yaqui refer to the past five hundred years, marked by the European invasion and ongoing colonization of the Americas, as "the epoch of Death-Eye Dog" because many people, "especially the alien invaders, would become obsessed with hungers and impulses commonly seen in wild dogs" (251). The emphasis on observation and forbearance in the elder's advice to the children might seem, at first, a rather passive response to such a desperate period of time for Indigenous people in the Americas. Yet, the story of the four children, and in particular the eldest girl's ability to recognize the danger of their situation (the old woman, if not exactly kind, certainly does not at first seem a murderer) and devise an escape plan, suggests something much more than passivity. As Yeome informs her granddaughters upon concluding the story, the children had also been told the almanac's "pages held many forces within them, countless physical and spiritual properties to guide the people and make them strong." And the book itself, with its powerful history of a people, "had saved [the children]" (252). The children's ability to observe, plan and escape their predicament, with the help of "physical and spiritual properties" embedded in the book of their people they carry, suggests the cautious philosophy they were tutored in is made of more than simple acquiescence, even if the senses of knowledge, agency, and temporality it denotes seem surprising.

The philosophy of the almanac, in addition to its non-Western ideas of agency, also productively complicates assumed Western models of linearity. Is it possible that patience is not synonymous with passivity? Does it in fact, from the Yaqui and broader Indigenous perspective, contain a more generative element? Could it be that, in this case, acceptance is not necessarily acquiescence? If not, then it is also likely the case that observation, in this sense, is operating in a manner other than Western empirical (removed and universal) objectivity. And this, in turn, suggests it is possible to construct an effective justice-oriented course of action based upon a framework that prioritizes awareness, discernment, and, yes, even patience. How different might this approach, gestured toward here in the story of the children's escape, appear as compared to dominant contemporary modes of progressive politics? Patience might not mean slower, as time unfolds in nonlinear fashion and new ways of seeing pick out suddenly apparent and ready paths. A distributed type of agency is quite likely more amenable to this precautionary approach, when one is aware that assemblages of forces are at work, rather than only the rational and autonomous human subject and/or a separate and random nonhuman agency. This approach, in which patience begets a type of situated and nonlinear relation to temporality, is an important element of the "material temporalities" to which this chapter's title refers. In her introduction to *Walking the Clouds: An Anthology of Indigenous Science Fiction*, Grace Dillon contends, "Historically, [science fiction] has tended to disregard the varieties of space-time thinking of traditional societies" (Dillon 2012, 2). Dillon, an indigenous studies scholar and member of the Anishanaabe Nation, includes, deploying a broad definition of science fiction, a selection of *Almanac* in her collection, and argues that, in the novel "the fight for Indigenous land reclamation and tribal sovereignty is a matter of planetary survival" (217).

I describe the temporality of that fight for "land reclamation" and Indigenous peoples' "sovereignty" as materialist because the revolutionary possibilities are depicted as deeply imbricated with both distributed agency and nonlinear temporality (which additionally exist in their own complex relation). In the following highly selective reading of *Almanac*, I expand the above observations regarding the children's narrow escape from death to the novel's larger preoccupations with the movements organizing to bring the epoch of Death-Eye Dog to a close. Or, put another way, its construction of a radical, effective, anticapitalist, decolonization movement in the Americas.

In the previous chapter, we noted that *Through the Arc*'s grasping for narrative closure (in keeping with the linear form and narrative constraints of the dominant novel form) leads to the unsatisfying reconstitution of a main character, Kazumasa, as the reformed, intentional, and rational actor. Kazumasa's intentional and rational *act* is itself actually a retreat, a self-imposed withdrawal from the mesh of complex, intersecting agencies he encounters. Recreating a pastoral ideal, he removes himself and his newly formed traditional family from the environmental catastrophe of extractive capitalism engulfing the Brazilian rainforest. In the end, this is really a disappointing, idealized, and nostalgic move, dependent upon a more humanist depiction of subjectivity, agency, and temporality. *Through the Arc*'s conclusion, as a result, dodges the questions—that, in fact, it itself raises via its depiction of distributed agency—regarding the relation between a decentered human subjectivity and the possibility for a distributed environmental politics capable of effectively grappling with environmental crisis in the Brazilian rainforest. In this chapter, on the other hand, I will suggest that Leslie Silko's famously dense novel engages with and cleaves a productive space for innovative thinking about political agency via the dual disorientations of postanthropocentric, distributed agency and material, nonlinear temporality; for this reason, I tend to approach Silko's novel as a theoretical intervention in its own right.

It is possible, at some level, that the Western assumption of linear temporality continues to limit much of posthuman and eco-theory's potential for fully thinking through the cascading impacts of distributed agency. On the other hand, the nonlinear storytelling in Silko's *Almanac*, while often disorienting for Western readers, sketches an alternative approach to existing modes of progressive politics. In Silko's material temporalities, rather than evoking simple passivity, patience becomes a form of slow down, a manner of being in the present without attempting to summon the future. This nonlinear and distributed, materialist philosophy operates outside the context of linear temporality and depicts agency in a way that reimagines the political act outside the narrow context of progressive political action (in which acting *now* is always understood as a summoning of a very particular future goal). Rather than leading to disconnection and inaction, a different sort of committed and attentive interaction arises with the given moment, the ever-present (even if always partially unknowable) now.

Material Temporalities

While it is now commonplace to note that Silko's *Almanac*, similar to the Mayan almanacs that in large part drive the novel's narrative, depends upon nonlinear temporalities, it is less common to explore this disruption of linearity while also engaging the question of nontraditional agency in the novel (particularly political organizing strategies and acts of resistance). To better grasp the novel's revolutionary political imaginary, the reading below begins by engaging the role of temporality in the novel and then places this nontraditional sense of time into conversation with the depiction of distributed agency. The three interlinked concepts of temporality, distributed agency, and intentionality then receive an increasing amount of attention as the chapter continues. This narrative of material temporalities ultimately disrupts certain assumed Western liberal democratic values and the ways in which social justice movements are meant to operate within prescribed modes of "progressive" theory and activism, thus highlighting the dependence of contemporary political organizing on a relatively limited understanding of agency and temporality. Furthermore, and somewhat surprisingly, the novel insists on a serious engagement with the value of taking a longer, expansive, transbiological view of temporality in the midst of dire social and environmental crises that seemingly beg for immediate and decisive action. This longer-view approach, however counterintuitively, enhances the characters' ability to see and engage in the present. The various revolutionaries in the novel, as a result, formulate and develop their movements within the context of nonlinearity to a similar degree with which they operate from posthuman and postanthropocentric subjectivities. The novel, in the end, productively disrupts expectations surrounding how the world changes and the temporality in which those changes unfold.

The almanac that the children carry north and which ultimately lands in the possession of Zeta and Lecha in Tucson, in tandem with the overall narrative structure of the book, presents a nonlinear understanding of temporality that contrasts with the Euro-American colonizers' view of expansionary progress and the project of Western civilization. Prominent environment and literature scholar Joni Adamson describes the almanac's central role within the novel as embedded in "the story of how the Mayan people resisted domination, held on to their culture, and survived into the twentieth century" (Adamson 2001, 139).[1] In this manner, the novel emphasizes the interdependence of the spiritual and the material, the human and the nonhuman, and the cultural, political, and ethical aspects of radical opposition to injustice and dispossession. The almanac's stories provide Yeome and her twin granddaughters, Zeta and Lecha, a way of seeing the world based in Indigenous cultural history, promoting an understanding of history and historical change outside the frameworks of colonial imperialism, transnational capitalism and Western scientific empiricism.[2] Past, present and future are less chronological, as the almanac tells the story, and instead become something more like simultaneous and continuous. Writing of the relation between knowledge and temporality in the novel, literary scholar Rebecca Tillett explains, "The bones of Silko's dead . . . have resurfaced to emphasize indigenous beliefs that the past is never truly past; that past events can never be fully forgotten; that the past will be always present" (Tillett 2007, 33). And, consequently, "the resurfaced bones indicate the impossibility of erasing either the past or the dead, who continue to live in a communal memory" (33). I think Tillett's astute observations, rather than clarifying the relation between knowledge formation and temporality in the novel, actually work to highlight the challenges that face these revolutionary characters. While the past is always present in the novel, it also seems the future is closer, or even occurring simultaneously, as well. The unsettling impact on the novel's revolutionary actors' sense of futurity—that is, the future is both now and also not quite yet now—shapes their approach to organizing strategies and actions in the present. This is distinctly different from the considerations of a political organizer operating through the lens of linear time. In contrast, how does one imagine their role in creating a particular, desired future after the decentering of the human subject and the disruption of linear time? Rethinking futurity, as much as history, may be an essential step.

While effectively drawing attention to the nonlinear aspects of narrative in the novel, scholarship on *Almanac* also often lays bare the difficulty of fully thinking through the relationship between nonlinear history and distributed agency. In "Envisioning a 'Network of Tribal Coalitions': Silko's Almanac of the Dead," for instance, Indigenous Studies scholar Channette Romero attempts to categorize the depiction of historical time in the narrative. The difficulty of this worthy project ultimately displays a telling and contradictory goal. In discussing the relationship between temporality and agency in the novel, Romero suggests, "Instead of a linear movement toward a transcendental future, time and history [in *Almanac*] are viewed as circular and continually returning. Because every time exists simultaneously and will repeat itself, people are urged throughout Almanac to remember past times and histories in order to avoid repeating the same mistakes and injustices" (Romero 2002, 629). While this assessment usefully highlights the privileging of nonlinearity in the novel, the trope of circularity is too quickly inserted in its place. This codification of non-Western conceptions of time would have us believe that there exists only a binary choice: linearity or circularity. However, the above quote itself displays how this false choice oversimplifies the novel's depiction of indigenous concepts of time. That is, Romero contends, within just these two sentences quoted above that temporality in the novel is at once "circular" and "continually returning" while also allowing that all time "exists simultaneously" for the Indigenous activists. There is clearly a difference we must attend to, however, between something like "circular" and "simultaneous" time. They are not exactly the same thing; but how exactly are they different and why might it matter?

Romero attempts to foreclose this question by privileging rational agency, which surreptitiously reasserts a linear temporality, one in which the past becomes a closed, knowable entity that humans can utilize in order to act more responsibly in the present and future. Quite simply, the knowledge of the past—whether in linear, circular, or simultaneous time—is limited to a deeply humanist role of informing the rational actor of the present. Romero contends that the nonlinear understanding of time in the novel is predominantly useful because it is another way to help humans "act" (more justly, or pragmatically) in the present.[3] The desire to connect nonlinear history to human (justice-oriented) agency is even more pronounced when Romero speculates on reader experience. She argues, "Rather than seeing themselves as one inferior step in a progression toward a more superior future removed from the earth, readers of the text are encouraged to take responsibility for their present actions as they are continuously related to the history and future of the earth and its peoples" (629–30). In this construction, the intentional subject is fully invested with the ability to choose—to listen and to heed history or not—and what is learned, according to Romero, is that they must "take responsibility" for their actions, exactly because the "present actions" of humans will determine no less than the "history and future of the earth." It is my sense that the above characterization of temporality and agency does not attend enough to the fact that human agency is not given such an unfettered role in *Almanac of the Dead*. The construction of both agency and historical time in the novel are much more complicated than existing scholarly accounts have entirely conceded.[4]

The myths of human exceptionalism and unfettered agency are fundamental aspects of the colonizers' culture and constitute a privileged position; therefore, disrupting these myths is clearly central to the movements organizing to end the era of Death-Eye Dog. However, the depiction of distributed political activism that aims to overthrow the colonizers, as depicted by Silko in *Almanac*, has at times left scholars wondering about the exact role of humans in this revolution.[5] The representation of distributed agency compels the reader to ask: Are these revolutionaries unfettered political actors learning from the past in order to construct a better future for all? Or are they bystanders, with little to no control, watching and waiting for an inevitable, or natural, sweep of history to unfold? In the end, the revolutionary organizers embody neither of these overdetermined constructions of political subjectivity and agency. The complex blend of human, spiritual, technological, and nonhuman agency that spurs the revolutionary spirit of Silko's incendiary narrative, I hope to show, is best understood if we attempt to think distributed agency and nonlinear temporality as deeply intertwined. This is even more strikingly clear when compared to *Through the Arc*, where collective political resistance from humans is practically nonexistent.[6] Although they are limited, contingent, and incomplete, Indigenous political and revolutionary movements in the novel offer an intriguing window of possibility for better theorizing the complex relation between distributed agency and nonlinear temporality.

The possibility of radical political agency is at the center of the novel's depiction of each Indigenous character and organization, as the various storylines of a long and ongoing insurgency against the European colonizers come to light. Angelita La Escapia, for instance, is a Mayan woman from Mexico City who has become a leader, along with the twin brothers El Feo and Tacho, of an Indigenous army calling itself The People's Army. Their goal is no less than the removal of Euro-Americans, along with their Western institutions and capitalist ideologies, from their people's ancestral lands and to build a more equitable and egalitarian society for Indigenous Americans and their allies. As a political leader, while certainly working outside the limits of either a simple rights-based discourse or a purely military revolution, Angelita looks to blend many aspects of Marxist thought, Indigenous knowledge and history, and contemporary geopolitical strategy in order to achieve one radical and revolutionary goal. She is extremely politically astute and therefore a lead intellectual and tactical figure in the people's revolution: "El Feo [her consistent political ally and somewhat less consistent romantic partner] left books and politics to Angelita, who was strong enough to stomach the poison about taxes, authorities, and the existence of states" (523).

Her strategy represents a flexibility that works within, and exploits, the dominant economic and political system to support The People's Army and its movement for decolonization. She wades her way through the "poison" of the institutions that originated and continue to reify the logics of capitalism and colonization in search of any advantage she can deliver to the army's cause. While fundraising, "If Angelita was talking to the Germans or Hollywood activists," for instance, "she said the Indians were fighting multinational corporations who killed rain forests" (514). On the other hand, "[I]f she was talking to the Japanese or the U.S. military, then the Indians were fighting communism. Whatever their 'friends' needed to hear, that was their motto" (514). Angelita's perceptiveness, shrewdness, and flexibility creates her success, however limited and constrained, in using the existing system of oppression against itself.

Joni Adamson, in her description of the novel's revolutionary construct, argues that, at their core, Angelita's goals are essentially concerned with what we have described earlier as social reproduction. That is, "Angelita sees herself as fighting for her people's right to practice their traditional culture and religion, and to derive a sustainable living in the places where they were born" (Adamson 2001, 153). The stakes for Angelita are no less essential than the social reproduction of her culture, or what constitutes a way of life construed as inextricably connected to emplaced human and nonhuman communities. It is simultaneously a local and global campaign, as the novel depicts "the fight for Indigenous land reclamation and tribal sovereignty is a matter of planetary survival" (Dillon 2012, 217). The radical nature of the Indigenous army's goals to retake the land coupled with their intricate understanding of the interconnectedness of spiritual, human, and environmental agency in their revolution challenges the reader to think beyond traditional political paradigms (whether those be reform- and rights-based discourses, nonviolent civil disobedience, or violent eco-sabotage).[7] "Indigenous resistance is not a one-time event," Nick Estes reminds us, "It continually asks: What proliferates in the absence of empire? Thus, it defines freedom not as the absence of settler colonialism, but as the amplified presence of Indigenous life and just relations with human and nonhuman relatives, and with the earth" (Estes 2019, 248). The goal is not only to end the epoch of Death-Eye Dog, but to build in its place a just and sustainable world in which Indigenous and poor people across the Americas have their land and are free to live upon it on their own terms. Nothing less than a successful decolonization of the Americas, and beyond, will make this possible.

Angelita's speech near the end of the novel, delivered before gathered villagers and activists in a remote mountainous community and just prior to the execution of the Cuban Marxist Bartholomeo (for his perceived treachery against the Indigenous movement for freedom), offers several insights into her vision for the revolution, the society that will take its place, and the path forward to realize these goals. Echoing the advice given to the young carriers of the almanac, which ultimately saved them from failure and death, Angelita consistently emphasizes how essential acute attention and careful preparation will be for the coming revolution.[8] This is also where the articulation of how nonlinear temporality and distributed agency operate together in the revolutionary theory of The People's Army becomes more clear. Angelita and her co-revolutionaries appear cognizant of how the distributed agency of historical change is co-produced by an inextricable mixture of human and environmental actions. From the beginning, for instance, they insist that many of the actants, the instigators of historical change, are already infused into the current colonial system of the Destroyers. As they see it, this complex, unfolding intra-action between Euro-American imperialism, the multifarious assortment of complementary and oppositional human social movements, and nonhuman, material agency will present an opportunity for The People's Army to add its contemporary revolutionary capabilities.

This view of a distributed revolutionary agency, meanwhile, is also clearly dependent upon a nonlinear concept of time. She explains, "The ancestors' spirits speak in dreams. We wait. We simply wait for the earth's natural forces already set loose, the exploding, fierce energy of all the dead slaves and dead ancestors haunting the Americas" (518). And, in even more clear terms, Angelita assures her listeners: "We prepare, and we wait for the tidal wave of history to sweep us along" (518). Her emphasis upon the "ancestors' spirits" and the earth's "natural forces" whose combined agency will "sweep" humans along with it can be misleading. It would be a mistake to read this as a passive approach in which The People's Army is asked to only "wait" for a "tidal wave of history," one in which they play no part whatsoever. We should note, instead, that Angelita suggests these natural forces are "already set loose" by a "fierce energy" of "dead slaves" and "ancestors." The energy, which Angelita depicts as comprising human, nonhuman, spiritual, and material components, is better understood as an inextricable mixture, an assemblage of force and energy, comprised of human and nonhuman (material) interaction. This assemblage is a force of its own that, while not exclusively human or human-directed, includes human agency and reconfigures our sense of time to include past actions of human/nonhuman actants as materially manifest (within the assemblage that accounts for historical change) in the present moment. It is a misreading, in other words, to see Angelita's speech through the lens of the nature/culture binary, which clearly she disavows; instead we need to remain cognizant that she is not using terms such as *nature, earth,* and *human* in the context of Western imperialism.

Reminiscent of our discussion of *Through the Arc* in the previous chapter, readers and scholars have rightly wondered if the emphasis on "natural disasters" bringing the epoch of Death-Eye Dog to an end implies there is no role at all for humans to resist social and environmental injustice; unless, that is, the humans become "natural forces" themselves.[9] In Angelita's own construction, for instance, the decentered human is *dispossessed* of any perceived or law-based ownership of nonhuman nature and is also then *disposed* of by the newly empowered earth. But this needs to be read as more than a simple nature-strikes-back trope. She argues The People's Army will, for instance, build upon the revolutionary potential present in Marxism: "They [Marx and Engels] had not understood that the earth was mother to all beings. But at least . . . [they] had understood the earth belongs to no one. No human, individuals or corporations, no cartel of nations, could 'own' the earth; it was the earth who possessed the humans and it was the earth who disposed of them" (749). Here, Angelita does posit humans and their institutions as dispossessed of intentional agency; however, the "earth" that disposes of them is no longer the traditional Other of the culture/nature binary. Instead, based on our reading of her speech above, Angelita's "earth" is best read as a complex assemblage of energy and force, comprised of human and nonhuman mixed-communities of distributed agency, including past, present, spiritual, and material actants. Readers are confronted, therefore, with a material and philosophical challenge to Western empirical and political traditions and the preparatory operations of activists working to create new portals toward (or launching points for) an until now mostly unimaginable future for the human and nonhuman communities of the Americas; the end of Death-Eye Dog era and the decolonization of the Americas. The People's Army creates a new, speculative political plane based in an Indigenous perspective of distributed agency and nonlinear, material temporality.

Angelita's revolutionary plans will also occur within a nonlinear concept of time, meaning that the "fierce energy" of distributed agency powering the movement is also always present, even when not yet physically manifest. And any inclination, therefore, to decipher between past and present acts, and their respective and exact impacts on the revolution, becomes very difficult. But the necessity of doing so, given Angelita's sense of material temporalities, becomes practically irrelevant. Historical change, the agencies building momentum toward revolution, as explained by Angelita, is an amalgamation of the entire history and present instantiation of colonization in the Americas itself; and this history is powered by an agency in which, from the Indigenous characters' perspective, there is no binary differentiation between the human and the nonhuman, nor the past and present. Crucially, the novel suggests that this reorientation to agency and temporality is not important because it contains a potential to simply inform an intentional political subject in the present moment, making her a more well-informed decision maker and ethical, influential actor. The subject herself, rather, will be fully reconfigured by this coalition of distributed agency and nonlinearity; the distributed political actor, as a result, will likely not think, plan, aspire, and act in necessarily and immediately recognizable ways.

This revolution to reclaim the Indigenous peoples of the Americas' rightful lands includes the construction of an economic and sociopolitical structure to replace the oppressive, destructive, and essentially failed capitalism of settler-colonialism. Angelita, for her part, clearly expresses her vision for what will replace the current state of economic inequality and colonialist oppression: "The dispossessed people of the earth would rise up and take back lands that had been their birthright, and these lands would never again be held as private property, but as lands belonging to the people forever to protect" (532). In this section of her speech, the reemergence of human agency is striking: Indigenous and dispossessed people will "rise up," "take back," and "protect" the land. Angelita's lover and co-revolutionary El Feo articulates a vision of revolutionary action that also privileges, at least in part, human action just as much as it clearly moves beyond traditional forms of advocacy or appeals to the state. His position makes even more clear that this movement must find ways to act effectually even as the state is nonresponsive to its members' claims to liberal humanist rights. El Feo's sense of their situation is described as such:

> The masses of people in Asia and in Africa, and the Americas too, no longer believed in so-called "elected leaders" they were

> listening to strange voices inside themselves. Although few would admit this, the voices they heard were voices out of the past, voices of their earliest memories, voices of nightmares and voices of sweet dreams, voices of the ancestors. (513)

This is not a sociopolitical movement aimed at political reform or electoral victories, nor a rights-based application to the state for certain types of recognition. Part of this revolutionary work, to be sure, must involve the unthinking of Euro-American political, economic, and social "ways of seeing" the world. The voices of their ancestors are with them now, and this is both a spiritual and a material reality for the underclasses of the world. Without dismissing the important role of spirituality, one also needs to recognize that Angelita and El Feo are describing and depending upon a revolutionary agency that is an amalgam of the spiritual and the material, as well as the past and the present. The "voices" are not simply ideas or advice from the past for the revolutionary actors to put into practice as intentional subjects but, rather, these voices are always already a member of the assemblage that is distributed agency in the material unfolding of El Feo and Angelita's movement for decolonization. The past, present, and future are simultaneously a part of the agential evolution of history in each moment of the material present; the entirety of earth and historical change, as Angelita explains in her speech, is a distributed agency that the revolutionaries must carefully watch, understand, and attempt to engage with in order to bring about the end of colonization in the Americas.

El Feo and his followers also understand their positionality as subjects to a colonizer government, rather than citizens of a democratic state. Though each insurgent seems to have their own version of how the revolution would begin, the following explanation is indicative of all the various suppositions provided across the almost eight hundred–page novel:

> The night the lights went out and didn't come back on, the tables would turn. The poorest, those living on the street or in the arroyo, they would laugh at the others because the homeless and poor lived every day without electricity or running water. Turn out the lights and the police had no computers, no files, no names, no spy cameras, and police radios went dead . . . they all had weapons and they all were ready to fight. Because if they didn't fight, they would be destroyed and Mother Earth with them. (748–49)

The opening phrasing, "the night the lights went out," leaves the catalyst and context for the revolutionary spark rather vague. This vagueness, as well as the sudden emergence of seemingly autonomous and rational actors in Angelita's and El Feo's descriptions of the revolution, points to the intense difficulty in articulating the specific causes of historical change in a posthuman and postanthropocentric framework that privileges distributed agency as the "engine" of history (rather than the supposed Euro-American agent and benefactor of civilization and history). Distributed agency and a nonlinear concept of historical change, nevertheless, do both remain central and fundamental to the revolutionaries' framework for victory. Futurity becomes something that is based upon an amalgamation, or assemblage, of human and nonhuman agency, as colonialism, capitalism, disease, droughts, and technological advances and failures interconnect and overlap, and the resulting "fierce energy" propels the Americas toward the demise of contemporary Euro-American domination. As we already know, however, this is also clearly not as simple as erasing all human agency or responsibility. For all that the characters talk of the coming demise of Euro-American civilization in the Americas as inevitable, it is a mistake to think that means it is not also the product, in some part, of human agency. The agency of the past and the contemporary work of the present are at once vital and not singular or determinative of the revolution (not in the manner liberal humanism would have us wish or believe it to be). Nevertheless, Angelita, El Feo, and the others clearly feel there is a responsibility to be attentive and active in this process, as well as in their ongoing debates about the best practices for what we might call an inchoate distributed environmental politics.

As we have seen, given a too-restrictive definition of what constitutes the human, the depiction of revolutionary agency in *Almanac of the Dead* might be perceived as entirely (or only) nonhuman. Or, in an attempt to locate the human role, it might be suggested that the novel only includes people in the revolutionary action by imagining them as natural forces themselves.[10] This construction, however, still problematically reaffirms the original binary by assuming that there is a clear delineation to be made between the agency of humans and so-called nature. Labeling revolutionary agency in this way would ask us to distinguish between people acting as humans (presumably, somehow unnaturally) or acting as nonhuman forces (i.e., naturally). We should not, of course, imagine the human actors as "natural forces," any more than we should see the "earthquakes" and "droughts" as somehow intentional, reasonable political subjects. Rather, in order to recognize a more fundamental point of the novel's depiction of agency, we must investigate the ways in which agency is co-produced in the mesh between, and across, human and nonhuman communities. The action unfolds within the materiality of distributed agency and nonlinear temporality, and working with the text via the broader concept of material insurgency allows for a more nuanced interpretation of the inchoate revolution itself as a type of distributed agency. Ultimately, the novel compels us to further explore the potential for understanding historical change as instigated by a complex set of human and nonhuman assemblages, in which humans are enmeshed in (and still widely accountable for) historical change but do not wield rational intentionality. The droughts, floods, and forest fires are all a result of a complicated intersection between nature-culture assemblages; that is, they are the distributed agency of extractive capitalism, ecosystem function, industrial agriculture, greenhouse gas emissions, and more. The continuing analysis of *Almanac* that follows, therefore, aspires to expand our understanding of what these reorientations might mean for forming effective sociopolitical movements capable of producing justice-oriented social reproduction.

Distributed Revolutions

Despite many intricate and complex variations across the revolutionary movements depicted in the novel, Zeta summarizes the generally accepted perspective among these diverse groups relatively succinctly: "War had been declared the first day the Spaniards set foot on Native American soil, and the same war had been going on ever since: the war was for the continents called the Americas" (Silko 1991, 133). This war is based upon a radical and straightforward principle: "There was not, and there never had been, a legal government by Europeans anywhere in the Americas. Not by any definition, not even by the Europeans' own definitions and laws. Because no legal government could be established on stolen land" (133). Among the various groups that are projected to participate and "retake the Americas," two revolutionary citizen armies, one comprised mostly of homeless war veterans and the other of Indigenous peoples, take on particularly significant roles. The Tucson "homeless army" is formed by Vietnam veterans Clinton and Roy, and the coalition of Indigenous peoples, the "people's army," as noted earlier, is led by Angelita and the twin brothers El Feo and Tacho (also known to his people as Wacha, and a spiritual leader).

Early in *Almanac*, we encounter the distrust that the homeless army's leaders reserve for both mainstream environmental and radical green preservationist rhetoric. For instance, we learn that Clinton, one of the group's founders and a man with African and Native American heritage, "did not trust the so-called 'Defenders of Planet Earth.' Something about their choice of words had made Clinton uneasy" (415). When the history of traditional mainstream conservationist values is considered, Clinton's concerns regarding the motivations behind certain types of environmental advocacy are understandable. For instance, "Clinton was suspicious whenever he heard the word *pollution*. Human beings had been exterminated strictly for 'health' purposes by Europeans too often" (415). It is not lost on Clinton that the rhetoric surrounding overpopulation is often deployed in some environmental circles as a diversion that allows for a disregard of other pertinent and more difficult issues, such as the uneven distribution of wealth and consumption within the developed world and globally. His concerns are not assuaged at all when he sees "ads purchased by so-called 'deep-ecologists.' The ads blamed earth's pollution not on industrial wastes—hydrocarbons and radiation—but on overpopulation" (415). This approach, consequently, criminalizes and silences the poor while naturalizing an environmentally damaging economic system built upon and fortifying that very socioeconomic inequality. Clinton is understandably concerned that this means mainstream conservation and radical back-to-earth groups value nonhuman nature more than humans themselves, and also—unwittingly or not—help to deflect blame for environmental degradation from industrialized Northern countries and multinational corporations.

Clinton's professed skepticism of deep green philosophy is a significant example of how the novel challenges the binaries that have traditionally underwritten mainstream environmental politics (especially prior to the book's publication in the early '90s). As Clinton sees it, "The Europeans had managed to dirty up the good land and good water around the world in less than five hundred years. Now the despoilers wanted the last bits of living earth for themselves alone" (415). Here, in just two sentences, Clinton decimates the pernicious focus on overpopulation found in significant amounts of environmental rhetoric. Interestingly, this sentiment echoes the Mayan almanac's predictions of the Death-Eye Dog's demise more generally; that is, that the overconsumption of environmental resources in the United States is simultaneously at the heart of Euro-American imperialism in the Americas and will be the cause of its downfall. Importantly, Clinton is actively seeking to cobble together a different approach to social inequality and ecological breakdown, one he hopes will more fundamentally challenge the sociopolitical and economic system that creates both environmental exploitation and a racialized socioeconomic hierarchy.

The novel begins, in these ways, to work through the entrenched historical differences between mainstream environmentalism, environmental and economic justice campaigns, and land-based, Indigenous movements, eventually drawing a connection between the needs and goals of the homeless army in Tucson and the Indigenous army in Mexico. Silko explores the contours of the relationship between radical social justice movements and environmentalism further through the inclusion of "radical eco-terrorists," a group calling themselves Green Vengeance (seemingly in a similar vein as Earth First!). Members of Green Vengeance surprise the attendees of the International Holistic Healers Convention to announce and display video of their recent destruction of a dam in the United States, accomplished with human suicide bombers, and to proclaim their support for the Indigenous people's uprising to retake their rightful lands. The spokespeople bring video evidence of "six eco-warriors . . . [giving] their lives to free the mighty Colorado" (728). Green Vengeance is quickly assessed as an opportune ally for the decolonization movement, based in the group's antistate radicalism and their official plan to destroy the energy grid of the United States. El Feo's prediction that the uprising would take advantage of "the night the lights go out" might then become a reality sooner than expected. Additionally, several leaders of the Indigenous community suggest, "Green Vengeance eco-warriors would make useful allies at least at the start . . . [because the organization] had a great deal of wealth behind their eco-warrior campaigns" (726). There is, therefore, potential for coalition via a shared vision of radical tactics, and an opportunity for the Indigenous revolutionaries to tap into the funding behind white radical environmentalism. The problematic philosophical history of ecotage groups (particularly in terms of their primitivist assumptions regarding a so-called return to nature), however, would leave some philosophical and material differences between the People's Army and Green Vengeance's plans for reclaiming the land from the state.

According to scholar T. V. Reed, Silko depicts a simultaneously diverse yet linked set of resistant movements, which are reminiscent of what Reed terms "decolonizing environmentalisms" (38). His argument for the value in "decolonizing environmentalisms" recognizes the historic, and in many ways still ongoing, barrier between environmental and social justice activism. Reed uses the concept to "indicate two interrelated processes: the decolonization of traditional environmentalisms and the creation of new decolonial environmentalisms that articulate the links between oppressed humans and exploited Nature via objectification, commoditization, and degradation" (38). In utilizing this term to describe the radical activism described in *Almanac*, Reed highlights the connectedness between environmental exploitation and the subjugation of the poor and Indigenous communities north and south of the U.S.-Mexican border in the novel. If, as Reed argues, "Almanac makes clear that only a thoroughgoing economic decolonization process can undo the social and environmental impact of the European imprint on the Americas," then the novel presents an excellent opportunity to consider the potential impact of seeing environmental and social justice activism in a more integrated fashion (38).[11] An alliance founded on strategic politics might open up space for productive conversations between Clinton and his homeless army, Angelita and other indigenous leaders, and the Green Vengeance eco-warriors.

Reed goes on to say that the end of colonial domination will present an opportunity for Native peoples to retake their land and create a society and political economy "in which human needs and the needs of the planet are aligned, and prosperity for some is not bought at the cost of poverty for others and environmental collapse" (33). Although the novel does narrate just such an opportunity, and I am interested in building upon Reed's cogent argument more generally, environmental scholars do need to be vigilant in avoiding any uncritical associations between Native American and sustainable cultures. Quite clearly—and I think Reed recognizes this as well—Silko's depiction of the sociopolitical movement to displace Euro-American colonialism in the Americas actively resists this problematic and primitivist depiction of Indigenous cultures. In the end, Reed's concept of decolonizing environmentalisms, in conversation with Di Chiro's explication of "social reproduction," seems a productive path forward for environmental justice scholars and advocates to move beyond the concept of "sustainability" (at least beyond its mainstream use in contemporary green capitalism) and toward a distributed environmental politics. The fight to promote social reproduction is, in part, a battle to privilege a noneconomic-based quality of life, equitable distribution of wealth, and long-term sustainable practices over a growth-based, expansionary economic model that produces socioeconomic inequality and environmental destruction. As outlined in chapter 3, the concept of social reproduction is most helpful in its emphatic emphasis on "mixed-community" (the interaction between human and nonhuman inhabitants of an ecosystem) and therefore helps to highlight nature-culture interdependencies. If we take the critique of global capitalism, central to Reed's point concerning alternative sustainable systems, and place it in conversation with the cultural and sociopolitical aspects of social reproduction in the context of mixed-communities, we find that the revolutionary work of both the Indigenous and homeless armies (and other subaltern subjects in the novel) points toward something much more interesting than a simple nature-strikes-back narrative. Seeing the sociopolitical goal in this way seems productive to me in that it offers a more dynamic account of the movement to retake Indigenous land than a simply Romantic, economic, or environmental account can individually muster.[12]

Much of what I am attempting to say above, by placing social reproduction and decolonizing environmentalisms in conversation to better understand The People's Army's goals, has been articulated most clearly and convincingly in the recent work of Indigenous studies scholar Leanne Betasamosake Simpson. In her most recent book, *As We Have Always Done: Indigenous Freedom through Radical Resistance*, she summarizes and builds upon Glen Coulthard's concept of "grounded normativity," which she explains are the "ethical frameworks generated by . . . place-based practices and associated knowledges" of indigenous peoples (Simpson 2017, 22).[13] It is, as she describes it, an Indigenous place-based ethics and community that remains open to tribal internationalism and, while appropriately critical, also to Western liberatory political theory (22). Grounded normativity strikes me as very much the basis for the future that Angelita envisions for the Americas after the Death-Eye Dog is eradicated. Simpson calls for a "refusal of dispossession that is generative" of a new world of Indigenous freedom based in "interdependence of land and bodies in a networked fashion rather than a gendered hierarchy" (44). Targeting settler colonialism as "the system that maintains this dispossession," Simpson urges Indigenous activists to be "clear that our attachment to land is not up for negotiation . . . and that a radical resurgence within grounded normativity means the dismantling of settler colonialism and the return of Indigenous lands" (44). The addition of grounded normativity to this conversation foregrounds the Indigenous place-based ethics that motivate/activate Angelita and El Feo's movement for decolonization and illuminates the world they envision in the place of settler-colonialism. This scholarship provides a radical and vibrant alternative to mainstream sustainability discourse, and grounded normativity clarifies any vagueness that might persist in social reproduction theory regarding whose ideas and which cultural norms will best suit a postcolonial reconstitution of a society based in social and environmental justice. As Simpson clearly states regarding her own scholarship and activism: "I'm interested in unapologetic place-based nationhoods using Indigenous practices and operating in an ethical principled way from an intact land base" (50). Silko's novel, as I read it, is a fictional narrative that explores the possibility of precisely this Indigenous potentiality.

Several important connections exist between the homeless army in Tucson and the Indigenous army forming in Mexico, and elsewhere in the Americas, and they help explicate essential elements of the distributed environmental politics within *Almanac*. Both sets of leaders are organizing revolutionary citizen armies by building their membership, capacities, and determination, as they watch for an opportune moment to "act." The opportunity, as the organizers come to understand and explain it, will be the result of a culmination of complex events, processes, and institutions: U.S. colonial domination, U.S. imperialism in the Americas and abroad, environmental and ecosystem crises. Both "armies," in somewhat different forms, also claim to recognize and hope to capitalize on the disruptive and revolutionary potential of this distributed agency that is unfolding within the violent framework of colonial domination. Both Clinton and El Feo, from their different perspectives on either side of the U.S.-Mexican border, describe the environmentally exploitative practices of the United States as an integral cause of its own imminent downfall. In many ways, they see the exact same forces of greed and exploitation that have created the current structures of power as also significantly contributing to that very system's demise.

While Clinton and El Feo never do meet in the novel, both are working to ready their prospective "armies" for the retaking of land and property from the Destroyers. How such disparate yet linked groups might effectively deepen this relationship and how to build an effective coalition as the time of transition rapidly approaches remain open questions throughout the novel. This fictional depiction of the work necessary to bridge urban environmental justice campaigns and decolonization Indigenous movements is reminiscent of the theoretical and practical challenge discussed by scholar Dina Gilio-Whitaker, who makes the case that an EJ movement inclusive of Indigenous peoples would need to construct "a model that can frame issues in terms of their colonial context and can affirm decolonization as a potential framework within which environmental justice can be made available . . . [and] also recognize that racism is imbricated with colonialism" (Gilio-Whitaker 2019, 25). These differences between the "armies" in the novel are not fully overcome, by any means, but what is more important is that the context of their relation to each other is changed. The disruption of nature/culture dualism allows for a broader perspective of environmental justice that emphasizes common cause between the two sets of revolutionary organizers, as both groups recognize that the oppressive forces they are fighting emanate from the joint structures of power created by capitalism and colonialism. As the novel ends with El Feo's unarmed, peaceful "army" of Indigenous people still marching northward, we can imagine a rendezvous with the Homeless army in Tucson as at least possible, if not probable. Recognizing the contemporary system as in a process of self-created devolution, Clinton and El Feo both draw attention to the self-destructive nature of white supremacy, hyper-consumerism, and extractive capitalism. Both groups continue to focus upon preparation and remain open to new and unlikely coalitions, readying their communities to take advantage of any tactical opportunities that might arise in the midst of this decomposition of the current order. It seems a radically flexible and opportunistic political approach, but also one likely to be discounted by many as unrealistic. It is not a simple challenge to determine how one is supposed to *plan*, exactly, for a co-produced sociopolitical uprising that is happening in nonlinear time; or, in other words, a distributed sociopolitical agentic emergence unfolding within material temporalities.

Through these storylines, Silko explores the intersections of social and environmental exploitation and the types of resistance that these acts foster across human and nonhuman communities. Clinton, in describing the trigger to the revolution for which his group is preparing, explains, "[T]he presence of the spirits—the great mountain and river spirits, the great sky spirits, all the spirits of the beloved ancestors, warriors, and old friends—the spirits would assemble and then the people of these continents would rise up" (425). Pointing to a proclamation similar to this one, Rebecca Tillett has pointed out, "Drawing upon his own complicated and paradoxical descent from both African slaves and slave owning Cherokees, Clinton explicitly comments on the dead inhabiting the

Americas" (Tillett 2007, 32). Consequently, the acts of colonization and imperialism upon which the United States is built, from this perspective, cannot be ignored and are still a constitutive part of the present. Clinton's mixed-race heritage and his apparent ability to build an intersectional critique of white colonial power in the Americas make his an essential perspective if we are seeking a logic for decolonizing environmentalisms in the novel.

We can note important similarities between Clinton's critique of power and El Feo's explanation of the inevitability of revolution, in that both foreground the neocolonial power's exploitation of North American resources. El Feo's perspective focuses on the profligacy and injustice of extractive capitalism:

> The United States allowed huge stores of grain and cheese to rot. El Feo had watched on television: the waste, great hills of discarded lumber and wire, and his heart had beat faster because he had realized someday the United States would spend all its money and sell off and strip everything that they could take from the land. Finally, the United States would be poor and broke, and all the water would be gone; then the people would see European descendants scurrying back across the ocean back to the lands of their forefathers. (523)

El Feo's insight into the overconsumption and economic inequality endemic to neoliberal extractive capitalism, operating within a highly racialized hierarchy in the United States, compels the reader to consider environmental degradation and social collapse as intricately linked catastrophes. Therefore, what at first appear to be two distinct movements for social justice—Clinton's battle for economic equality and the overthrow of a system that profits from war, crime, and homelessness, and El Feo's radical movement for retaking Indigenous lands in Mexico and the U.S. Southwest—are brought together here through Silko's emphasis on the interconnectedness of social reproduction and grounded normativity as political organizing goals that connect movements actively opposing the power of settler-colonial capitalism. Moreover, and perhaps somewhat obviously, both of these radical movements advocate for fundamental restructuring of political, economic, and social aspects of society through that nimble and flexible blend of nonviolent protest, backed by the threat of violence, and full-on militarized revolution.

El Feo's political motivations are probably the most single-minded of any character in the novel in that the clear and absolute goal of his activism is to take back Indigenous lands. In fact, the narrator explains, "El Feo did not believe in political parties, ideology, or rules," and that, in the end, he only "believed in the land" (513). For him, "All that mattered was obtaining the weapons and supplies the people needed to retake the land" (513). El Feo travels from village to village tirelessly recruiting members for the growing Indigenous army as well as enlisting practical support from the villagers to ensure solidarity as well as practical help such as safe houses and trustworthy messengers. He accepts his role with undying energy and relentless commitment, as "El Feo understood he had been chosen for one task: to remind the people never to lose sight of their precious land" (524). This unwavering commitment to the retaking of Indigenous lands is, to his mind, the first step in a larger economic and sociopolitical change that will subsequently occur. He is certain that with "the return of the land would come the return of justice, followed by peace" (513). Seen in this way, El Feo's single-minded concentration on the land takes on a broader progressive vision of promoting equality between humans as well as between human and other-than-human communities. His vision is actually one that bridges the social and environmental. And, upon further inspection, it is also certainly much less simple (or singular) than El Feo might initially suggest to his audiences.[14]

Most of the representatives of the various movements for social, economic, and environmental justice finally gather together, near the end of the novel, at the Holistic Healer's Convention held in Tucson, Arizona. The convention "had been called by natural and indigenous healers to discuss the earth's crisis" (718). In these climactic scenes, the reader is presented with a fuller picture of the scale of the revolutionary changes these disparate, yet increasingly coordinated, radical activist groups hope to achieve.[15] "As the prophecies had warned, the earth's weather was in chaos; the rain clouds had disappeared while terrible winds and freezing had followed, burning, dry summers" (718). The prophetic nature of these coming transformations adds another layer to the novel's exploration of distributed agency and nonlinear temporalities. For example, in the short chapter "Prophesy," El Feo and Tacho, his twin brother, describe the approaching revolutionary moment as such:

> What was coming could not be stopped . . . what was coming was relentless and inevitable; it might require five or ten years

of great violence and conflict. It might require a hundred years of spirit voices and simple population growth, but the result would be the same: tribal people would retake the Americas; tribal people would retake ancestral land all over the world. This was what earth's spirits wanted: her indigenous children who loved her and did not harm her. (712)

Though it might be tempting to suggest the Indigenous activists are pointing to Fate when they assume to know the "tribal people would retake the Americas," that would be a reductive move, ultimately allowing for a Western, empirically based discounting of their prediction as a sort of superstition. Rather, if seen through the lens of Angelita's and El Feo's speeches discussed above, indicating that the People's Army's decolonizing aspirations speak to an approach of sociopolitical organizing that operates within a framework of distributed agency. Tacho actually suggests this very thing: the "pilgrims" participating in his nonviolent march north to the U.S. border would be "protected by natural forces set loose" and "forces raised by spirits," yet, "among these forces would be human beings," and the "people would dream the same dream, a dream sent by the spirits of the continent" (712). This is a revolutionary amalgamation of entangled spirits, humans, and more-than-human forces. Echoing his twin brother Tacho, El Feo himself recognizes the complex multiplicity of approaches that will be necessary to achieve it: "All across earth there were those listening and waiting, isolated and lonely despised outcasts of the earth. First the lights would go out—dynamite or earthquake, it did not matter. All sources of electrical power generation would be destroyed. Darkness was the ally of the poor. One uprising would spark another and another" (513). The prophetic (spiritual), the technological (or lack thereof), the nonhuman and human agency are all present in various ways in this description of historical change. Clear distinction among each of these forces is not possible, and is not deemed necessary in these descriptions of the uprising to come, as the revolutionary agency builds as an assemblage of forces from its very conception.

Back in Tucson, Clinton and Roy also attempt to build their "army" of homeless people while not knowing exactly what will trigger the revolutionary moment they hope is approaching. Each in his own way, however, does recognize the potential in developing a network of urban-based communities of resistance across the country. In this context, building their numbers and increasing their outreach to other underserved and disenfranchised groups are practical steps of preparation, while both continue to preach patience to each other and their allies. Roy and Clinton help form organized homeless camps around the city and construct a network of shared information and goods. As the state does decide to finally confront and remove the growing homeless encampments, the police and SWAT teams use "armored vehicles to smash down the cardboard and tin lean-tos and tents pitched under the mesquite trees" (740). When they come to the one encampment comprised almost entirely of veterans, it appears it is the veterans' turn to endure this state-sanctioned violence. However, as the police approach, the SWAT team suddenly stops and appeared "paralyzed by the sight of the homeless war veterans standing at attention in their raggedy army-surplus uniforms without any weapons. Clinton would never forget that moment" (741). And, though seemingly a symbolic victory at best, this moment is one Clinton believes will only add to the revolutionary momentum. The symbolic act of the homeless army takes on a more material form, too, when seen through the joint lenses of distributed agency and nonlinear time:

> [Clinton aspires to] . . . the patience of the old tribal people who had been humble enough not to expect change in one human lifetime, or even five lifetimes. Maybe not tomorrow or next week, but someday Clinton knew, the other homeless people would remember the defiance of the homeless vets. . . . Like little seeds, the feelings would grow, and the police violence that had rained down on the people would only nurture the growing bitterness. (741)

While the nurturing of "little seeds" in hopes of future growth might fit comfortably in contemporary humanist models of social movement organizing, the deep-time sense of futurity and the meaningfulness of present acts in the absence of clear near-term rewards seems indicative of something more unique. "Other homeless men and women had witnessed the face-off between the SWAT team and the veterans," and Clinton had "detected a flicker of recognition" across their faces (741). The witnesses detect, in this small moment of qualified victory, a possible community that respects all of its members and refuses to devalue and dispossess people based on nonsensical hierarchical structures of race and capitalism. These visions of the possible may operate much as the "voices" of Angelita's ancestors, providing another layer of agentic capacity to fuel the revolution.

The relationship between the organizing strategies of the Homeless Veterans Army and the Indigenous People's Army continually calls our attention to the pivotal, yet contingent and partial, role of human action in constituting historical change. Each group, as outlined above, attempts to strike a balance between patience (without complacency) and opportunistic action (unchecked by preconceived expectations or limitations). Patience, vigilance, imagination, and opportunism are privileged in the hopes of cultivating knowledge, skills, insight, and momentum that might just prepare them for the right moment—when the lights go out!—to destroy the current colonial system of the Death-Eye Dog and facilitate the creation of social structures that promote a justice-based social reproduction for Indigenous peoples and other poor and dispossessed communities.

A Patient Urgency

In *Almanac*, as in *Through the Arc*, it is extremely difficult to locate, map, and/or define political agency if we insist on asking for an intentional subject and the linear organizing of a traditional political movement. In order to think beyond the liberal political subject, and to instead locate a postanthropocentric and distributed environmental politics, it is helpful to identify a few key elements that seem elemental to this inchoate, alternative political agency. As we have seen, much of the political work in the novel echoes the task of the children, the young protectors of the almanac on its path north, as they tried to save its sacred pages. The various approaches are certainly opportunistic, as well as flexible; they move beyond traditional political strategy and target goals through their willingness to embrace a vision that promotes radical social and political transformation. The various movement leaders, to a person, embrace a distributed agency comprised, to various degrees, of human, spiritual, and nonhuman elements. And this similar foundation helps to propel the movements beyond a rights-based advocacy, at least in part, due to its material conception of agency and temporality. The various revolutionary activists in the novel are able to relate their own seemingly limited day-to-day work of observation and preparation to a massively optimistic and transformative, yet to them very realizable, goal of a decolonized America in part because of a nonlinear conception of time (not in spite of it). These movements resist, and also at times outstrip, contemporary formulations of progressive linear politics.

Within the context of contemporary environmental politics and its discourses of emergency, it is particularly interesting to note the strategic prominence of preparation and patience in *Almanac*'s revolutionary movements. Increasingly, all things related to climate change activism are presented as "working against the clock" and meeting deadlines to beat the "point of no return," or the "tipping point," of runaway global climate change. And there is good reason to be concerned—or infuriated—with the inaction of national and international institutions, particularly in the contemporary U.S. political and economic climate (as noted, in fact, in the first chapter).[16] In this context, with literally the planet as we know it on the line, coming at the problem touting patience seems almost heretical. Unless, that is, and as we would do well to remember, this *patience* is not equivalent to *passivity*. The nonlinear and material temporalities that shape the Indigenous revolutionary work in *Almanac* operate on vastly different time scales and time lines than liberal humanist models. A patient-urgency is sustainable, it generates persistence against great odds. And it is essential that environmental scholars and activists do not discount this approach as somehow limited to a particular indigenous way of thinking, or only relevant to an irrecoverable preindustrial past. Within this type of reorientation, those who aim to build a radically postcapitalist, postcolonial, socially and environmentally just society in the Americas might see the unseeable, conjure the unconjurable.

In closing this chapter, I want to focus on one specific instance of nontraditional agentic capacity—a wonderful example of impossible conjuring, actually—that puts several of this project's animating questions into relief. This is a particularly fascinating and fantastical scene that takes place, far from the U.S.-Mexico border, in a Yupik village in Alaska. Lecha, Yeome's granddaughter and Zeta's twin sister, meets an elder woman in an Alaskan Yupik village, where she is visiting and staying with a friend, who is known for her special and unique spiritual knowledge and powers. Lecha's friend Rose coordinates an opportunity for her to witness the least-known, but most powerful, spell this elder can perform. In the recreation room late one evening, Lecha witnesses a fantastic event: she watches as the old woman rubs "special fur pelts" against the villagers' shared television set, speaks into the screen as she tells old tribal stories, and begins to create and somehow guide a "natural electricity" capable of traveling great distances. These "fields of forces," Lecha is told, will adversely impact both the weather and the electronic instruments on planes passing overhead, quite often resulting in the plane crashing. In this case, the television screen actually depicts the final frantic moments of a plane crashing until the "screen goes white" (157). In this striking story, the Yupik elder actively repurposes the colonizers' tools in a fantastic and violent resistance to dispossession and resource extraction. Rather than being overwhelmed or dismissive of the technologies introduced by the U.S. government and transnational corporations to discover, extract, and transport its natural resources, she turns the tools of extraction and oppression against those who presume to control and benefit from their use.

Lecha becomes understandably fascinated while watching the woman enact her seemingly impossible form of resistance to extractive capitalism and the colonizing state. "White people could fly circling objects in the sky that sent messages and images of nightmares and dreams," Rose explains to her as they watch, "but the old woman knew how to turn the destruction back on its senders" (156). The Yupik woman's fantastical craft, through which she has "realized the possibilities in the white man's gadgets" (155), prefigures the concept of distributed agency, which is at the center of the philosophy motivating the Indigenous army's rebellion later in the novel. "The old woman had gathered *great surges of energy* out of the atmosphere, by summoning spirit beings through recitations of the stories that were also indictments of the greedy destroyers of the land. With the stories the old woman was able *to assemble powerful forces* flowing from the spirits of ancestors" (156; my emphasis). The woman's "plane-crashing spell" blends the technological, the natural, and the supernatural with a deep spiritual and material response to the colonization of the Americas (156–57). The spirits that her stories evoke, in fact, are described as "furious and vengeful" and apparently quite ready to lend a hand against the colonizing forces (157).

On her flights back to Anchorage and then Seattle, directly following her witnessing the Yupic woman's work, Lecha meets a "well-dressed white man with a briefcase" (158), an "insurance man" whose industry is profiting from the growing resource extraction in Alaska. He informs her of "dozens of unexplained plane crashes" across the state (159), and as a member of the insurance industry, these accidents are of course professionally significant for the man. The microcosm of the relation between settler-colonial society and the colonized cultures of Indigenous people in the Americas is set in the recognizably claustrophobic space of a small passenger plane. Lecha can even smell the alcohol-laden breath of the insurance man, who himself cannot sense (no matter how closely he might currently be sitting to one of its originators) the rising power of a network of Indigenous decolonization groups. He drunkenly explains that "whiteouts" are occurring suddenly in otherwise fine weather conditions and relays rumors that a new sort of Bermuda Triangle is forming between Bethel and Nome, Alaska. Before falling asleep into a deep, alcohol-induced slumber, he dismisses, however, any sort of nonempirical explanation for the crashes: "None of that stuff is true. It can all be explained" (160). Lecha has just witnessed the old Yupik woman's power for herself, of course, and is just now learning of the wider range of her actions (as well as considering the loss of life in the crashes as well). On the other hand, the insurer has been aware of the myriad incidents, and their extraordinary elements, for some time but is unable, or unwilling, to accept any explanations that deviate from his own empirical view of the world. In economic terms alone, the increased level of risk is central to his profession's ability to capture wealth from the ongoing extraction of resources in Alaska, and the better the industry understands the problem the more likely it will be able to set insurance rates appropriately (ensuring a consistent profit model). Yet, he still discounts any possibly pertinent information not provided to him in purely empirical terms. Meanwhile, "Lecha had seen what the old Yupik woman could do with only a piece of weasel fur, a satellite map on a TV screen and the spirit energy of a story" (158). She has her own evidence to go on, she knows what she experienced in the Yupic village's recreation room.

Juxtaposing Lecha and the insurance man as they sit beside one another on a plane returning to the continental United States highlights their opposing senses of agency and knowledge-formation practices. The impact of this experience on Lecha is clear, though: she has "never forgotten" the old woman and "learned something" important from her experiences with the Yupic (158). Part of this lesson for Lecha, no doubt, is the power of assemblages themselves and the repurposing of the Destroyers' technologies as a potentially powerful form of resistance. The question of intentionality seems particularly important in the context of this small episode in the novel, hinting toward the larger questions of political efficacy that my reading of the novel engages. To what extent does the old woman's ability to "gather" and "assemble" these forces leave us with a resistance to colonization that simply coopts the rational agency of the colonizers? And, after any necessary assembly, to what degree is the Yupik woman able to *control* this assemblage of forces? Though the woman indicates she is able to direct these forces well enough to decide for herself whether or not to actually crash a particular plane (159), the question of intentionality is still left somewhat open. While it's obviously not the point to look at the Yupik woman's actions as a type of blueprint for resistance, it may act as a valuable stimulant for redefining the possible. At the very least, the distributed agency of the Yupik woman's epic and fantastical defiance of extractive capitalism operates as a story, or as a representation, that materially unsettles contemporary norms and expectations that account for a political "act" and its component parts. The astounding inexplicability of this power opens up a space in which to think the impossible, where the unimaginable now becomes a distinct aspect of Lecha's imagination (and our own). Whether or not the woman wields her mystical power with intentionality, and whether this power is even "real," Lecha has now been introduced to the power of assemblages as a distributed agency of resistance.

Lecha's experience with the Yupik woman might also remind us of the key difference between the representations of social movement organizing in Yamashita's *Through the Arc* and Silko's *Almanac*. In the former, there are no justice-oriented, alternative movements ready to fill the socioeconomic and political void left as the Matacao plastic city crumbles and disappears due to the distributed agency of insurgent bacteria. Instead, we are left to assume that new global capital projects will move in to replace that one industrial marketplace, and the safest thing for Kazumasa and Lourdes is to retreat into an apolitical, pastoral plantation life. Additionally, *Through the Arc*'s striving for narrative closure allows traditional humanist agency to reformulate itself, even if in the form of Kazumasa's rejection of modernity and supposed retreat to a pastoral life. We see in this incomplete depiction of distributed political agency just how difficult it is to imagine political organizing and directed historical change beyond the norms of unfettered, rational human agency. Whereas in *Almanac*, although the cliffhanger style of the ending leaves us with only circumstantial and suggestive evidence, it is clear, at the very least, that a multitude of distinct yet interconnected radical social movements are readying to take advantage of what might be a series of imminent tactical opportunities in order to transform society and reconstruct healthier systems of social reproduction. Consequently, the possibility for effective social justice organizing within a framework of distributed agency is more fully apparent in Silko's work. The image of Lecha and the white businessman is a case in point: Lecha, her mind on fire with radical potentialities, and the insurance man, drugged and bloated with alcohol nodding off to sleep, sit close to each other in their cramped plane seats while representing two worlds on divergent paths. The clarity of thought, energy in action, and the optimism of belief in the novel, as it is seen in the words and deeds of Lecha, Angelita, El Feo, Clinton, and others, is always with the revolutionary figures, despite the fact that their movements seem so overmatched by dominant systems of white America's institutions and structures of power. Yet, in this scene the white insurance man, as representative of settler-colonial institutions and extractive capitalism, is disdainful and overconfident in his ignorance while, on the other hand, Lecha is coming to realize the potential transformative power of assemblages.

The past two chapters have been working toward a general contention that the challenges of our posthuman and postnatural moment require a reformulated and justice-oriented environmental politics; a system that must become more comfortable acting within a context of uncertainty and limited human agency while at the same time expanding its capacity to address, rather than recoil from, challenges such as climate change and environmental injustice with both creativity and boldness. Yamashita's and Silko's related yet unique depictions of revolutionary social movement organizing—contingent, nonlinear, and coproduced with agency dispersed across the human and nonhuman—offer posthuman and environmental scholars a window through which we glimpse several potentialities, as well as limitations and challenges, for thinking environmentalism as a social movement operating within the framework of distributed agency and nonlinear temporality. As environmental scholars unsettle humanist conceptions of time and agency, intentionality is placed under a rather intensive pressure and scrutiny. Politically, it seems dangerous to too quickly banish the autonomous actor and the rational act. In the novel, however, we find new coalitions and unexpected opportunities seized, as an ever-attentive patient-urgency emerges as a new temporality for radical organizing. Silko's nonlinear representation of a patient/active organizing method is another surprising assemblage of seeming contradiction. It is postanthropocentric and nonlinear; galvanizing a new way of seeing and engaging with the present that is not trapped inside the dream of causal relations and rational intentionality. It is progressive, without relying on Progress. When we consider the intense intra-actions of distributed agency and nonlinear temporality, the deeply embedded inextricability of act and time, this is what I term *material temporalities*.

In the era of climate change, the clock is ticking and the time for action was already years ago, and some who are calling for patience are acting in bad faith, certainly. So, is this era of environmental crisis really the time to let go of linear progress and rational agency? Could it possibly be a good idea to ditch anthropocentrism in the Anthropocene? It most likely is not really a choice at all. But to do so won't be easy. We next turn to the burgeoning genre of climate change fiction to further explore why this is necessary, how and why it won't be easy, and what practices of imagination might be necessary.

5

(Dis)intentional Politics and Its Limits

Crisis and Innovation in Nathaniel Rich's *Odds Against Tomorrow* and Chang-rae Lee's *On Such a Full Sea*

> Without progress, what is struggle?
>
> —Anna Tsing, *The Mushroom at the End of the World*

When examining fictional representations of political subjects and social movements through the combined lenses of other-than-empirical knowledge formation processes, post-rational agencies and nonlinear temporalities, it becomes increasingly necessary to imagine possible forms of political organizing that operate beyond linear, progressive, future-oriented, and goal-based narratives. The impacts of these reorientations upon social movement organizing, operating within the logics of distributed political agency, remain stubbornly opaque. Thinking deeply about distributed agency and its consequences for political efficacy, it appears, has led us to a rather odd-sounding question: What would it mean to organize a sociopolitical movement without an intentional goal? I come to this unusual query via the radical indeterminacy inherent in recent theorizations of the decentered human and distributed agency. Exploring agency without intentionality opens up two important conversations that I hope will prove productive for working through this uncertainty. First, the counterintuitiveness of *disintentional organizing* itself points out the vastly new terrain on which posthuman political subjectivity places us, reminding us how mistaken we would be to assume that the decentered human subject is automatically a more ecologically minded one. Many of our assumptions about progressive politics must be unsettled before we can reimagine political agency without the bounded, rational actor. Second, trying to envision something such as disintentional politics, as this chapter will attempt to chronicle in its reading of two recent works of climate fiction, helps us recognize that distributed environmental politics—though not intentional in the sense that liberal humanism would suggest—is not doomed to despair and passivity, nor to total chaos.

I intend for disintentionality, as a concept of political agency, to operate as an imaginative and open-ended construct within which we might develop a path in the liminal space between intentional and unintentional (or, between rational intention and the uncertainty of unintended consequences). It is most helpful, then, to approach disintentional politics as the phrasing of a problem, as a theoretical and operational challenge, rather than as some type of new political program or plan. The concept, in fact, challenges the viability of the traditionally understood organizing plan. A *distributed* environmental politics might then also be a *disintentional* politics. The distributed political subject finds themselves working in a context of reimagined material relations to mixed-communities and agentic assemblages, thinking from positioned and relational rationalities, and operating in temporalities unbound from causal relations. A disintentional politics would recognize the fatal conceits of rational intentionality while simultaneously reimagining meaningful and impactful acts within distributed agencies of intra-active assemblages. Deploying the term *disintentional*, as opposed to *unintentional*, is a purposeful attempt to defamiliarize the idea, hoping to avoid certain unhelpful, humanist assumptions we might harbor about acting without intention as, at best, reckless and, at worst, dangerous and even immoral. Disintentional agency assumes there never has been a rational, intentional actor anyway—at least not as Humanism would have us believe—and, as a result, it is now incumbent upon us to rethink the relation between act and result beyond the binary of intentionality/unintentionality.

A disintentional approach to environmental politics demands the posthuman, disanthropocentric political subject develop new ways of operating effectively, without assuming humanist configurations of intention, linear progress, and futurity: that is, methods for engaging agentic assemblies in ways that enable social and ecological justice (without a traditionally defined, future-oriented endpoint or overarching, goal-oriented approach). Distributed organizing must operate outside linear constructs of modern Progress, and this is a daunting task for reimagining agency and temporality. As Anna Tsing has poignantly reflected: "Progress felt great; there was always something better ahead. Progress gave us the 'progressive' political causes . . . [and] I hardly know how to think about justice without progress. The problem is that progress stopped making sense" (Tsing 2015, 24–25). Tsing's openness here resonates strongly with me; I also hardly know how to think "justice without progress," but I do think many of the fictional narratives analyzed in this book offer essential insights, warnings, and even some hope.

This chapter intends to examine exactly how the social, economic, and political disruptions of climate change, and the narrative fiction it is inspiring, press us to produce a political agency and efficacy that is difficult to imagine from our contemporary humanist viewpoint. In particular, these texts will allow us to explore several fictional characters and communities who find themselves asked to participate in the molding of a better future while simultaneously knowing they will not progress through this future in exactly the manner modernity has always promised. Can we forge a progressive politics without Progress? "It is in this new dilemma that new tools for noticing seem so important," Tsing concludes, "Indeed, life on earth seems at stake" (25). We have already been working through some "new tools for noticing" in previous chapters, from Thoreau's Relational Knowing to the patient-urgency of The People's Army in Silko's *Almanac*. Now, turning to Nathaniel Rich's *Odds Against Tomorrow* and Chang Rae Lee's *On Such a Full Sea*, and their respective depictions of climate-impacted futures, the selective readings to follow provide inchoate representations of a disintentional politics based upon distributed modes of being, knowing, and acting.

My reading of *Odds Against Tomorrow*, first of all, interrogates Rich's depiction of a newly decentered human and how this distributed subject might react to the sudden realization that while human agency is partly (and consequentially) responsible for climate change, humans will also find their power to control, or even manage, the resulting weather-related events and their socioeconomic impacts significantly partial and limited. Mitchell Zukor, the novel's main character, is a white, upper-class male, and recent college graduate, who also happens to be a math wizard of Wall Street. When he finds his assumptions of human exceptionalism disrupted via a massive hurricane that floods the island of Manhattan, he does not suddenly and smoothly discover a progressive environmental politics, nor does he transform into an ideal ecological citizen. Instead,

Mitchell isolates himself from friends, family, and community and, in a struggle with depression and anxiety, begins to build a literal wall of storm debris to surround his squatter's palace. The narrative opens up questions that I have argued are sometimes obscured by environmental scholarship, if it too quickly assumes that the disruption of liberal humanist subjectivity, and its dominant assumptions of anthropocentrism, will inevitably lead individuals toward a presupposed path to ecological consciousness. *Odds Against Tomorrow* implies, instead, that the physical and psychic disruption of anthropocentrism might have much less predictable results; the novel struggles to imagine how unintentional acts might become disintentional politics, and there is much to learn from the novel's ultimate failure of imagination.

The chapter then transitions to Lee's *On Such a Full Sea*, with an eye toward the narrative's construction of a (partial) political imaginary of disintentionality. This novel's politics emanate from the materialist premise that each individual exists in physical and psychic interrelation with a larger ecology: an ecology that should be understood to include the cultural, institutional, and nonhuman environment (in the vein of Di Chiro's mixed-community concept explored in chapter 3). The motto that both inspires and challenges the newly formed political consciousness of the B-Mor residents is quite succinctly, but rather cryptically, expressed as "where you are." Within this deceptively complex expression, much repeated even as the characters remain unsure of its meaning, the inhabitants of B-Mor explore political possibilities that focus intensely on the present moment, and attempt to organize that intensity without a strategic plan, or some particular future promised land, in mind. I will suggest that this ambiguous phrase attempts to politicize the distributed agency of the decentered posthuman subject, or the distributed political actant, of which we have, to this point, caught only fleeting glimpses.

In the end, neither of these climate fiction novels, in the midst of their extended representations of postanthropocentric political subjectivities, is quite able to produce a commensurate and coherent version of futurity without Progress. Both novels, instead, sketch a certain political resonance for disintentionality, particularly via the characters' newfound attention to the material connections between the human and nonhuman environment in the present moment (however disrupted the social and ecological systems of these interconnected worlds become). Both narratives explore a type of political agency that functions within the myriad distributed networks of the present, without relying upon a particular future goal; and while neither approach quite finds its way, the failures are instructive.

Wasting Away on the Land

A preoccupation with futurity dominates the plot of *Odds Against Tomorrow*, or, as the title implies, the lack of it. Its near-future setting, its contemplation of agency in the Anthropocene, and the almost obsessive preoccupation with the unpredictability of the future (and the present, for that matter), opens a space to explore the limits of contemporary eco-theory's often overly optimistic attitude regarding the political potential of postanthropocentricism. The narrative is driven by two crisis-inducing events that draw attention to the scripting of agency and futurity in the novel. The first, revealed in a flashback to Mitchell's college years in the opening chapter, is a massive earthquake in the Pacific Northwest that flattens Seattle, severely damages the region's infrastructure, and kills a significant number of residents. The second, serving as the main narrative event of second half of the novel, is a hurricane that brings intense flooding to New York City, kills many of those who do not (or cannot) evacuate, and effectively shuts down the city for weeks. The earthquake, while portrayed as deeply tragic and unsettling to the nation as a whole, more readily fits into the modern humanist view of environmental catastrophe. That is, it is understood as a forceful reminder of the unpredictability of natural systems and the random nature of natural disasters. Hurricane Tammy, on the other hand, more clearly registers as a disaster induced by both human and nonhuman factors, in large part due to the recognized role climate change plays in the drought preceding the storm, the strengthening of the storm over the Atlantic Ocean, and the subsequent storm surge and flooding. This ultimately allows readers to consider the flood as the result of a distributed—that is, an inextricable mixture of the human and nonhuman—agency.

These multiple registers of agency are intimately linked to temporality and anxiety about the future in the novel. Mitchell Zukor, a recent college graduate from the Midwest, is in the early but lucrative stage of a career developing algorithms that predict the odds of various potential disasters becoming actual ones. Later, however, Mitchell breaks with this predominantly empirical style, utilizing a more subjective, imaginative, and even quasi-religious approach that develops into what he comes to call a "cult of fear" (Rich 2014, 71–73). Eloquently capturing the essence of this character, Lawrence Buell describes Mitchell as "a neurotically inventive Chicken-Little doomster with a pathologically heightened environmental risk consciousness who finds an unusual, corporate niche in the accelerated deregulated capitalism of the post-Reagan era" (Buell 2011, 276). I would be hard pressed to put it better. Even given the many future-oriented concerns regarding possible economic and geopolitical crises, it is the nonhuman force of the San Juan fault off the northwest coast and the distributed agency of Hurricane Tammy that drive the novel's exploration of individual and societal responses to an increasingly uncertain and prediction-resistant future. Buell, also noting this element of the novel, suggests that "the uncertain future semiotically and materially [becomes] the determining factor" in Rich's depiction of a contemporary moment where "uncertainty . . . is fundamental" (282). The anxiety caused by the uncertainty manifests in Mitchell's personal life and also the society as a whole, where corporate leaders become obsessed with mathematical attempts to quantify risk. It is smart business, sure, but it also clearly becomes a sort of therapy for the wealthy. In fact, as Mitchell studies the residents of Manhattan, he begins to notice that a "feeling was building. An urban malaria, a future-effected anxiety disorder. Whatever kind of disease it was, it had become infectious" (Rich 2014, 51). Ecocritic Antonia Mehnert, reading the novel in relation to Ulrich Beck's theory of risk-society, points out that this "disease" in the novel stems from "a society confronted with threats beyond its control" (Mehnert 2016, 128). This future-oriented anxiety, to phrase it another way, becomes a central preoccupation of the novel's plot as it investigates the possible individual, cultural, and institutional reactions stemming from an increasing lack of confidence that the environmental, economic, and political context of the near future will resemble that of the present moment. It is not only that the future becomes unimaginable, but that the unpredictability of that future begins to impact the present moment in psychological and material ways. Mitchell, much like the broader society he inhabits, ultimately struggles to find ways to live in the present that might assuage his deepening future-oriented anxiety.

After the earthquake in Seattle, but before Hurricane Tammy hits the northeast coast, a company surreptitiously recruits Mitchell away from his original employer and introduces him to their plan to commodify this rising anxiety about the future. The company, named FutureWorld, essentially offers their corporate clients indemnity against future catastrophes by utilizing a loophole in the laws of New York State, in which a company that makes "reasonable" efforts to prepare for catastrophes cannot be sued by employees (Rich 2014, 28). As the company founder, Alec Charnoble, explains to Mitchell, FutureWorld plans to "fill the void" left after insurance companies refused to fully cover the companies in a post-9/11 world. Their slogan: *FutureWorld: Find Out What the Future Will Cost You* (19). And with the man at the helm named Charnoble, not so subtly calling to mind the disaster at Chernobyl, one would guess it is going to be costly in more ways than one. The job suits Mitchell, though, who will now be paid handsomely for what he has already been doing for most of his young adulthood: running the statistical probabilities of various worst-case future catastrophes, or black swan events, and mapping out best-case survival plans in the event they actually occur. Companies are paying millions of dollars for Mitchell and FutureWorld to simply help them retrieve their sense of confidence in the future. The average stressed-out denizens of the city, of course, have no such access to what is really a very expensive confidence boost in human exceptionalism and the promise of futurity. If the companies are willing to pay FutureWorld exorbitant sums of money and sit through a series of Mitchell's worst-case-scenario presentations, they also cannot be held lawfully responsible by their employees, citizens, or other institutions for any catastrophe their operations might be linked to in the future. The dream of never-ending economic expansion and the promissory future becomes an expensive illusion for the wealthy. Mitchell comes to realize, "Those in power wanted to be told that everything will stay just as before—as long as you purchase a little insurance. And this was the service that Future Days would provide. In the short term it would be a lucrative business" (236). And, for Mitchell, "[T]he short term was all that mattered. He was beginning to think there would be no long term" (236). The palpable anxiety in New York City, even before Tammy arrives, speaks to the intense discomfort that results from contemplating an increasingly unpredictable future.[1]

Once the storm does arrive, Mitchell finds himself working in the city while his clients, Charnoble and the city's elite, use many of his detailed escape plans to evacuate the island. After a harrowing night holed up in Mitchell's apartment, he and Jane Eppler, his co-worker and emerging love interest, are forced to evacuate by canoe. Paddling through an entirely flooded Manhattan, the pair find themselves on a water tour of horrific destruction and death, until they pull into a Red Cross camp on the Jersey side of the Hudson River. This traumatic event rips away any last remnants of Mitchell's confidence in Baconian conceptions of human dominance over nature. In fact, after this experience, he muses, "The idea that man could order the world to his own design was the most pitiful tale ever told. An empty house, left alone for just a single year, begins to return to the earth. It starts with a storm, a ceiling leak" (236). This is a crisis of subjectivity and consciousness that environmental theorists and activists would do well to think about more thoroughly. After the storm, Mitchell comes to realize that "the long term was now upon them . . . over the next several decades, things would not be as before. Things would be, for starters, a lot wetter. The floods would keep coming, more and more frequently. Soon the coastal cities would lose the will to rebuild the old seawalls and levees" (196). In this manner, the novel provocatively raises questions about contemporary conceptions of futurity and how individuals and communities might respond to the realization that global climate change is at once a (substantially) human creation and (partially) beyond human control. The novel's increasing, almost suffocating, focus on Mitchell's struggle to come to terms with his uncertain future and unknowable present moment is indicative of the challenge the Anthropocene presents for the humanist worldview. With his positivist and anthropocentric worldview disrupted, Mitchell at first struggles to see a viable future of any sort: in large part because his conception of intentionality cannot withstand the "innovative" powers of weather systems in the age of human-induced climate change. Upon further reflection, for instance, he concedes: "Tammy was worse than anyone could imagine. . . . And what was human imagination, after all, but the reconfiguration of past events? Tammy . . . was an innovative disaster. Its horrors were unprecedented. It created images that man had never seen before, but once seen, could never be unseen" (234). The impacts of these overwhelming realizations upon Mitchell lead to a stripping away of his confidence in rational scientific prediction.

As Manhattan remains flooded and uninhabitable for week after week, and after a short but harrowing stay in a FEMA camp for evacuees, Mitchell decides against any return to Manhattan. He instead sets up his own camp in an abandoned and waterlogged area in the outskirts of Staten Island, close to the Long Island Sound. The government has decreed certain areas "Dead Zones" and is contemplating not rebuilding the most damaged, and often the poorest, neighborhoods. As a result, the former neighborhood of Flatlands, now designated by city officials as a Zone 5 area (lowest priority for rebuilding), is likely to be left by the city's policymakers and engineers to revert back to its natural state. Mitchell moves into the abandoned Carnarsie Bank Trust Building in Flatlands, in search for an "unmediated relationship to the land" (Mehnert 2016, 133), and others slowly begin to arrive in the neighborhood as well, populating abandoned churches and some of the other larger and more structurally sound buildings. That this community dedicated to simplicity and self-sufficiency will be built in a place that is most vulnerable to future storms and sea level rise, itself a phenomenon of distributed agency instigated by the complex impacts of the industrial and technological revolutions in the era of late capitalism, is not lost on the attentive reader. In fact, in the novel, Flatlands is not zoned for rebuilding exactly because it is determined to be most helpful to Manhattanites as marshlands, to buffer the city against future storm surges. It is also certainly not irrelevant that the now destroyed Flatlands neighborhood is a diverse and distinctly working-class neighborhood (in the actual world and presumably in the novel as well, though the narrative does not address it), and lacks the political power of the Manhattan elite. Whether or not the power brokers of Manhattan's revival will care that an emergent community of squatters is becoming an aspect of this buffer landscape remains unclear.

The Dead Zone settlers that begin to appear in the weeks following Mitchell's arrival increasingly aspire to build a functioning alternative community that operates outside existing political and economic structures. It never becomes clear if this community might forge a truly oppositional politics in any practical sense and, even less generously, might be read as an example of libertarian escapist fantasy. Mitchell isolates himself from these new neighbors, on the other hand, and focuses with obsessive passion (one of his hallmark traits, actually) upon projects that will improve the chances of his own individual survival in the Dead Zone, thus limiting his commitment to community building (and furthering the newcomers' tendency to view him alternatively as an oracle or unstable hermit). Mitchell's attempt to make a personal fortress out of the Carnarsie Bank building is in part an intense desire to simplify his world in the face of complexity, destruction, fragility, and mortality. By a stroke of luck, the bank building is itself the best protected building in the neighborhood, as it butts up against a marsh that acts as its own natural barrier between Mitchell and the Sound proper. In response to this sudden loss of trust in an empirical and human-centered worldview, safety and privacy become overwhelming concerns for Mitchell. Through this simplification, he hopes to regain some level of confidence in his ability to shape his own world. For instance, when the first young couple arrives to settle down in the Flatlands, sporting backpacks and outdoor recreation clothing, he instantly panics. His focus must remain on his own progress, because "what Mitchell was after—an impregnable, self-contained, self-sustaining fortress—would require . . . dedication. No place would be reserved for anyone else" (Rich 2014, 289). Since he can only see tragedy ahead for society, Mitchell shrinks the scale of his world all the way down to the individual, in hopes of conjuring the future again. In this manner, Rich concentrates his exploration of this transformative experience in one single character (in this case it is a character embodying the many privileges of being a straight, white, wealthy male), and only begins to suggest how this individual change might relate to more systemic societal revolutions.

We are certainly not meant to take Mitchell's hunkering down in a self-imposed hermitage in the old bank as a fully fleshed-out plan for surviving the Anthropocene, but rather as a process of deep and difficult individual metamorphosis. This is a crisis of subjectivity and agency in the face of the immense scale of climate change and its myriad and complex impacts upon human society. When Mitchell does attempt to "dream forward," his confidence is strikingly limited for someone recently renowned (and well remunerated) for mathematics-based, acutely specific predictive capabilities. He constantly reaffirms his decision to isolate himself as the only option. "In the Carnarsie Bank Trust he would create his own self-contained universe. This was a future. It might not be the best possible future or even a particularly comfortable future, but it was a future he could see" (287). To contemplate a future beyond what "he could see" immediately in front of him, however, seems utterly impossible. He remains hopeful, in a certain way, but his desire to "see" an immediately knowable future is emblematic of the anthropocentric conceit of human exceptionalism and progress. That is, the assumption that humans are now and will always be the rightful and dominant subjects of history (and futurity) on earth (and beyond), and will utilize that subjectivity to direct the future in foreseeable and beneficial ways. He dreams wistfully, "There had to be a big perfect thing right ahead, some pursuit more vast and profound than fear prediction. Now that his old way of life was gone, nothing remained. . . . So there had to be something larger up ahead, because if not, then the only thing was destruction and chaos" (253). Without an envisioned future goal, a future-oriented plan to help construct the present moment, Mitchell is set terribly adrift. To varying degrees, many readers might relate to this feeling; it is, after all, quite reasonable for someone to want to feel as though one generally knows, if not what *will* happen, the general contours of the world in which it will happen. But climate change is making this increasingly impossible.

Mitchell's struggle to operate in the present moment without the sense of an intelligible future is then indicative of the challenge environmental activists face in the Anthropocene. Does the immensity of the challenge of global climate change, combined with the uncertainty of distributed agency, leave activists adrift in the present? Or, is there an opportunity in this disorientation to forge a new type of non-progress-oriented politics that can be impactful in the uncertain present without relying upon the comfort of a knowable future? Mitchell seems to be struggling with a form of this question himself as he builds his castle amid the debris of the Dead Zone. One response suggests that a back-to-nature mantra, reminiscent of rugged individualism, will persist throughout his experiment of regeneration. For instance, we can note its significant presence in this passage in which Mitchell questions whether he is actually prepared for the task:

> He was under no illusion. Out here in the neighborhood formerly known as Flatlands . . . he wouldn't unearth Eden, or even some agrarian ideal. Most likely his work here wouldn't amount to very much at all. He knew nothing, after all, about farming, fertilization, engineering, construction. Problems would arise that he could not anticipate and he'd be comically unprepared to fix them. The weather would only become increasingly erratic. The fields might go fallow or flood. Winter would be excruciating. And a single serious injury or illness would force him to give up. (286)

Comparing himself unfavorably to an "ideal" settler and cultivator of the land, and due to this lack of experience and capacity for an "agrarian" existence, he admits that he is not setting out to build a lasting entity. The physical aspects of his work in the Flatlands are tied up in a more existential project: one that delves to the core of what it means to be human, to labor, and to dream in the posthuman and postnatural world of the Anthropocene. What are the future-oriented expectations of his present labor? And how might he invigorate the process of foundation building within the contours of distributed agency? While the others joining him in the Dead Zone do seem more intent on building the foundations of a communal existence with longevity, Mitchell remains predominantly focused on his immediate and individual circumstances. In addition to the problematic back-to-the-land agenda, a major impediment to the emergence of a productive social project is the very fact that Mitchell and these other predominantly (entirely?) white "settlers" are recreating the settler-colonialism and dispossession at the heart of the history of the United States. Ecocritic Matthew Schneider-Mayerson has recently explored this issue in the novel very cogently, accurately pointing out Rich's lack of critical engagement with Mitchell's many layered privileges, as well as the problematic erasure of people of color and social justice issues in the novel overall.[2]

The climax of Mitchell's crisis of individual consciousness arrives in the marsh surrounding his bank fortress. It begins as he walks into the swamp with his axe, a "powerful weapon," with the intent of gathering driftwood from his "domain," thus signifying his desire to reformulate a recognizable agency through both possessive individualism and Baconian taming of nature. It ends, however, with a temporary relinquishment of all agency, including his desire to even move at all or, possibly, to continue living (290). He eventually comes across a large tree deposited by the storm that, he figures, once broken into "think stumps" could be used to "reinforce his wall's foundation" (291). However, while preparing his axe he notices that while the log "had appeared . . . dead," it was actually "everywhere crawling, munching, slurping, rotting, liquefying, cannibalizing—a grotesque insectopolis" (291). When he kneels down closer to further examine the "insectopolis," he begins to question his intentions for the log and, more generally, for his future life in Zone 5. "Did he really want to obliterate this festering micro-universe? Or might it be nicer simply to join it? To stretch out under the sky until night came and all the creeping things mistook him for a second log to explore and infest" (292). In the end, he finds himself unable to either destroy the log or join with it. Though he cannot literally become a tree himself, he might, however, very well be mistaken for one by the insects. He and the decomposing log are interconnected, but not the same entity; they impact each other, but cannot become *one*.

Despite his desire to "join" the decomposing log, this is demonstrably more than a cliché moment of "oneness" with nature. As he studies the log, Mitchell feels nauseous as its state of decomposition makes him think of his friend Elsa's apparent, but unconfirmed, death. And, eventually, he turns inevitably to his own mortality. Reminded of a close friend's death, his own insignificance, and the finite nature of his own existence, he felt "he was going to throw up" (292). Mitchell's intense interaction with the nonhuman—one that unsettles anthropocentric norms and presses questions of the very distributed nature of existence—leads to something quite different from a sublime bliss or ethical humility; he has, instead, gone from a weapon-wielding, powerful owner of the land to a creature of apparent depression and definite torpidity. Mitchell's feelings of helplessness up against the immensity of what appears to be a climate gone crazy, and his close encounter with decomposition in the marsh, lead him to quite seriously consider a sort of suicide through inertia. As he lies on his back next to the tree, Mitchell ponders what it might be like to simply do nothing at all. I read this scene as an excellent reminder of both the inherent weakness and the powerful endurance of humanist models of subjectivity and agency. Once the assumptions behind the rational and autonomous human individual have been disrupted deeply enough, it is not necessarily simple to see what remains, or might be devised, to help guide decision making in the posthuman and postnatural world.

Mitchell seems to feel that if he is no longer able to maintain a semblance of control over the future then the only other choice is to relinquish all agency. This is reminiscent of the fears climate organizers feel when discussing the realities of climate change, that they might actually frighten people into surrender. Mitchell's contemplation of decomposition is a key scene for understanding the novel's representation of one individual's interaction with a postnatural and posthuman world, and his experience of recognizing the resulting decentered human subjectivity it necessitates. Rather than providing definitive answers regarding the results, however, in the culmination of *Odds Against Tomorrow* we discover an incomplete but productive meditation on the difficulty of this process itself. It is apparent that Mitchell will need to engage with both the growing Dead Zone community and, soon enough, the relevant state and corporate institutions. Mitchell finds the spectrum of individualist options, from possessive to rugged to escapist individualism, as exceedingly difficult to see beyond, and an alternative community based in anything other than "back to the land" naturalism as almost unimaginable. At the same time, the novel's conclusion suggests there is really no such thing as individual or societal retreat from a changing climate. Wherever you go, there you are—still in the postnatural Anthropocene; still in the (increasingly higher and saltier) marsh waters.

Engaging these challenges is difficult enough that many readers might find themselves sympathizing with Mitchell's desire to melt into the marsh, to just "waste away" on the land. This response is indicative of a crisis of subjectivity that I have been suggesting environmental theorists and activists would do well to think about more thoroughly. Mitchell, as a privileged member of Western hyper-consumer culture, laments the loss of a knowable world when faced with the newfound uncertainty of his suddenly decentered subjectivity and limited agency. Braidotti dedicates an entire chapter of *The Posthuman* to what she calls "Life after Death." She explains her "vitalist notion of death is that it is the inhuman within us, which frees us into life. Each of us is always already a 'has been,' as we are mortal beings" (Braidotti 2013, 134). The transition from human to posthuman subjectivity, she contends, occurs in relation to a new understanding of the relation between life and death. "The full blast of the awareness of the transitory nature of all that lives is the defining moment in our existence," she contends, "Being mortal, we all are 'have beens': the spectacle of our death is written obliquely into the script of our temporality, not as a barrier, but as a condition of possibility" (132). Mitchell now finds himself in the liminal space between life and death, as well as between a human and posthuman subjectivity, and seems to stall for a while—unsure of who to be and how to act. His contemplation of decomposing in the marsh is a fascinating representation of the potential and the limits embedded within the transition between the human and posthuman subject. "Becoming-imperceptible," Braidotti writes, "is the event for which there is no representation, because it rests on the disappearance of the individuated self" (137). The decomposing log compels Mitchell's affinity and disgust simultaneously, and this resonates with the character's struggle to move beyond his humanist worldview overall, in that embracing a posthuman subjectivity would entail a fuller acceptance of his own "multiplicity and . . . [his] relational connection with an 'outside'" (138).

In the novel, we follow Mitchell's intense desire for a comprehensible future and, even in the aftermath of a catastrophe such as the flooding of Manhattan, mere survival is not sufficient. In the end, the novel leaves us to consider three fundamental themes related to Mitchell's existential crisis of subjectivity in the swamp: ownership, agency, and futurity. Each of these themes is fundamental to the dominant sense of the humanist and capitalist form of subjectivity and agency. And this section closes with brief, hopefully suggestive, final thoughts on each. The novel presents these themes as central to Mitchell's struggles to reimagine his post-Tammy existence, as he looks to chart a path forward through the uncertainty of his present and near and long-term future.

The first issue of significance is *ownership*. Even in his inert state in the swamp, Mitchell holds on to his mindset of private property and possessive individualism. His desire to relinquish agency altogether seems related to the inability to think outside logics of the market and private property, even as he claims his squatter rights in the Dead Zone. For instance, the emphasis on proprietary rights as he contemplates his suicide through inertia is telling: "Even as the swamp flies . . . started flapping around his eyes, as the bark beetles scaled his bare arms and the grass scratched at his neck, he would stay there. *This was his land now*" (293; my emphasis). Clearly, Mitchell is very aware that he is actually a squatter and holds no legal ownership over the land, but he is not yet able to articulate his growing attachment through anything other than the lens of possessive individualism. "If he wanted to lie on it all night long, or even for weeks, until he wasted away . . . if he wanted to lie there for eternity, nobody could stop him" (293). In his work at FutureWorld before Hurricane Tammy, he essentially operated as a shield to ensure transnational capital's legal and economic security in the face of uncertain impacts of climate change. And now in Zone 5, as others look to build a community, Mitchell is building physical and figurative barriers around himself. Especially considering this neighborhood was a working-class and minority community before the storm, Mitchell's claims to ownership take on an even more pernicious quality as dispossession in action, another form of settler-colonialism for the age of climate disruption. This possessive individualism infuses even Mitchell's contemplation of death, and certainly forestalls any motivation he might have for living in a posthuman entanglement with his human and more-than-human neighbors.

The second theme is *agency*: or, put another way, even if Mitchell does nothing, *stuff* still happens. If he were to die in the swamp, for instance, his decomposing body would quite rapidly become a part of the thriving and generative "insectopolis" that originally arrested his attention. Therefore, the distributed nature of subjectivity, intentionality, and agency is central even to his desire to not act at all: or to decompose and distribute his body, quite literally, across the swamp. Mitchell contemplates this death as, at least, a definable future. While tantalized by its supposed definitiveness, he ultimately turns back to a much less certain posthuman life in a postnatural world. What, then, lies between the impossible disavowal of all agency and the improbable humanist claims to the autonomous and rational self? From his desire to predict everything—to exert his rationality to predict, and therefore exert influence and control over, the future—Mitchell has now swung to another extreme, to pass all agency and control over to the process of decomposition. And, as he ultimately realizes, neither path is tenable. Mitchell's personal crisis and inchoate transformation, in this manner, narrates the process of the struggle to comprehend and internalize the distributed nature of agency.

Third, we arrive at the question of *futurity*. The narrative's troubling of anthropocentrism and humanist concepts of agency is intimately linked to a disruption of linear progress, and these linked disruptions are fundamental to the novel's exploration of individual and societal reactions to climate catastrophes. The Dead Zoners project is ongoing, really barely beginning, as the novel comes to a close. Even while Mitchell continues to barricade himself in the Carnarsie Bank, new members arrive and commit to the monumental project of building a resilient and sustainable society on the outskirts of the ultimate modernist and capitalist metropolis. Can the "Dead Zone" become something more than a short-lived reprieve from the disaster of neoliberalism and the vagaries of climate change? Is there a resiliency, an affirmative postanthropocentric politics, to be forged in the abandoned neighborhoods of New York City? If they want to begin their work forging a postcapitalist community in which they can survive (and even thrive), it will occur in the wreckage of their known world. The Dead Zone is not entirely independent of the reforming, post-disaster economy of New York City, as Mitchell himself is still accepting—and appears relatively dependent on—funding and supplies from Jane Eppler's new futurist business, back up and running in Manhattan (305). The novel concludes, then, in the midst of multiple projects to reimagine community unfolding at multiple scales and various modes of interdependence, but its speculative audacity is limited.

For the Dead Zoners, the persistent focus on the present, and operating in the now without grasping for certainty about the future, represents a terrifying but necessary process. The temporality of this balancing act will also be necessarily different, possibly resembling what Tsing has called "salvage rhythms," which follow new "forms of temporal coordination" (Tsing, 131). That is, she explains, "Without the singular, forward pulse of progress, the unregularized coordination of salvage is what we have" (Tsing 2015, 132). The Dead Zoners will need to create their community through a process of salvaging and recuperation, all while accepting they do not fully know their own intentions and cannot pretend to entirely predict the reasons for, and the ramifications of, their next act, response, failure, or compromise. This is the context of their project, rebuilding something from the wreckage of unbridled capitalism and the climate emergency in the abandoned zones of a drowned economic capital. "To know the world that progress has left us," Tsing reminds us, "we must track shifting patches of ruination" (206). A politics without progress, a disintentional politics, does not clearly emerge in *Odds Against Tomorrow*. The reader is presented, instead, with a series of disorienting challenges to any one individual's capability to build this new world on their own. Individualist notions of ownership and agency, and related linear orientations to temporality, limit Mitchell's imagination. While he knows that he does not want to return to the lucrative business of futurism in a society that may have no future left worth predicting, he remains unsure of whether to join the patchy, ruined community of the Dead Zone or to instead lay down with a decomposing log. And without intention, in what ways do decisions like these come to matter anyway? To press this question, we now move to another novel of climate fiction, one much more earnestly interested in the relation between the individual and community.

Organize "Where You Are"

Chang-Rae Lee's *On Such a Full Sea* unfolds more than a century into the future, and a blend of authoritarianism and neoliberal market logics, rather than any recognizable democratic government system, dominates all aspects of society. B-Mor, a community located in the area of present-day Baltimore, Maryland, produces seafood and vegetables for an upper-class citizenry that resides in various private, selective, and secure Charter societies. B-Mor, on the other hand, is ruled by a seldomly seen authoritarian government, referred to only as the Directorate. The citizens are descendants of a community of people from "New China," who were forced to immigrate en masse when, in the midst of an environmental breakdown, their city was bulldozed in service to a major infrastructure project. Readers experience this vast and complicated geographic and cultural landscape via a mysterious plural narrator, who is prone to nebulous and opaque discourses on the cultural and political questions facing the B-Mor society. The voice appears to be that of a nonmaterial, community spirit of B-Mor (rather than an actual human denizen of the city), though other scholars have suggested it might be a singular voice speaking for "like-minded people" in B-Mor, or even a "group of scholars" studying the history of B-Mor (Page 2017, 93).³ As the narrative unfolds, having no liberal democratic norms to draw upon, the residents find themselves rather awkwardly initiating a sociopolitical movement almost entirely from scratch. They gather together to petition for expanded economic opportunity, upward class mobility, and more accessible health care, among other similarly mundane requests. They also appear to be dreaming, however, of something more: an idea of community, and its possible becoming, which they cannot yet fully articulate.

In the following pages, I selectively read Lee's novel with an eye toward the narrative's construction of a (partial) political imaginary and its limitations; in fact, I suggest this novel presents a unique opportunity to explore political subjectivity and agency beyond the limits of humanism. Lee's presentation of the B-Mor citizens' burgeoning political consciousness can be read as a materialist approach to social and political engagement with their world. This is a politics of materiality that, at least in part, begins with the premise that each individual exists in physical relation to a larger ecology; an ecology that should be understood to include the social, institutional, and nonhuman environment. The motto that both inspires and challenges the newly formed political consciousness of the B-Mor residents is a simultaneously simple and cryptic expression: "where you are." Contributing significantly to the depiction of an intra-active, distributed nature of agency in the novel's politics, this expression emphasizes, rather than a bounded, rational, and intentional agent, a political subjectivity constituted through an engagement with the material world that emphasizes the dispersed, embedded, and networked embodiment of posthuman subjects.

This increasingly ever-present concept—"where you are"—emphasizes, I will argue, each inhabitant's very material and inextricable relation to their immediate present moment in space and time, rather than a universalized citizen-subject of an abstracted ideology. In terms of temporality, the attention to one's immediate surroundings also suggests a particular type of focus on the present moment that eschews goal-oriented, or future-oriented, planning. Building from the revolutionary nonlinear temporality explored in Leslie Silko's work in the previous chapter and furthering our exploration of the quandaries inherent to disintentional organizing in *Odds Against Tomorrow*, Lee's novel presents us with an opportunity to think through the relation between distributed agency, nonlinear temporality, and disintentional political organizing. Though in the end incomplete, the novel does explore an intriguing experiment in which social movement organizing is (at least partially) redefined in posthumanist and disintentional modes.

The novel unfolds across several regions of the former United States of America, including what is today the Mid-Atlantic region, Appalachia, and New England. In an environmentally decimated and politically fragmented society, a new sociopolitical structure has taken the place of democratic liberalism and its variants. There are three different classifications of societies across the east coast of what we now know as the United States of America: the Charter towns, the Facilities, and the Open Counties. The Charters are comprised of the wealthiest percentile of society, the Facilities are the production zones that supply the Charter towns with food and other material necessities, and the Open Counties, lawless and environmentally compromised, stretch across the remainder of the degraded landscape. A disease referred to only as "C" is omnipresent. Everyone, other than possibly one or two individuals in each generation, is born with the early vestiges of this seemingly cancer-like disease. "Our tainted world lives within us, every one," the narrator explains (Lee 2014, 65). Not everyone experiences this internalization of the polluted environment in equal ways, however. Those living in the Charters, in particular, are able to utilize their access to the best pharmaceutical treatments to live long and mostly healthy lives, while the Facilities residents receive limited medical attention (seemingly just enough to keep the working population sustainable) (101). Meanwhile, the closest thing we find to a doctor in the Open Counties is Quig, a former Charter veterinarian now running a makeshift, for-profit hospital out of a fortified compound in the Appalachian Mountains.

The Charter residents live a fast-paced, competitive, and luxurious hyper-consumer lifestyle under the rules of extreme neoliberalism, where market logic rules and citizens operate as individualized human capital, markedly similar to Wendy Brown's theorization of the neoliberal subject, in a "tireless drive for excellence" (179). Each individual is responsible to ensure his or her own economic success, and parents do everything possible to ensure their children's opportunities from the earliest developmental stages. In this sense, as will be explained further below, Charter residents might be best described as what Brown has termed "financialized human capital," rather than traditional citizen-subjects (Brown 2015,

33). When financial-subjects understand themselves as "human capital," Brown suggests, the task becomes "to self-invest in ways that enhance its [the subject's] value or to attract investors through constant attention to its actual or figurative credit rating, and to do this across every sphere of its existence" (33). In *On Such a Full Sea*, there is no public "safety net" of any sort, of course, and being sent to the Open Counties is essentially a death sentence, since few Charters are equipped with the skills and knowledge needed to survive outside the confines of their luxurious communities. If subjects fail to secure themselves a career path via the annual academic exams, for instance, they will be relegated to a service-oriented job such as nurse, driver, waiter, or teacher. And, as we might predict, while the Charters place a highly utilitarian emphasis on education as career training, the educators themselves are left undercompensated and little appreciated. These service workers live within the Charter walls as second-class citizens in dorm-style, high-rise buildings, with little opportunity for home ownership or other paths to upward mobility. Even more severely, those who fail to achieve financial security or are caught in criminal activity are simply banished to the so-called Open Counties.

The Open Counties consist of a mostly lawless and environmentally wrecked landscape. Readers experience the recognizable but significantly altered landscape as they follow the main character, a young woman named Fan from the B-Mor facility, who travels through the Open Counties for the first time. As she finds herself, for instance, somewhere in the northern Appalachian Mountains, "It was mid-September, still the heart of summer, the foliage of white oak and black cherry and hemlock ... [is] distressed and washed out by the fierceness of the light" (Lee 2014, 79). Summers are longer, wildfires are common, resources are scarce and community solidarity is weak in the Open Counties. Small towns are the only organized institutions and these are generally run by a local authoritarian acting as a blend of warlord and mob boss. There is no formal coordination between the towns, though the various small-scale authoritarian leaders entertain and debate the idea of forming a political alliance of sorts from time to time (usually as a result of some pressure from their local communities during times of particularly unbearable conditions). These discussions apparently never culminate in fundamental change, however, as the various power brokers are loathe to compromise their own positions for the possible broader benefits to the open counties residents (132).

In between these two extremes, the Facilities operate as the production centers necessary to provide essential goods to the Charters. The structure of society within the Facilities is presented predominantly via the narrator's own description of the city, especially via the story of Fan and her boyfriend Reg (and their home, social, and professional lives in B-Mor) and the changes that unfold in B-Mor after their twin departures. B-Mor is a food production center specializing in a highly advanced and unique form of aquaponics, producing mostly fish and various vegetables. They live in what are known to be renovated row houses from the original U.S. city of Baltimore, and the neighborhoods are structured around extended family kinships (18–19). Receiving what appears to be only limited schooling, young people are then provided extensive training in jobs for which their skills seem most suited. Daily life is comprised of work, family, modest consumerism, and extensive media technology (a mostly passive intake of stories and news is described, rather than an active social media interaction). The Directorate holds authoritarian power over the facility, leaving the residents with a constrained freedom consisting of limited options for spending free time and small amounts of expendable income.

This limited but comfortable and safe existence is generally seen, by the denizens, as a necessary sacrifice to an unforgiving economic market that might otherwise significantly disrupt their lives. In fact, the narrator explains that "self-sacrifice is a hallmark of life here in B-Mor, one of our original and most cherished norms" (52). The small but unrealistic dream of upward mobility operates alongside a desire to maintain the comparably comfortable facility life (the real and perceived horrors of the Open Counties are constantly reinforced in the facility) in order to keep the B-Mor residents in line. Expulsion to the Open Counties seems much more likely to occur than any sort of ascension to the Charters; only the tiniest fraction of a percent of Facility residents are accepted to Charter life (determined by almost impossibly high scores on an academic test they can only take once as preteens). For the B-Mors, thinking too much about Charter society is akin to "worry[ing] about the life cycle of the nearest star" (53) and everyone is aware "[t]here is no leaping of worlds" (51). In fact, B-Mor was "conceived and developed" in order to "obviate the need for . . . purposeful dreaming" (32). It is important to note how much "purposeful dreaming" resonates with progressive political campaigns and, since their world is instead purposefully built to dull exactly this type of intentional imagination, the political spirit that later emerges in B-Mor emerges from a place that those habituated to Western liberal democratic norms will not find easily recognizable. The B-Mors, if they are to do it at all, will have to build their political culture from scratch, experimenting and learning as they go, without the well of any political history, let alone the specificities of Western liberal democracy, from which to draw.

The Directorate has recently taken to limiting essential social services, such as health care, and generally a round of austerity is ongoing. As a result, a prevalent but mostly unspoken concern is growing, particularly concerning their health care system, among B-Mors: "[E]very person we know has had to make . . . compromises, most not leading to horrific consequences, but the truth is you can't help but wonder where this will lead, what new reforms will be instituted next year, or in ten, and to what extent the quality of life in B-Mor might someday come to resemble the conditions outside" (53). The inside-outside and self-other binary construction evident in this quote becomes important later in the novel. There was one scare, for instance, in which the B-Mor-produced seafood was suspected of contamination, and the Charters' resulting refusal to buy the product, even if just for a matter of weeks, placed B-Mor's entire future in jeopardy. It seems quite likely that if the issue had not subsided as quickly as it did, many, or even all, of the residents might have found themselves suddenly subject to life in the Open Counties. Their value and very existence is dependent upon their usefulness to, and production of goods for, Charter society. In this manner, the B-Mor citizens are themselves a type of "human capital," valuable only in their ability to produce goods for the Charters; however, as we will explore below, the depiction of their inchoate political consciousness, which grows in fits and starts throughout the novel, also suggests their societal predicament cannot be fully understood through the lenses of either neoliberalism or liberal democracy alone.

The political questions of most interest in the novel are ultimately found in the narrator's explanation of an increasingly visible yet undefined political movement in B-Mor. It is initially inspired by Fan and her decision to leave the facility, along with the concurrent set of directorate decisions targeting basic quality of life in B-Mor. Fan's departure is sudden and an act without clearly defined motivations. She is a young woman, barely beyond her teenage years, who works in an important role in the food production system as a fish tank diver and lives with her extended family in a small row house. Though no one has willingly left a Facility in recent memory, Fan suddenly—and shockingly—poisons her fish tank at work and walks through a guarded gate in disguise. One motivation for her surprise absconding is fairly obvious: her partner, and the father of her unborn child, Reg, was recently taken by the directorate for study, under suspicion he might be a rare person who is cancer free, and she is intent upon finding him. However, as the narrator explains, "It couldn't have been just Reg she had gone to search out. She had no real leads as to where he might be, or if he was even alive. So why would any sane person leave our cloister for such uncertainties?" (60). The possibility that Fan is acting upon desires larger than romantic or individual goals remains distinct (probable even), though the nature of these less obvious goals remains mostly speculation. Reg "was the impetus, yes, the veritable without which, but not the whole story" (61). The rumors and interpretations of Fan's departure, which spread across B-Mor with great import, represent the inchoate political consciousness the novel suggests might prove possible within this overly economized and antidemocratic future world.

Fan's departure from B-Mor is slowly politicized by a previously apolitical society. While it might be tempting at first to dismiss this as a cult of personality, the B-Mor society's flirtation with political activism is more productively approached as an exploration of the emergence of a distributed political subjectivity that looks to outstrip neoliberal economization of the citizen. The starting point is a final phrase, an instruction of sort, which Fan leaves in her wake. As mourners gather for the funeral of a young boy who was once friends with Reg (before his recent and sudden disappearance), and just before her own surprising getaway, Fan turns to the crowd and says simply, yet cryptically: "where you are" (31). Whether these were even her exact words is actually never fully verified; however, that this was a sort of final directive to the community before her famous departure becomes the accepted version for most. The meaning of Fan's instruction is of course debated among her increasing number of devotees, and is also left open to the reader's interpretation.

The narrator describes a desire among B-Mor's residents to foster a more politicized relation to their world, and a hesitant and inchoate movement of sorts ensues. Their utter lack of a historical or cultural connection to liberal democratic traditions leaves the B-Mors floundering for organizing principles and, especially, for tactics and intentional goals. Fan and Reg quickly become figures of myth and legend, and a rising political consciousness slowly builds from the original, unexpected impulse to care for, and about, the star-crossed couple. The narrator explains, "As conceived, as constituted, we may in fact be of a design unsustainable. Which is why we needed Fan, in both idea and person. For within her was the one promise that could deliver us, the seed of all our futures, Charters' and B-Mors' and even of the shunned souls out in the counties" (104). The "design unsustainable" in which they live cries for change and they become inspired by a "seed," that is within the "idea" and "person" of Fan. Rather than a developed and preconceived future world toward which to dream, the seed that inspires exists in the present moment. Her final words to her neighbors, the enigmatic expression "where you are," is quite clearly different than a call to imagine where you will be, or could be, or even want to be. Fan, as the seed of something fundamentally unknowable to the B-Mors, urges her neighbors to remain attentive to the present moment and their immediate surroundings, rather than any particular image of her own or the society's future. The current "design unsustainable" itself must hold their focus: seeing, knowing, and interacting with this present "design" differently is the "seed" of the future they desire. The B-Mors, Fan seems to be suggesting, need to look closely and recognize their entangled world for what it is in the right there and then, and somehow forge new ways to engage with this current construction of place. Now, it is true that the narrative later reveals that Fan is pregnant when she leaves B-Mor, and this could lead to a rather limited reading of the above quote as simple foreshadowing, and that it is her unborn baby that holds the key to this world's future. However, if you will bear with me, I would like to refuse that reading and its limiting and savior-complex heavy themes, for something I hope will be—while less instantly gratifying—more theoretically consequential.

Reading Fan's pronouncement of "where you are" in conversation with another familiar proverb in B-Mor, that one should "behold a fire from the opposite shore," provides more insight into the novel's exploration of distributed and nonintentional, or nonpurposive, politics. Prior to Fan's ascendance, the dominant moral compass of the Facility operates, in part at least, under the influence of an expression generally attributed to B-Mor's "Originals," the founding generation of their facility, that suggests it is always best to "[b]ehold a fire from the opposite shore" (239). The narrator admits this expression appears contradictory to the Facility's proclaimed ethos of community and togetherness, but has "remained in currency" nonetheless (239). Yet, the expression's longevity might be ascribed to how it is actually indicative of a community-based, binary differentiation, and the familiar construction of a Self-Other binary, or us-versus-them duality. This is the creation of the *Other* through the bounding and bordering of the B-Mor community. And this just might also be a key element of the "design unsustainable." Remember, Fan might hold the key to a new life for more than just the B-Mor residents, as the narrator suggests Fan's story, and its potential to be a catalyst for change, is relevant for the Charter and Open Counties as well. This implies that part of what it means to follow Fan's advice to focus upon, to live in, or to build from "where you are" is to allow this attentiveness to place, to the present, to the immediacy of their interdependency with the more-than-human world to unsettle the bounded individual and bounded human society that the Self-Other binary endorses and sustains.

The construction of community up and against an outsider, an Other, however, appears strong in most of the communities in the novel, where survival depends upon the ability to remain useful and accepted by one's own peers. The members of B-Mor work and live together, for instance, in a system that privileges efficiency, calm domesticity, and willing repetition, and when certain abnormalities arise, the so-called fires, the tendency is to put one's head down and keep on keeping on (calmly and efficiently). To this point, the narrator offers this explanation: "The way we love one another is cast by the form of our excellent contiguity, a rigorous closeness that only rarely oversteps its bounds" (88). This tight-knit community and the cultural expression condoning a blind eye to the misfortune of "others," completes this antagonistic relation to the outsider. That is, the B-Mor residents understand that members of their Facility "labor and prosper together, or else tread at [their] lonely peril" (238). In the end, the togetherness is promoted as long as everyone is on task and contiguous, and their patience for individuality is thin. The B-Mors prove effective in ostracizing any irregularities (in most any form but particularly anything hinting at defiance of norms or formation of political consciousness), and this is equally paramount to B-Mor's corporatized community's sense of Self and Other. Indeed, the narrator concedes that the long popular expression "of course . . . means to indicate that one can rightly look after one's own, that you are not obligated to address the plight of others" (239). Where the line is drawn to distinguish between one's own body and the environment and one's own community and the outsider, the Other, informs the community's sense of self up and against the unfamiliar, and the inevitably lesser.

While the workings of the international governmental institution that connects the world's many Charter towns are not especially clear, the Directorate that holds authoritarian power over B-Mor is somewhat more fully explicated. This institution's main function appears to be to strike a balance between maintaining the moderate quality of life expected by B-Mor residents with the demands of a more global market (for which it provides food). The Directorate's decisions are presented by the narrator, and understood by the community, to be necessary actions based upon global market realities. The entirety of life in B-Mor is understood, in fact, through the lens of the community's economic value as a producer of quality food for Charter societies. B-Mor might be best understood as an extreme articulation of what scholars are coming to understand as the impact of neoliberalism on social and political life. In our own stage of late capitalism, neoliberalism already reconfigures "democratic political principles of justice into an economic idiom, transforms the state itself into a manager of the nation on the model of a firm . . . and hollows out much of the substance of democratic citizenship and even popular sovereignty" (Brown 2015, 35). In the novel, each of the three levels of society is the imagined endgame of contemporary neoliberal policy, in which the 1 percent live lavishly in the Charters, a portion of the society still necessary to production work and reside in limited but comfortable, nondemocratic conditions in the Facilities, and the Open Counties are the warehouse of the unnecessary (or trouble-making) souls.

Wendy Brown's exhaustive analysis of neoliberalism as a sociopolitical "rationality," rather than a set of particular economic policies only, provides a powerful lens for analyzing community life in B-Mor. Brown, building from and expanding upon Foucault, understands neoliberalism to be "a form of normative reasoning remaking state, society, and subject, generating social policy, positing truth and a theory of law" (69). One of Brown's more pertinent arguments is that this "hollowing out" of the political elements of liberal democracy leaves citizens within neoliberal rationality with less and less recourse to the political foundations (particularly those forged through liberal democratic institutions and practices) necessary to move beyond the limits of neoliberalism. This then limits, according to Brown, the people's ability to imagine (let alone construct and enact) more radical democratic responses to the economization of social and political life (17). As she asks several times and in different forms throughout her analysis, once *homo politicus* has been replaced with *homo oeconomicus*, "Why would peoples want or seek democracy in the absence of even its vaporous liberal democratic instantiation?" (18). Recognizing the novel's depiction of a neoliberal future in an environment deeply impacted by climate change adds important context to the way in which it scripts political subjectivity and agency. If Brown is correct to argue that "replacement of citizenship defined as concern with the public good by citizenship reduced to the citizen as homo economicus also eliminates the very idea of a people, a demos asserting its collective political sovereignty" (39), then Lee's novel can be read as attempting to imagine how exactly political subjectivity might reconstitute itself in a world where liberal democracy is no longer a foundational concept. That is, "one of the important effects of neoliberalization is the vanquishing of liberal democracy's already anemic *homo politicus*," precisely because "neoliberal rationality hollows out both liberal democratic reason and a democratic imaginary that would exceed it" (42). Brown's theorizing of neoliberalism and its impact on liberal democracy proves helpful for examining the inchoate movement in B-Mor: through this lens, one might suggest the B-Mors are attempting to reimagine *homo politicus* while struggling to navigate existent tensions between individualism and community, the economic and the political, and the abstract versus material representation of political citizenship.

The novel attempts to imagine the B-Mors' burgeoning sociopolitical movement without necessarily relying upon liberal democratic norms, to which they have no connection or relation. The expression "where you are," while it does hail the individual "you," quickly draws this individual into a relational and entangled existence with the "where." This is not the abstract individual citizen-subject of liberal democracy. Fan asks her neighbors to commit their time and energy to engaging with the complex relationality between people, place, and time, rather than promoting abstract individual freedom from those relations. The emerging political subjectivity and agency of Fan's "where you are" is dependent upon interconnection rather than bounded isolation and hopes to inspire the B-Mors to move beyond the "bounded world" of the Self-Other binary inherent in their cultural commitment to "behold a fire from the opposite shore." These two seemingly contradictory cultural expressions—"where you are" and "behold a fire from the opposite shore"—are in tension throughout the novel and their relation becomes increasingly important as we consider their meaning within the context of materiality and embedded subjectivity. The commonplace cultural expression that one should "behold a fire from the opposite shore" points to a binary differentiation in which the community draws a boundary around itself; the *other* remains the point of reference for their own culture, to be described and known from a distance in order to differentiate the original B-Mors as unique, central, and cohesive. Fan declares, "where you are." And, in so doing, challenges the notion of the unitary actor and the bounded community, instead implying a certain entanglement, connectivity, and inseparability between the subject and her environment. Fan asks her listeners to explore intimacy and network, rather than individuality. It is not even clear who the "you" actually refers to, as Fan's motto passes through the community via whisper and rumor. The "you" itself increasingly becomes an entanglement of characters, rather than any one bounded individual, who find themselves always already enmeshed in their mixed-communities.

Rather than asking her neighbors to imagine themselves as liberal humanist subjects moving unbounded, as they please, across systems, institutions, and landscapes, Fan's directive, "where you are," forces each person to reflect upon the very embeddedness of their subjectivity first and foremost. This directive assumes a certain interconnectivity, and a resulting limitation upon human agency, that is indicative of a more posthuman and postanthropocentric conception of subjectivity and agency. When assessing the implications of "where you are" as a principle or motif in this context, it is more difficult to imagine oneself as outside or above, somehow unrelated or not responsible for, the surrounding human and nonhuman community.[4] If abstract individual political freedom, a model of political identity underpinning the past two hundred years and more of modernity, is no longer viable (if it ever was), we will need different ways of imaging political actors and agency. In B-Mor, there is no recognizable political tradition for the community to draw upon, and the Directorate rules without resident input; this is similar, one might argue, to the challenges of political organizing in our own moment where traditional models of protest are often ineffective and the state appears unresponsive to the public will. Denizens of B-Mor abide by the Directorate's rules seemingly more out of fear of the city's dissolution (if determined to be more trouble than their value to the Charters is worth) than any actual consent to the Directorate's legitimacy or sense of shared cultural vision with the ruling elite.

What happens next is less clear, of course, and Lee himself at times seems unsure of what to do with this directive from his own fictional heroine. But, in fact, the incompleteness of Fan's declaration also lends to its disruptiveness; that is, this is an expression of political potential that is yet to be fully conceived, as it inspires a movement still yet to be fully realized. The novel enacts this incompleteness, first of all, in its depiction of the B-Mor residents arguing over what exactly Fan meant and then again in their initial, awkward and hesitant attempts to produce political gestures of their own. It is as if the nascent activists are asking: "Do what 'where we are'? How? With whom and to what end?" These are understandable questions that are raised when one attempts to engage with social movement organizing in a manner that requires conjuring as yet undefined forms of distributed political subjectivity, temporality, and agency.

Disintentional Organizing

The increasing politicization of B-Mor's laborers initially emanates from the simple idea that it is wrong for the Directorate to take Reg away from his family and community (they assume he has been taken because he is one of the all too rare C-Free persons) and that Fan, by breaking facility law (committing sabotage on the aquaculture operation and illegally leaving the compound), is not necessarily in the wrong. As a result, some rather random acts of politically tinged misbehavior emerge inside of B-Mor. "Free Reg" graffiti tags begin to appear each morning, for instance, before being painted over quickly by facility employees. Groups begin to meet and discuss these issues in public, a previously unheard-of type of public gathering. And, somewhat strangely, a group of unrelated people spontaneously decide to litter an impossibly pristine pond in a local park, endangering the beautiful prize fish that inhabit the water (Lee 2014, 93–95). These awkward, unfocused, and tentative gestures begin to create a surge of feeling in the people, as explained by the narrator, that individually and communally there is something lacking in their lives. Something about how these acts express tangential support for Reg and Fan, no matter how ineffectively, begins to constitute an increasingly serious threat to the status quo. Even if this emerging social movement is not exactly sure what they are doing or why, and its participants would certainly not self-identify as activists of any conceivable kind, the narrator explains it is "as if we each had a solitary desire that should not be named but whose expression, once sparked, was so instantly enacted that it felt as pure and instinctive as fleeing from a house fire" (95). The "solitary desire" of each individual is explained as "pure and instinctive," and one method for reading Lee's depiction of emerging political consciousness might then be to see the B-Mor's new political "expression" as an activation of their "natural" rights as liberal democratic citizens. Consequently, a more mundane reading of the novel might suggest the B-Mors are searching for an expression of an innate individuality that has been suppressed in the authoritarian facility structure.

The narrator considers this possibility, certainly, while exploring the meaning of the individual in traditional B-Mor society, and in its newer more politicized iteration. In addition to the passage above, the narrator's description of Fan's commanding presence at the funeral, where she utters her famous phrase to the mourners, also seems enamored with the power of her individual presence. "[W]e B-Mors—and maybe now you, too—respond more deeply than the rest to someone's determined gaze, or the way they move across a room, or simply stand there, as Fan did that day at young Joseph's wake, with such solidity that you might think the world and everything in it was, for a flash, turning around them" (243–44). The centrality of the individual here hints toward a cult-of-personality politics, an anthropocentric conception of the political actor at the center of their world. It is moments such as these that lead literary scholar Amanda Page to understandably argue that Fan is, in the end, simply a "fantasy of liberal universal humanism. She is the lone imagined holdout in a world that has given up on freedom" (Page 2017, 106). This reading, while plausible, risks the problematic naturalization of individualism and of too quickly forcing the novel's weirdness back into a humanist straightjacket. Based on a reading of Fan as liberal humanist, Page then is left to assert, "The failure of the B-Mor resistance movement, inspired by Fan's legend, then, might be inevitable because all they really have is an idealized story of true individual freedom—an amorphous hope that there is an escape from the rigid social and economic structures by which everyone is bound" (106). I am not convinced, however, that the movement is entirely a failure, first of all (and I'll show why later). Nor, for that matter, am I willing to allow that Fan's message is merely a reference to idealized individualism and abstract freedom.

The narrator continues to explore, in a worrying tone, whether or not the "Free Reg" movement, which of course is related to Fan's lionization but also becomes its own distinct campaign (and one with a clearer goal, as well), is creating a B-Mor where people think too much about themselves (Lee 2014, 293). Displaying an uncertainty around the role of the individual in political life, more generally, the narrator openly wonders if the more individualized protests are a good or bad omen for the movement, musing: "Are our thoughts angling as much toward ourselves as to our household or clan? Have we become as primary as the collective rest? Such an indication may be in what we have begun to hear and see of the concern for Reg. B-Mor remains focused and worried about his whereabouts and welfare; there are growing calls for official information" (293). The narrator seems to be considering whether the B-Mors must become politicized individuals first, in order to then be capable of becoming more thoroughly organized. Is the demand for Reg's release, and even the sanctification of Fan, really just the rights-based discourse of liberalism (in this case, a liberalism being invented anew, without precedent in B-Mor's recorded history), or is it something different altogether? The emphasis on Reg's release seems based upon a realization that individual lives have meaning and a demand for his rights to be respected; and, interestingly, it is directly following this concern being raised that the narrator describes a particular act of civil disobedience that is the first to use a familiar protest tactic. "There was even a lie-in at one of the main intersections of the settlement, in which a thoroughly organized group of younger people spelled out his name on the asphalt with their bodies, causing a jam that took some hours to undo, an inconvenience for sure but one we abided" (293). This disruptive protest, a time-honored practice of drawing attention to your claims by inconveniencing your fellow citizens, but also, and most importantly, displaying the protest's ability to throw sand in the gears of capitalism, is "abided" by the community. The fact that the Directorate continues to ignore the campaign, however, is the more important point.

When we look beyond the traditional political actor as bounded individual, however, there are several key scenes and passages in the novel suggesting an incipient form of subjectivity that outstrips anthropocentric and humanist notions of individualism, and I find these much more compelling. These alternative constructions of the individual suggest a recognition that each member of the movement does not act in isolation, but in intimate interactive modes that blur the boundaries of where one ends and another begins. The potential for an organizing model dependent on something other than a collective formed of otherwise individuated subject-actors is tentatively expressed by the narrator as such: "We think each of us has a map marked with private routings and preferred habitual destinations, and go by a legend of our own. Yet it turns out you can overlay them and see a most amazing correspondence; what you believed were very personal contours aligning not exactly but enough that while our via points may diverge, our endings do not" (95). This perception of the individual as moving across and within a layered and dense human (and I would suggest nonhuman) community is more fully resonant with the narrator's broader explanation of the distributed, rather than hierarchical, infrastructure of the movement. With only a limited emphasis placed on leaders and hierarchy, much of the movement appears as dispersed, local, and horizontal. A key scene in which a spontaneously appearing rally exposes the limit of the technological state surveillance is even more illustrative of this point. The narrator explains,

> [S]omeone with high access leaked a security vid of the rally, the face ID predictably focusing on the organizers first and their deputies next and then systematically sectioning the crowd, but the drone's zoom and pan kept moving too slowly and then too fast, perhaps not programmed for such large and dense and shifting numbers, and in the end the vid was rendered unviewable, jittery and useless, until it zoomed out to capture the entire massing. It turns out we are one, if not ever how we expected. (292)

Something about this particular rally exceeds the capability of the surveillance technology, but what is it? The suggestion that the technology is "not programmed for such large and dense and shifting numbers" places an emphasis on the interconnection—the crowd's "dense" consistency—and the distributed agency of the political action—the "shifting" flow—rather than simply the number of individuals participating. The state is unable to pierce the flowing density, or the intricate layers and their constantly shifting relationality, of the protesting mass. As the "vid" zooms out to capture the "entire massing"—a useless angle to the authorities—the narrator refuses to describe the full gathering of B-Mors, in what would be a simple abstraction, as a democratic citizenry, the public manifest, or the demos. Instead, that seemingly logical leap is disrupted: the protestors are "one" but not how they "expected." The power of this "massing" to overwhelm the state observational apparatus is not held by one individual and it is also not in their unity as a large group alone. Their ability to remain a threat to the state, while evading its systems of punishment, is in the liminal space between individual and community.

If the B-Mors are not yet ready to declare their organizing goals within the given language and logics of liberal democracy, it seems essential that readers also leave some space here for something slightly different as well. The political discussion, tentative public gatherings, and the new communities they create are all implied to be imperfect but powerful steps in the formation of a new relation to each other and their world; and it is a relation that they cannot themselves yet define. It could simply be that they do not yet have the language of liberal democratic norms, or, as I would like to suggest, it might actually be because their approach to organizing—within the framework of Fan's directive "where you are"—is not amenable to those existing progressive constructs of social movements. Indicative of the tension between the immediacy of their actions and the lack of defined objectives for those very acts, the B-Mors themselves remain aware that they are not exactly sure what it is they are attempting, nor for what ends. What are we to make of the B-Mors' undefined goals? Is it implied that the B-Mors are not organized because they do not have goals, the imaginative capacity to ask for self-government? Or is the lack of a defined goal endemic to a new sort of sociopolitical organizing that might emanate from the depths of neoliberal ideology?[5]

In a world ravaged by climate change, ruthlessly organized by neoliberal logics of capital, and in Facilities controlled by an authoritarian Directorate, the B-Mors interrogate the possibilities of their current moment and material experiences without defining exactly where they "wish to go," outside of some individual, but by no means negligible, demands that would free Reg and improve their individual quality of life in practical ways (such as improved health care). The B-Mors seem most invigorated by the practice of engagement, however, and what they experience, learn, and become in the process of the community organizing. That is, the narrator explains, "if we resolve not to quell ourselves, to keep up the talk, to preserve the good picture of the pair in our minds no matter how contrary to the designs of the Directorate it might be, this practice alone invigorates us, raises us up, even if there is nowhere we wish to go" (104). The practice of disrupting the old models that emphasize bounded actors and communities, and teasing out the new, emerging models—which urges for a situated and relational engagement with the immediate, overlapping, conjoined, socio-material structures that constitute the body politic of B-Mor—becomes a speculative act of resistance in spite, or possibly because, of the very experimental nature of their engagement.

They do not yet know where they "wish to go," so they begin with interrogating "where they are." Will the B-Mors need a dream of a utopian future to propel their movement, a goal-oriented progressive agency? Or can they gather and sustain momentum in a commitment to the "now," a critical engagement with their present, not necessarily motivated by a future place, or a defined goal, to which they aspire?

They are tasked with creating a new political culture where there has been none, and not via a shared and overarching goal, but by engaging together in the present, continually in the present moment, one after the next. The dreamlike quality of this material and disintentional political work may very well be the ability to suspend belief in the future but remain motivated to act, fight, and organize in the present. This seems necessary in the novel exactly because the citizens of B-Mor are constructing their forms of organizing in full knowledge that the state power—the Directorate—is not empowered by their consent and, therefore, does not need it. As Cherniavsky points out, "[I]f the power of the state no longer operates on a claim to represent [the citizen] . . . then the agency of the citizen protestor, as well as the contexts and horizons of protest are also fundamentally transformed" (Cherniavsky 2017, 139). In the context of the novel, when faced with the particular type of power wielded by the Directorate, it does not necessarily make sense for the B-Mor laborers to construct themselves into citizens as understood under liberal humanism. I think it is fair to argue they are looking for something else, the B-Mors' engagement with Fan's "where you are" pronouncement instigates a movement that trusts in no particular future, but avoids fatalism.

When the humanist assumption of intentional agency is disrupted, we must also imagine political organizing in a context other than linear progress. This search for new patterns of disintentional organizing is then one way to make manifest a through line in this book's approach that has led us from Thoreau's quest for Relational Knowing, to Silko's nonlinear revolutionary activism of patience, through to this chapter's focus on disintentional politics. The ways of thinking, the relation to temporality and the sense of how our actions create the future are intertwined in these reimaginings of liberal humanist traditions. And "without the driving beat [of Progress]," Anna Tsing has suggested, "we might notice other temporal patterns" (Tsing 2015, 21). Finding progressive political agencies outside of progressive temporality will mean looking for "patterns of unintentional coordination [that] develop in assemblages" (21).[6] Building from Tsing, I am suggesting that a disintentional politics might help us frame the challenges and opportunities embedded in thinking agency and intentionality in ways that privilege distributed ways of knowing and acting in a world of mixed-communities and complex assemblages. Fan's directive of "where you are," resonates greatly with Tsing's own call for a new and specially honed curiosity: "The curiosity I advocate follows such multiple temporalities, revitalizing description and imagination . . . [so] we might look for what has been ignored because it never fit the time line of progress" (21).[7] I am also then suggesting that a disintentional politics might animate a curious and experimental politics for a justice-based, global climate change environmentalism, one that does not succumb to fatalism because it is not about the future; it is about the present. This is reminiscent of a point Leanne Simpson has made in regard to her theoretical and practical investment in the Indigenous movement for decolonization: "I don't want to imagine or dream futures," she declares, "I want a better present" (Simpson 2017, 246).

On Such a Full Sea, ultimately, ends with a whimper rather than a revolution as the economic recession eases and the Directorate repeals the harshest elements of their austerity campaign. The fire subsides, but is it fully extinguished? Fan is in hiding, presumed to be preparing to have her baby and continue her search for Reg, and the B-Mor residents return to a seemingly apolitical and semi-content existence balancing their work responsibilities and family-oriented personal lives. The novel then does not articulate a fully formed new political consciousness, but instead depicts the challenges and possibilities that might confront a society attempting to build a political subjectivity and agency from the apolitical well of neoliberalism. The movement is even somewhat dismissed in the final pages as only a "period of disturbance, which, from really anyone's perspective now, would appear to have passed" (Lee 2014, 337). This is not entirely convincing, though, and the narrator quickly hints that a second look might lead us to a different conclusion. The politics of "where you are" yet might still manifest as a movement, even as the random outbursts and recognizable protests quiet down. Changes are evident and a new awareness persists in the everyday life of B-Mor's citizens. The narrator continues:

> Some of us still tap our fingers to the rhythms of those street-filling chants, or can see, when no one else can, the shape of the signs still ghosted in our minds. . . . It's not common, not at all, but every once in a while someone will rise up from a

chair in an eatery or tea shop . . . and face the blithe crowd with half-open arms and without having to utter a word say to all: So what is this? (337).

How do the B-Mors conjure something they need before they know what it is? It seems that their only chance—and possibly our own as well—is to feel for the rhythms, patterns, pulses, the material temporalities of "where you are," recognizable to us only when we engage the distributed network of relations and agencies made manifest by the current materiality of the present moment.

In *Odds Against Tomorrow*, Mitchell struggles to find meaning in his life when there appears to be no "long term" for human society, and it is unclear if he will recognize the potential for alternative community building with the Dead Zoners; he is depressed, anxious, and vacillating between self-preservation and self-annihilation as the novel closes. In *On Such a Full Sea*, the B-Mors struggle to sustain a movement without defined goals, but certain ways of seeing, and nonlinear material temporalities, do leave vestiges of something new in their communities, as the rhythms of their everyday lives seemingly return to normal. Are these "salvage rhythms," in the spirit of Tsing's scholarship that searches for new forms of living in a postcapitalist society? These fictional cliffhangers are both reminiscent of Tsing's concept of "latent commons," or "fugitive moments of entanglement in the midst of institutionalized alienation. These are sites in which to seek allies," she suggests. They remain latent, according to Tsing, because though they are "ubiquitous, we barely notice them, and . . . they are undeveloped" (Tsing 2015, 254). New forms of curiosity, new ways of noticing, and building relationships across difference will be necessary. "We need many kinds of alertness to spot potential allies," Tsing suggests; "The hints of common agendas we detect are undeveloped, thin, spotty, and unstable. At best we are looking for a most ephemeral glimmer. But, living with indeterminacy, such glimmers are the political" (254–55). Building coalitions of indeterminacy, organizing without a goal, and acting without an intention might all seem simply incongruous, but it might just be in these types of unlikely, even seemingly incompatible, unions that we discover the efficacy of distributed agency.

6

The Unknowable Now

Passionate Science and Transformative Politics in Kim Stanley Robinson's Speculative Fiction

> An extraordinary social and psychological change is taking place right in front of our eyes—the impossible is becoming possible. An event first experienced as real but impossible . . . becomes real and no longer impossible (once the catastrophe occurs, it is "renormalized" perceived as part of the normal run of things, as always already having been possible). The gap which makes these paradoxes possible is that between knowledge and belief; we know the (ecological) catastrophe is possible, probable even, yet we do not believe it will really happen.
>
> —Slavoj Zizek, *Living in the End Times*

Near the conclusion of Kim Stanley Robinson's *Science in the Capital* trilogy, the newly elected U.S. President, a former Democratic U.S. senator from California named Phil Chase, suggests that the crisis of climate change will call upon human society to "become the stewards of the earth" (Robinson 2007, 517). He also, however, admits "that we [will] have to do this in ignorance of the details of *how* to do it" (517; my emphasis). In other words, Chase inspires his constituents to accomplish, rather than just the unthinkable, what we might term the *unknowable*. This final chapter explores that challenge, as outlined by Chase, within the context of the following questions: What does it mean for humans to be "stewards of the earth" while simultaneously admitting we do not know "how to do it"? In what ways will this look necessarily different from traditional environmental concepts of stewardship and more recent capitalist conceptions of a green economy? And, finally, how will society grapple with not only the crisis of futurity brought on by climate change, but also the simultaneous destabilization of knowledge formation and political agency in the contemporary moment?

Robinson places his trilogy in a near-future United States, with a predominant portion of the narrative unfolding in Washington, D.C., which is undergoing drastic changes due to the unfolding of an abrupt climate change event.[1] This scenario is based on studies of earlier shifts in climate, particularly the Younger Dryas, in which a drastic change from warm-wet to cold-dry weather occurred in a matter of years, rather than decades or centuries. The climatic shifts that occur create at least one major catastrophic weather-related issue in each novel (for instance, the major flood event in D.C. at the end of *Forty Signs of Rain*) and operate as a type of "liberating crisis" for Robinson's narrative.[2] In this manner, the trilogy is an experiment in possible futures in which the dominant assumptions of science, politics, and consumer culture are radically challenged. President Chase's call for experimentation, therefore, is based in a rethinking of what it means to comprehend, accept, and adapt to a highly unstable climate. He searches for a method of governing the country through a crisis instigated by an entity scholar Timothy Morton has termed, in his provocative scholarship, a *hyperobject*. According to Morton, a hyperobject is an "enormous entity" that, through its unique blend of unfathomable dimensions and impossible intimacy, "causes us to reflect on our very place on Earth and in the cosmos" (Morton 2013, 15). Abrupt climate change, as a type of hyperobject, provides the catalyst through which Robinson's trilogy explores new concepts of scientific practice and political efficacy in a near-future moment, as it demands action while simultaneously appearing, for all practical purposes, unknowable by traditional empirical means.

The manner in which Robinson configures the relation between individual and societal transformation, as well as between reformist and revolutionary political struggle, is of particular interest. As Roger Luckhurst astutely points out, the near-future depicted in Robinson's trilogy "is still one hemmed in by the political forces of neoliberalism" (Luckhurst 2009, 171). And, he continues, "It is 'our' contemporary science and technology that has to deal with catastrophic climate change: there are no science-fictional mitigations invented in the course of the 1500 pages; they all sit inside the horizon of current scientific research" (171). Because the trilogy depicts a near-future climate crisis that occurs within the framework of early-twenty-first-century political, economic, and scientific (so-called) realities, the question that motivates my reading of the trilogy then becomes: What is suggestive and possibly unique regarding its presentation of the relationship between scientific knowledge and distributed political agency? And, furthermore, is it a potentially productive critical model? In this final chapter, I first explore these conceptual challenges via a consideration of Robinson's critical representation of objectivity and the scientific method within the *Science in the Capital* trilogy. Next, I examine how this newly configured scientific practice, one termed a "passionate science," relates to other proposed social, economic, and political transformative possibilities in the novels. In particular, I will suggest that reading the trilogy's depiction of "passionate science" in relation to the alternative lifestyle of "optimodality"—as experienced through the scientist Frank Vanderwal's individual adoption of an alternative urban-nomad lifestyle—reveals the trilogy's most significant and suggestive attempt to imagine a radical transformative politics, one based within a framework of distributed agency and in the midst of a severe climate crisis. And, finally, I make the case that Robinson's trilogy is uniquely attuned to the manner in which distributed agency and the situated, decentered human offer a possibly transformative opportunity for social and environmental justice, as these theories simultaneously present a potential crisis for dominant conceptions of political subjectivity and intentionality that challenge our contemporary understanding of knowledge formation and social movement organizing.

Positioned Rationality as "Passionate Science"

Frank Vanderwal is a professor from UC San Diego in the midst of a one-year appointment at the National Science Foundation (NSF). His immediate supervisor, Anna Quibler, is the director of NSF's biomathematics division and together they manage casework for the foundation and oversee the approval of grants via the institution's peer review process. Though he struggles to explain why, Anna's approach to scientific practice unsettles Frank. Ultimately, he admits that it is "the way her hyperscientific attitude combined with her passionate female expressiveness to suggest a complete science, or even a complete humanity" (Robinson 2004, 17). Perhaps unsurprisingly, what makes him so uncomfortable is how much it "reminded [him] of himself" (17). Despite this partial identification with Anna's approach, Frank still sees these two sides of himself (the objective and subjective) as irreconcilable. In fact, he thinks of himself as "too stuffed with extreme aspects of both rationality and emotionality" (17). According to Frank, however, it appears that Anna has found a way to make passionate science work. In this way, a link between the two colleagues, centered around this perceived contradiction between the expectation of rationality in their professional lives and the intense subjectivity of being human, is formed early in the trilogy.[3]

Frank is uncomfortable with what he sees as disparate qualities within himself and at first resists what might be best described as a type of fragmented subjectivity. Instead, integration, or holism, remains Frank's objective. Letting go of this preoccupation with a whole and uniform sense of self becomes a significant part of Frank's transformation, as the three novels increasingly emphasize the necessity of embracing the fragmented nature of subjectivity. Frank will come to practice a style of nomadic living that he terms "optimodality"—an embrace of life's "perpetual change" and his own internal multiplicities—that eventually leads him to live in a tree house, befriend a community of squatters, and track escaped zoo animals in D.C.'s Rock Creek Park, all while maintaining his day job at the NSF working on a science-based approach to climate change mitigation and adaptation.

Along with the destabilization of Frank's empirical and humanist sense of self, the trilogy problematizes traditional views of the nature/culture binary. In his earlier *Mars* trilogy, Robinson presents the process of planetary scale geoengineering on Mars as a complex confluence of human and nonhuman agency. Early in the second novel of that trilogy, the process, termed "areoformation," is explained as such:

> [A]ll the members of a biosphere evolve together, adapting to their terrain in a complex communal response, a creative self-designing ability. This process, no matter how much we intervene in it, is essentially out of our control. Genes mutate, creatures evolve: a new biosphere emerges. . . . And eventually the designers' minds, along with everything else, have been forever changed. (Robinson 1994, 3)

The red planet's impact on the new human colonizers is more than simply physical in nature, although this is certainly important (as in the effect of lower gravity on their muscle mass). An even heavier emphasis is placed on the physical environment's impact upon the social development of a new Martian culture. Rather than the human community and the Martian landscape impacting each other in a type of causal relationship, the *Mars* trilogy instead refuses the initial separation. In this manner, agency is depicted as always already distributed across the human and nonhuman. The *Mars* and *Science in the Capital* trilogies are both thought experiments on the types of scientific practices and cultures (economic, political, and social) that might help inform the creation of a technologically advanced, socially just, and utopian society. Robinson's narratives are, in certain ways, reminiscent of Donna Haraway's more theoretical feminist and posthuman critiques of objectivity and empirical science. Haraway's "situated knowledges" and what Robinson, somewhat more mundanely, refers to as "passionate science" both have, at their heart, an emphasis upon knowledge formation as a process of multiplicity, embodiment, and subjective positionality.

Similarly, in an analysis of Robinson's 2009 novel *Galileo's Dream*, Sherryl Vint suggests the novel presents "science as an 'articulated structure of hope'; that requires us to see reality fully" (Vint 2012, 46). She continues, "This is the kind of amodern science advocated by Latour, which refuses an artificial separation between science and society, one that recognizes that the values by which we organize our social and material lives will also shape the kind of science we have and the futures it can help us produce" (46). While my reading of the representation of science in the trilogy aligns in many ways with Vint's cogent analysis of *Galileo's Dream*, I will suggest that the *Science in the Capital* trilogy makes a provocative connection between knowledge-formation practices (such as a passionate science) and the distributed nature of agency. In *Galileo's Dream*, Vint contends that "the world remains the passive object to be known" and consequently "a better future" can be forged by "human agency" alone, rather than an "assemblage of vibrant matter" (49). In Robinson's *Capital* trilogy, on the other hand, I will argue the relationship between situated knowledge and distributed agency is more nuanced. In particular, I suggest reading the trilogy's depiction of "passionate science" and "optimodality" in relation to each other unveils a vivid articulation of what is often termed a "successor science"—one that is particularly attentive to distributed agency—in Robinson's work.

To begin, it is essential that we first clarify Haraway's representation of the egalitarian possibilities that emerge from within a successor science. The concepts of situated knowledges and positioned rationality, both in theory and practice, must account for what Haraway calls the "god-trick" of objectivity. In *Simians, Cyborgs and Women*, she writes:

> The science question in feminism is about objectivity as positioned rationality. Its images are not the products of escape and transcendence of limits, i.e., the view from above, but the joining of partial views and halting voices into a collective subject position that promises a vision of the means of ongoing finite embodiment, of living within limits and contradictions, i.e., of views from somewhere. (Haraway 1991, 196)

The scientist, in this approach, recognizes her own subjective partiality, her own "situated" self, and allows a new embodied process of knowledge making to become an important step toward relinquishing the quest for the god-like claims of objectivity. That is, to let go of the impossible dream of being nowhere and, therefore, everywhere. Importantly, Haraway goes on to say, "[R]ational knowledge does not pretend to disengagement . . . to be free from interpretation, from being represented, to be fully self-contained or fully formalizable. Rational knowledge is a process of ongoing critical interpretation among 'fields' of interpreters and decoders. Rational knowledge is a power-sensitive conversation" (196). Robinson attempts to present these very qualities, highlighted by Haraway, in the scientific work, coined "passionate science," that becomes fundamental to the personal and sociopolitical revolutions in the trilogy. This articulation of a scientific method, based in multiplicity, experimentation, and nonhierarchical structures of power, seems central to much of these novels' focus upon the possible intersections of science and culture. Of course, according to Haraway, "[W]e are . . . bound to seek perspective from those points of view, which can never be known in advance, which promise something quite extraordinary, that is, knowledge potent for constructing worlds less organized by axes of domination" (192). When representing the possible "construction" of just such a world, Robinson explores the relationship between these situated knowledge formation practices and distributed agency.

It is important to note that there is a fundamental connection between the scientific approaches determined best practice for climate change mitigation and the embryonic yet suggestive socioeconomic transformations in the novels. Gib Prettyman rightly points out that, for instance, in Robinson's trilogy, "geomediation is not a silver bullet, but one element of a cultural and economic shift as well . . . even the science itself that Robinson imagines is different due to its incorporation of human bias, politics" (191). This difference in the *Capital* trilogy's depiction of the relationship between the scientific and the socioeconomic responses necessary to respond to the challenges of climate change are exactly what makes this series and, for that matter, the Mars trilogy before it, such an interesting depiction of geo-mediation. Rather than seeing geo-engineering as simply another expression of human power and control over a passive nonhuman environment, the approach sketched in the trilogy is open to an examination of the multiplicities and contingent agencies involved in all human projects. As McKenzie Wark notes, while discussing Haraway's alternative approach, "[Situated Knowledges] is about reconnecting the making of observations to the scene of their making. There's a limit to how far an observation can be abstracted from the situation that produces it. A thorough witnessing sees also the means by which it sees what it sees, and knows what it knows" (Wark 2015, 145).[4] In Frank's slow adoption of a passionate science, readers are presented with a fairly incisive critique of the assumptions from which the scientific world operates when it continues to worship at the altar of objectivity, or the god-like, disembodied "everywhere and nowhere" that Haraway, Latour, and others have so thoroughly elucidated.

The alternative model offered in the trilogy, as we will find, is inevitably flawed and somewhat incomplete (particularly in its inability to imagine a science operating more considerably outside of the profit motive). However, Robinson does offer a provocative vision of Haraway's situated knowledges, as newly conceived scientific method, and how it might affect U.S. politics, economics and culture as the society confronts increasingly complex and dangerously unstable climatic changes. Two critical events, in particular, catalyze Frank's eventual search for a situated, applied, and passionate scientific method. The first is his reaction to Rudra Cakrin, a brown-bag lunch speaker at NSF and visiting Buddhist monk from the climate-threatened, fictional island nation of Khumbalung. The second, and certainly more physical, transformative moment is the result of a surprise punch to the nose.

The theme of Rudra Cakrin's speech, the importance of compassion in all human endeavors, including science, impacts Frank profoundly. The guest speaker pointedly informs the group of NSF scientists gathered for the informal talk and luncheon: "An excess of reason is itself a form of madness" (Robinson 2007, 244). From the initial sketch of Frank's rather uncritical faith in objectivity outlined above, we can see why, taken seriously, these words would provide a profound shock. And, fittingly, Frank leaves the lunch in the midst of what can only be described as the beginning of an existential crisis. Afterward, he thinks to himself: "An excess of reason. Well, but he had always tried to be reasonable . . . Dispassionate; sensible; calm; reasonable. A thinking machine. He had loved those stories when he was a boy. That was what a scientist was, and that was why he was such a good scientist" (247). Frank's thoughts then return to his colleague Anna Quibler's more subjective approach to science; however, he still hesitates to fully accept that reason alone is not a sufficient device for bridging the gap between science and culture (or science and policy). "That was the thing that had bothered him about Anna," he goes on to himself, "that she was undeniably a good scientist but she was a passionate scientist too, she threw herself into her work and ideas, had preferences and took positions" (248). It was readily apparent she "cared which theory was true," and that, to Frank, just "wasn't science. To care that much was to introduce bias into the study" (248). Despite this lingering skepticism, Frank remains undeniably struck by Cakrin's argument highlighting the impossibility of a purely rational self. His image of himself as a "thinking machine" is fundamentally disrupted.

While ruminating over these epistemological questions, Frank decides to forego his return to San Diego, his teaching position, his pastime of surfing, and a possibly lucrative advisory role with a biotech start-up called Torrey Pines Generique. He elects, instead, to stay at the National Science Foundation, and commits himself to investigating what an applied and passionate approach to science might be able to accomplish in regard to climate change mitigation. In a letter to NSF director Diane Chang, he calls out the institution for remaining too reserved and nonpolitical. Chang, in a pointed response, challenges him to put his own ideas to work by outlining a new scientific approach to climate change mitigation (296). Slowly recognizing failure in his quest for objectivity in his professional and personal life, Frank turns toward, and is pulled along, a transformative path leading toward something akin to Haraway's concept of "positioned rationality." Robinson, in this way, draws the reader's attention to the problematic nature of objectivity, particularly its assumption of the scientist's ability to achieve a disembodied, universal, and god-like status of observation. And Frank, along with many of his NSF colleagues, begin to explore how "passionate science" might develop new approaches to climate change mitigation.

Going Optimodal: Transformations in the Anthropocene

In the second novel, *Fifty Degrees Below*, Frank begins to adopt a lifestyle that he terms "optimodality" and slowly creates a routine that revels in multiplicity and contradiction. His embrace of optimodality signifies a process through which he might eventually accept his own fragmented subjectivity. No longer searching for an integrated self, he instead begins to redefine his relationship to the human and nonhuman elements of the city in a manner that, just weeks earlier, would have been completely uncharacteristic. He allows his apartment lease to run out and buys a van in which he plans to live. It is not long, though, before even the van itself proves too much a separation from the nonhuman environment. So, Frank builds a well-hidden tree house in Rock Creek Park (which was officially closed after the flood at the end of *Forty Signs of Rain*) to call home. Frank's daily experiences are radically changed by his decision to "go optimodal" and to embrace the fragmentary and segmented aspects of his daily life. In so doing, he begins to embrace both the natural and human-built environments of a city he had failed to get to know, or even begin to see, in his first year in D.C.

He is enticed by an article in *The Washington Post* that chronicles the story of homeless folks camping in the park, and Frank terms it, in true romantic fashion, a "return to wilderness." Drawn to the park in search of a version of this traditional wilderness experience, Frank is initially motivated by the myth of "uninhabited" and "pristine" wilderness as a truer, or better, type of nature. Once in the park, however, the solitude and peace he seeks is quickly disrupted by two men arguing nearby. His response is telling: "Frank didn't want to deal with any such people. He was annoyed; he wanted to be out in a pure wilderness, empty in the way his mountains out west were empty" (Robinson 2005, 14). There is an interesting connection here, which unfortunately Frank does not seem to recognize, between his beloved and supposedly "empty" mountains out west, emptied via the dispossession of Indigenous peoples who were the earliest inhabitants of these regions, and the "not-empty" city park, where those dispossessed of proper housing in various ways now come to dwell in D.C. Frank's initial reliance on these environmental, and outdoor recreationist, tropes regarding the restorative qualities of pristine nature (as well as the idea of wilderness as a place outside of, and separate from, human culture) are slowly unsettled by his so-called optimodal existence. Instead, and more interestingly, Frank's transformation becomes an investigation into the highly fluid boundaries between the second-nature of the built city park and the third-nature of the human-built environments of D.C. In this way, Frank's life begins to blur the artificial lines too often drawn between the *real* wilderness, its urban green-space *simulations*, and the *actual* city.

It is important to note here that the trilogy clearly does not engage thoroughly enough with hierarchical structures of power based in race, gender, and sexuality. Frank certainly needs to be read as an embodiment of multiple sets of privilege (white, male, straight, and able-bodied) that are, to my mind, never adequately examined in the novels. On a given day, Frank will wake up in this tree house at dawn, walk along Rock Creek in search of exotic animals let loose from the zoo during the flood, exercise and shower at a local city gym, work on the scientific and political implications of geoengineering during the day at the NSF offices, eat at his favorite international restaurant for dinner, and finally return to Rock Creek for an evening fraternizing with his fellow squatters in the closed park. Frank's varied experiences and the new communities of people he meets begin to have dramatic effects on his understanding of society, economics, ethics, and even the scientific method itself. It also, however, highlights the privilege of physical and social mobility that he enjoys. While Frank's transformation is depicted as a movement away from the most problematic and violent assumptions prevalent within contemporary structures of capitalism, his multiple levels of privilege are never fully and effectively examined in the novels. Many of his transformative experiences are, at least in part, dependent upon the privileges of mobility and access afforded to him by his whiteness. Frank's willingness to live in and freely roam around the officially closed Rock Creek Park is based upon a certain type of (over)confidence indicative of white male privilege: he remains (mostly) free of fear, for instance, from a violent assault and/or becoming a victim of police harassment as he constructs and inhabits his illegal tree house deep in the park's forest.

While issues of class and economic inequality do factor in Robinson's representation of D.C. society and politics to some degree, it is noteworthy that race, somewhat conspicuously, does not. This silence on matters of race in the trilogy is particularly problematic, as the narrative's distinct lack of engagement with the experience of Black citizens in D.C. ignores the reality of a constituency that comprises a significant percentage of the city's inhabitants.[5] Additionally, the trilogy's disinterest in racial justice issues associated with climate change, seems to suggest that issues of institutional racial inequality in D.C. will be attenuated by the broader structural changes enacted upon scientific, economic, and political systems and institutions. On the importance of attending to the intersections between systems of racial injustice and environmental degradation in urban settings, environmental theorists from across the disciplines have quite rightly argued that, as well summarized here by political theorist Damian White and cultural geographer Chris Wilbert: "a just urban socio-environmental perspective must consider who gains and who pays and ask serious questions about multiple power relations . . . [because] environmental transformations are not independent of class, gender, ethnicity, and other power struggles" (White and Wilbert 2009, 75). While not taken up in the novels in a substantial manner, this perspective would need to be an integral part of an effective distributed environmental politics.

When Frank does eventually find himself the victim of physical violence in the park, it is only after he chooses to intervene in a scuffle, upon finding a group of homeless men he has befriended under attack from unknown assailants. As he admits, "The bros [as he calls his homeless friends] were under a different kind of surveillance than he was . . . with consequences much worse than Frank's (one hoped)" (Robinson 2005, 278). This recognition of his privilege compared to the police harassment the homeless face is admirable, but the difficulty of grasping its full ramifications becomes evident in his final aside, "(one hoped)." That is, while Frank has recently become aware that the government's secret intelligence agencies may be watching him due to his recent unusual activity, he also understands that jail is an unlikely result of this investigation. In fact, as a mid-level government official, he here clearly "hopes" that his privilege will hold up, if necessary. Possibly feeling the need to justify why exactly he should receive better treatment than his "bros" if they are all busted for trespassing, he reminds himself: "They had police records, many of them extensive. Technically much of what they did was illegal, including being in Rock Creek Park at all" (278–79). While the "bros" are outright trespassing in the park, Frank relies upon a document from the National Zoo that indicates his volunteer status as a tracker of the many escaped animals still roaming the park. These two sets of institutional forms, the bros' police records and Frank's zoo pass, offer the flimsiest of blinders (paper-thin, one might say), which allow Frank to keep his privilege essentially unexamined at any level of real significance.

Frank's inability to fully engage the logics of his privilege points toward a certain unknowable aspect of privilege itself (from the perspective of the privileged, that is). There is a way in which this refusal resembles large segments of society's inability in the novels, and arguably in our contemporary moment, to fully *know*, or deeply and fundamentally grasp, the climate crisis. When it comes to either the refusal to recognize white privilege or climate change denialism, these forms of denial remind us that it is possible to become *aware* of an event, fact, or entity but remain somehow incapable of *knowing* or *understanding* it. It is exactly this phenomenon, in fact, to which Zizek's quotation, in the epigraph to this chapter, gestures. Similarly, many of Frank's colleagues in the science community will become frustrated by the slow social and political reaction to the climate crisis, bemoaning the fact that, as they see it, "we know but can't act." Others, on the other hand, attempt to grapple with the very unknowable nature of the climate crisis itself and, therefore, in order to chart a cautious path forward, move to challenge and reformulate the fundamental humanist concepts that assume a direct correlation between human knowledge and agency (i.e., causation and intentionality). Exactly how to understand human agency's role within these transformative changes (that is, what we might call the potential and crisis of distributed agency) is difficult to determine and necessarily entails a rethinking of political subjectivity.

In Frank's case, the applied, practical, and subjective nature of his own experience leads him to further disown the concepts of objectivity and universality that he once treasured as the keys to *good science*. To this point, Prettyman argues, "Through the story of Frank and his transformation, Robinson suggests that for science to be potentially revolutionary or utopian, it first must change its own forms of thought significantly" (Prettyman 2009, 188). The significance of Frank's optimodality, therefore, is at the center of the broader political, social, and economic changes that Robinson depicts by the culmination of the trilogy. In other words, none of the environmental, political, or economic changes we find emerging in the trilogy could come to pass if humans, and particularly those living in Western capitalist countries such as the United States, do not begin to reassess their relationship to the nonhuman world (and therefore the knowledge making practices they deploy to gain information about—and supposed control over—environmental processes). For Frank, at least, "each blustery afternoon changed his life. That was autumn, that was how it should feel, Frank saw, the landscape suffused with the ache of everything fleeting by. A new world every heartbeat." (Robinson 2005, 268). His time spent exploring a more material and interconnected relation to the human and more-than-human communities from Rock Creek Park to the hallways of the NSF, prompts Frank to recognize the importance of observing and engaging with the uniquely fluid assemblages of the present moment. "He had to incorporate this feeling of perpetual change, make it an aspect of optimodality. Of course everything always changed!" (268). Rather than uttering a platitude lifted straight from any high school yearbook, Frank is expressing the surprising experience of inhabiting place from a decentered, disanthropocentric perspective.

The potential embedded within this individual transformation and how it might be mapped onto the societal is an integral question raised by the trilogy and something we will look at more extensively below. During a long cold spell (the temperature is between zero and fifty-below for more than a week in the usually mild D.C. area) that dominates the narrative of the aptly titled second novel *Fifty Degrees Below*, Frank's expertise in outdoor recreation and living proves quite an asset. More accustomed to outdoor conditions than most city dwellers, a serious "gearhead," and lover of technological advances in cold-weather clothing, Frank volunteers his time, during the week-long freeze, to help wherever he can. He outfits the homeless with extra winter gear that either he does not need himself or can find cheap at secondhand outdoor shops, and goes from home to home in nearby neighborhoods to check on those in need. He even joins a volunteer group chopping up fallen trees that are blocking roads and downing power lines around the city. This severe weather event offers Frank the opportunity to practice the Buddhist maxim of "always generous," and, importantly, continues to disrupt the reflexive binary thinking that has previously led him to accept the dichotomy of subject and object, society and nature, or, even, city and wilderness. On one particularly cold day, we find Frank

> [k]icking through piles of fallen leaves . . . the cold air struck him like a splash of water in the face. It felt good. He had to laugh: all his life he had traveled to the mountains and the polar regions to breathe air this bracing and heady, and here

> it was, right now in the middle of this ridiculous city. Maybe the seasons would become his terrain now, and winter would be like high altitude. (282)

The idea that Frank's remove to Rock Creek Park might be something akin to the romanticized wilderness experience of the Western environmental tradition is significantly disrupted in this passage and several others like it. Even if it is still a "ridiculous" city to Frank, we can see the beginning of the end for his traditional view of nature as a place without humans. Whether it was the "mountains" or the "polar regions," the empirical Frank *knew* he had to travel *away* from human society to find Nature. At this point, the newly "optimodal" Frank begins to understand that the divide between city and wilderness, much like the divide between individual and community and humans and the nonhuman environment, is less than absolute.[6]

By depicting the changes in a character such as Frank, one who at the outset seems the least likely to renounce the power and possibility of reason and objectivity, the trilogy disrupts a series of assumptions that have stymied the political effectiveness of the environmental movement. First, it exposes the limitations of deep green politics advocating a "return to Nature" by revealing the concept of a primeval, pristine Nature as a fully socially constructed idea. Second, not content to then restrict the nonhuman world to social construction, Robinson insists that the reader take seriously the importance of his or her very situatedness in the environment. Frank is very much located in an environment and it is this *positionality* that he realizes inflects his view of the nonhuman environment. Not only is it subjective, it is also as complex and fluid as the seasons; and this is not to be feared but embraced. Robinson, in a 2004 interview conducted while he was writing the trilogy, describes Frank's transformed life as an "escape from and an assault on capitalism, on the individual level" that is "more active than renunciation . . . [and] a form of celebrating reality in the form of our bodies and the immediate home and landscape around us" (Szeman and Whiteman 2004, 188). Frank begins to accept that, as a result of this new deeply emplaced perspective, the existing systems of thought and institutional structures of power will not provide the necessary tools to respond to the climactic crisis befalling the planet. It is helpful, once again, to briefly return to Haraway here to better understand Frank's explorations into the multiplicity of environments, experiences, and communities that galvanize his optimodality.

Haraway, as explored above, has famously investigated the relationship between Western concepts of self and the fantasy of the unitary individual subject in order to effectively extend her critique of objectivity. In the end, she argues for the benefits of what she terms "splitting" rather than the dominant image of "being," and does so in order to further articulate an alternative to the patriarchal and racist underpinnings of Western empirical knowledge. She writes:

> The split and contradictory self is the one who can interrogate positioning and be accountable, the one who can construct and join rational conversations and fantastic imaginings that change history. Splitting, not being, is the privileged image for feminist epistemologies of scientific knowledge. "Splitting" in this context should be about heterogeneous multiplicities that are simultaneously necessary and incapable of being squashed into isomorphic slots or cumulative lists. (Haraway 1991, 193)

The "heterogeneous multiplicities" that become Frank's every day, allow him to let go of his desire for a fully integrated self, a world of strict empiricism, and a belief that he can or should perform science in such a manner. Frank's personal transformation into the optimodal life results in a radical repositioning and, most interestingly, highlights the multiplicity of positions and/or perspectives, from which the scientist attempts to view and understand the physical world. Of course, for Haraway, positioning is "the key practice grounding knowledge organized around the imagery of vision, as so much Western scientific and philosophic discourse is organized. Positioning implies responsibility for our enabling practices. It follows that politics and ethics ground struggles for the contests over what may count as rational knowledge" (193). The positioned rationality that Haraway describes above highlights the potential of Frank's personal transformation to radically impact his scientific practice. There are also, in Frank's optimodality and inchoate successor science, echoes of H. D. Thoreau's attempts to develop a system of knowledge formation based in relational knowing. Additionally, Thoreau's remapping of Walden, which emphasizes the material interconnection and hybrid-objects of Walden pond, the railroad line, and his small cabin home (as explored in chapter 2), is best understood as a practice of positioned knowledge production. In these ways, Thoreau's commitment to borders and hybridity, his acute awareness of his balancing act at the intersection of nature-culture assemblages, during his time at Walden Pond is itself a type of optimodal lifestyle and a version of passionate science. No wonder Frank, via his regular visits to emersonfortheday.net, finds such inspiration in Thoreau!

It is correct to point out that Frank's optimodal lifestyle, to some degree, is only a sort of short-term experiment (as was Thoreau's time at Walden), and also an opportunity that is broadly based in his privilege of mobility as an educated, professional, white male (again, as was true for Thoreau). The results of these experiments, however, instigate an important reformulation of self that reorients these historical and fictional characters' unsatisfied desire for god-like objectivity and universal truth, and both are interested in more than only individual consciousness change. As Luckhurst astutely points out, "this personal crisis coincides with Frank's recommitment to the NSF and his call for an institutional paradigm shift indicates how we are to map the personal onto the collective" (Luckhurst 2009, 177). As such, via the link drawn between Frank's optimodal lived experience and his professional practice of passionate science, Robinson begins to imagine the relationship between individual and societal transformation. Again, Luckhurst: "Reformulating subjectivity will itself be part of the conjectural changes required in the permanent climate crisis of advanced capitalist nations" (177). Frank's individual transformation is not solely a singular experience but is, rather, connected to broader reformulations of scientific, cultural, and economic worldviews. This repositions the scientist-human, the "passionate scientist" who is ready to engage with her work from the embedded position of a "split and contradictory self," who now finds herself inside a constantly open and interacting relation with, rather than separate or outside, human institutions and the built and unbuilt nonhuman environment. In other words, we come to know things through relations, and we are, as well, always already inside these relations ourselves. The passionate science that Frank is beginning to comprehend and practice is Robinson's answer to the overdetermined objectivity that Haraway criticizes as the "god-like everywhere and nowhere." Instead, emotion, and therefore subjectivity itself, is a central characteristic of a science that promotes social justice, economic equality, and environmental health.

In this vein, the trilogy successfully destabilizes the concepts of scientific objectivity, the integrated and rational self, and the nature/culture binary through the "grounding knowledge" Frank accrues via his optimodal existence. Consequently, we can recognize Frank's optimodality as a type of productive posthuman subjectivity with implications for broader societal transformations. Rosi Braidotti's conception of posthuman subjectivity is edifying in this regard, as she explains:

> I define the critical posthuman subject within an eco-philosophy of multiple belongings, as a relational subject constituted in and by multiplicity, that is to say a subject that works across differences and is also internally differentiated, but still grounded and accountable. Posthuman subjectivity expresses an embodied and embedded and hence partial form of accountability, based on a strong sense of collectivity, relationality and hence community building. (Braidotti 2013, 49)

Through Frank's optimodal life, *Science in the Capital* explores the possible consequences of such transformational changes at the level of the individual and society while placing a particular focus upon how individual transformation might link to broader social change and "community building." At the risk of simplification: the singular becomes communal due to its inherent relationality.

Robert Markley has drawn attention to the important connection between Frank Vanderwal and the character of Sax Russell in the Mars trilogy. Markley points out that both characters begin the respective trilogies as symbols of professionalized scientific objectivity and, more generally, white male privilege; and their transformations lead them to integrate subjectivity, emotion, and politics into a scientific method they originally saw as distinctly unique from everyday life and emotions (Markley 2005, 378). Interestingly, each character's conversion is complicated (or possibly facilitated) by a physical injury to his brain. Sax's injury is inflicted by torture at the hands of the private police force employed by the corporate conglomerate vying for political and economic control of Mars. Markley tells us that Sax must "relearn the intricacies of putting thoughts into words. Sax's efforts to regain his speech metaphorically underscore his emergence as a symbol and practitioner of a science committed to the ethical imperatives of . . . eco-economics" (378). Therefore, the transformation that Sax undergoes after his injury causes the practitioner of pure science to recognize the integral relationships between politics, economics, social movements, and scientific practice. In this manner, "Science, for Sax, loses none of its commitment to exploring the cosmos but, transformed and embodied, redefines the relationship between objective values and ethical commitment. Science creates rather than simply describes"

(378). For Sax, after his injury, the knowledge making process of empirical scientific practice is most useful when understood as more fully imbricated with the social. According to both Markley and Elizabeth Leane, Robinson's representation of this "successor science" in the Mars trilogy is one that generates the potential for political, economic, and social change as well. Leane describes Sax's transformation as part of Robinson's larger interest in the promotion of a utopian science, referring to it as a successor science to the objective scientific method that Sax is originally committed to practicing. She writes, "Sax's conversion represents . . . a move towards a science which refuses the colonial and patriarchal impulse to naturalize and objectify the other" (Leane 2009, 54). Extrapolating from the *Mars* trilogy to the more recent *Science in the Capital* trilogy, it becomes possible to read Frank's conversion as a continuation of these transformations, now situated in a very near-future context on Earth. In Frank's case, his physical injury emanates from a blunt-force blow to the nose at the hands of an unknown assailant, as he attempts to defend his homeless companions from a seemingly unprovoked attack in Rock Creek Park.

The timing of Frank's injury, just about halfway through the 1,500 page trilogy, creates a sort of tipping point in Frank's metamorphosis. The injury impairs his decision-making abilities rather than, as with Sax, his power of speech. Prettyman also reads this injury, much like Sax's, as integral to Frank's transformation in that

> [i]t forces Frank to combine the habitually abstract observations of science with a fully-engaged emotional involvement, so that the understanding of material reality (the hallmark of scientific method, properly conceived) is situated in the fullness of lived reality, rather than wielded as a "rational tool." . . . Both Frank and Sax discover that becoming more fully-human and effective scientists is a never ending process. (Prettyman 2009, 190)

Rethinking an earlier, uncritical acceptance of his privileged position as observer, he now comes to realize that he cannot move through these social spaces (Rock Creek Park, the ferals' squatting communities, etc.) undetected or unchanged, that in reality he cannot be, and does not want to be, an invisible spectator. The alternative, he realizes, is that he is instead "situated in the fullness of lived reality" (190). The perceived lack of agency he experiences during his recovery, the acute indecision, and the emotional swings brought on by the injury to his brain leave

Frank struggling with the usually unconscious aspects of his thought process. He has trouble trusting his judgment and is surprised by his lack of conviction. This is a meaningful depiction of the disconnect between the assumed rational sequence of deliberation, decision, and action that is also inherent to distributed agency's disruption of unlimited and intentional human agency. Frank struggles to trust in this process uncritically and is forced to relearn, as Sax relearns language in the *Mars* Trilogy, how to best operate ethically and effectively from this positionality somewhere between intention and indecision (reminiscent, in fact, of the processes for disintentional politics explored in the previous chapter). While Frank remains positive about the potential for his optimodal lifestyle, the injury leaves him frustrated with the limitations that seem to come along with this new distributed sense of self and agency. It is quite possible, however, that these operate, to some degree, as productive limitations.[7]

Through detailed depictions of Frank's personal and professional transformation, including his attempts to redefine his own relationship to various human and more-than-human communities in and around D.C., the trilogy builds a world in which the strict binary relationships of human versus nonhuman, subject versus object, and city versus wilderness break down in potentially productive ways. At this point, it is important to consider the scale and durability of the changes Robinson foretells through Frank's transformative process. For instance, some scholars have argued, mistakenly I think, that Frank's optimodality is only a temporary response to a crisis situation. Luckhurst, for instance, claims that the novels "seem to suggest that optimodality is the subjectivity of a time of crisis, but that the readjustment of nature and culture that comes from a committed ecological politics will allow a more holistic sense of self to emerge" (Luckhurst 2009, 178). This analysis, however, appears to accept a humanist conception of normalcy, while all too quickly discounting the trilogy's persistent and trenchant critiques of holism as simply a coping mechanism during a time of crisis. To suggest that Robinson presents a simple "readjustment" followed by a quick return to "holism" is certainly an underestimation of the trilogy's ambitious narrative. While at first Frank's optimodality is a useful survival skill in a time of catastrophe, it also becomes the core ingredient allowing for the broader and more systemic social, scientific, and political changes that are crystallizing by the end of the final novel, *Sixty Days and Counting*. As we have seen, optimodality itself is a practical and revolutionary development infused with Haraway's critique of objectivity and Braidotti's outline of a posthuman subjectivity. Consequently, Frank's parcellated social life is one part of a larger emphasis on situated knowledges in the trilogy,

Frank begins to advocate for passionate science at the NSF, arguing it is the best approach to develop, and put into practice, the scientific community's limited knowledge for addressing climate change. Frank and his NSF colleagues begin to team with world leaders to fund and approve several large geoengineering projects, including a massive operation to dump enough salt into the Atlantic Ocean to stabilize the northern Gulf Stream. These projects reveal the trilogy's interest in depicting techno-fix scientific approaches to climate change that are derived from outside the logics of traditional empirical science and capitalist profit motives. It is Frank's acceptance of a split, or posthuman, subjectivity that informs the passionate science and scientific government, which the trilogy foregrounds, as necessary to any appropriate geo-mediation projects aimed at climate change mitigation. The extended crisis of abrupt climate change is far from over as the trilogy comes to a close, and the challenges of adapting to climate change are only beginning. Therefore, optimodality is central to Frank's critical rethinking of his relationship to science and the nonhuman world, and this subsequently motivates his attempts to recalibrate NSF's response to climate change and geo-mediation in fundamental and lasting ways.

It is worthwhile to contemplate the narration of crisis more broadly within the trilogy insomuch as it foregrounds the centrality of Frank's personal transformation within the novels' broader socio-environmental themes. In a recent interview included in his co-edited collection *Green Planets*, Robinson himself explains, "It seemed as if the story was going to have to be told as some kind of daily life, which in narrative terms meant it could not be a thriller" (Canavan and Robinson, 245). When he included scenes of a "protagonist frolicking in the snow with his toddler son" or performing mundane but necessary acts such as "changing diapers," he suggests that it was "a stab at representing how it might feel to live during climate change" (245). Rather than abrupt climate change itself, according to Robinson, the "biggest crisis in the story is . . . the scientist Frank going through a change of consciousness. For any of us that is always a big crisis" (245). And, he goes on to explain that "while writing the novel I found that even in the [climate] crisis, abrupt on geologic scales, events still resolved to individual humans living variants of ordinary life" (244). Attention to Robinson's own conception of Frank's transformation, as articulated above, surely requires the reader to recognize optimodality as less a survival tactic and rather a more fundamental, long-lasting, and suggestive "change of consciousness."

Let us interrogate, for a moment, the concept of crisis a bit more. In the introduction to *Green Planets*, co-editor Gerry Canavan speculates on the efficacy of dystopian science fiction as a narrative device for climate change fiction. He speculates, "If capitalism has always been, in K. William Kapp's memorable formulation, 'an economy of unpaid costs,' then the growing recognition that the bill is coming due can represent a kind of nascent revolutionary consciousness. Looking through the lens of apocalypse . . . we might, even now, act" (12). If we take the crisis, or thriller, narrative model to be dependent upon anxiety, suspense, and fear, then we might also be reminded of Frederic Jameson's thoughts regarding science fiction's ability to help readers conceptualize an imperiled future. In regard to the beneficial aspects of fear itself, Fredric Jameson writes, "This would be a good deal more intense than the usual rhetoric about 'our children' (keeping the environment safe for future generations, not burdening them with heavy debt, etc.); it would be a fear that locates loss of the future and futuricity, of historicity itself, within the existential dimension of time and indeed within ourselves" (Jameson 2005, 233). In fact, Robinson's own reflections on the trilogy both recommend and put into question the supposed efficacy of crisis as a narrative tool. While he admits to using the concept of abrupt climate change to structure the narrative, he also emphasizes that what he found most compelling were the everyday stories of his characters. Frank's trial-and-error adoption of optimodality, while a crisis of consciousness certainly, plays out on a different register than that of fear or anxiety. Rather, his transformation is based in a more affirmative mode of practice that highlights a sort of playful experimentation with new opportunities brought forth by the disruption of abrupt climate change.

The optimistic qualities of optimodality are reminiscent of Rosi Braidotti's own skepticism regarding fear, particularly one based in shared vulnerability, as a motivation for collective responses to contemporary environmental and social challenges.[8] "The posthuman recomposition of human interaction that I propose is not the same as the reactive bond of vulnerability," she clarifies, "but it is an affirmative bond that locates the subject in the flow of relations with multiple others" (Braidotti 2013, 50). Braidotti finds the "reactive" response to vulnerability too negative for creating the necessarily "affirmative" bonds necessary to vastly reimagine and reorganize community-based relationships (within and across species) in a posthuman and postnatural condition. She, therefore, is inclined to look for more formidable and fundamental ways to conceive a posthuman collectivity capable of creating new and less hierarchical institutional systems and cultural structures that allow for a life of sustainable and rewarding experience. A new conception of posthuman connectivity, according to Braidotti, "actualizes a community that is not bound negatively by shared vulnerability, the guilt of ancestral communal violence, or the melancholia of unpayable ontological debts, but rather by the compassionate acknowledgement of their interdependence with multiple others most of which, in the age of anthropocene, are quite simply not anthropomorphic" (100–101).[9] Frank's optimodal existence, with its emphasis upon place-based processes of knowing and acting, operates as one example of the potential for positive and hopeful engagement with crisis in which the strength of the response is not based in fear and vulnerability as much as in opportunity and flexibility. As we have been suggesting, however, individual consciousness change will not be enough, and it must be coupled with political leverage capable of systemic change. How then does Frank's optimodal lifestyle help us think beyond the liberal democratic political subject?

To more fully explore the effects of Frank's optimodal life and practice of passionate science upon the entrenched politics and capitalist interests depicted in the trilogy, we need to transition our focus to another setting of scientific experimentation—the laboratories of Torrey Pines Generique, a biotech start-up in San Diego working in the field of biotechnology. Early in the trilogy, Robinson uses the Torrey Pines company to explore the expanding private scientific economy, particularly the biotech industry. This particular lab is searching for the insertion technique that would allow for gene therapy in humans. Later, when Frank and the NSF help to transform the Torrey Pines facility into a publicly funded research institute, it operates as an example of a more open and public practice of science dedicated to contemporary social justice and future environmental sustainability. However, when we first meet one of the lead scientists at Torrey Pines, Leo Mulhouse, he is entrenched in a competition for private patents with other start-up biotech companies that leads to high levels of secrecy and spy agency–level security measures.

The profit motive, private patents, and trade secrets are a part of the everyday fabric in the laboratories of these research companies. Intense security is "all standard in biotech now, after some famous incidents of industrial espionage. The stakes were too high to trust anybody" (Robinson 2004, 30). Leo's predicament highlights the lack of transparency that, elsewhere in the trilogy, is central to the scientific method Frank advocates. After a fairly successful study is completed, for instance, Leo needs to wait for approval from the firm to publish his results because "they want to find out what they can patent in it" before it is made public (93). Leo himself is a contradiction who wavers between fantasizing about the great economic potential of his work in biotech and a more idealistic vision of science for the sake of knowledge and human health. He hopes the biotech industry might become "like the computer industry in terms of financial returns" (31). He also, however, believes that "private science, secret science . . . wasn't science . . . which was [or should be] a matter of finding out things and publishing them for all to see and text, critique, put to use (93). He admits, though, that secret science was becoming "standard operating procedure" (93). Frank is a small investor in the firm and even acts as a part-time consultant as a professor at San Diego State University. Consequently, as he uses his growing powers at NSF to help shape the work on climate science and geo-mediation, Frank eventually creates a publicly funded and essentially open laboratory at Torrey Pines that operates as a bridge between government research and the California university labs. The idea, as he puts it, is that "the new institutes [are] in full control of their scientific results. No private trade secrets or patents" (Robinson 2005, 235). In this way, the trilogy sketches a new scientific approach, new methodologies for practicing science more resistant to capitalist profit motives, that will also reshape the structure of scientific practices and the institutions themselves (both public and private).

Clearly, the trilogy advocates for the potential benefit of what some of the characters, including Frank, call a Manhattan Project to discover and promote technologies designed for climate change mitigation. While the novels do entertain and explore the future possibilities of a sustainable economics beyond the profit motive, the narrative most heavily relies upon capitalism (especially in the new directives of Democratic president Phil Chase) to ratify what is termed a win-win approach to climate change mitigation. That is, the opportunity to address the worst effects of climate change and make money in new green economies and terra-formation projects simultaneously. In a conversation with his environmental advisor, Phil Chase reminds Charlie Quibler, "Right now we have capitalism. So we have to use it" (Robinson 2007, 374). When presented with a skeptical response to capitalism as a potential cure to environmental degradation, Chase continues to press his case: "For one thing, capital has a lot of capital.... It runs into the trillions of dollars. They want to invest it. At the same time there's an overproduction problem. They can make more than they can sell of lots of things. And so all capital of all kinds is on the hunt for a good investment" (374). Chase's reformist approach, as compared to the more transformational and postcapitalistic approaches sketched in the *Mars* trilogy, is not as clearly committed to a radical environmental politics.

The attempt to strike a balance between public works projects and private investment in climate mitigation might reasonably be attributed to the trilogy's commitment to a realistic, near-future approach. Or is it simply a capitulation to the intractability of neoliberal policies in the early twenty-first century? And, in what ways, if any, is it different than the sustainability movement, green capitalism, or corporate greenwashing with which readers are already well familiar? If President Chase argues for a more politically palatable and reformist approach, Robinson offers us a more strident voice for radicalism in Anna's husband, and environmental advisor to the president, Charlie Quibbler. In one important scene in the final novel, Charlie represents the new administration in a meeting with IMF and World Bank leaders. Charlie lays out a plan of climate mitigation, international in scale and vaguely socialist in contemporary political parlance, to which the world's economic leaders are steadfastly and unanimously opposed. Charlie, in a fiery speech, accuses the economists of ignoring the exteriorization of costs, building private profit while adding to public economic and health costs. He argues it is essentially a false system and comes to the realization that

> being economists, they were still exteriorizing costs without even noticing it or acknowledging such exteriorization had been conclusively demonstrated to falsify accounts of profit and loss. It was as if the world were not real—as if the actual physical world, reported on by scientists and witnessed by all, could be ignored. (202)

In this case, Charlie emphasizes the role capitalism plays in structuring both the science and politics of climate change and mitigation techniques. While Senator, and then President, Chase argues for the need to utilize the profit motive at the center of neoliberal economic policy to combat the worst effects of climate change, other characters, such as Charlie and

Frank's colleague Edgardo, attempt to sketch a future economic system that incorporates environmental costs into its budget equations.

It is in these sections of the trilogy that Robinson's narrative is most successful in imagining alternative economic, social, and political systems that focus on environmental sustainability and social justice rather than perpetual growth. In one particularly interesting scenario, Edgardo, in a memo to this newly politically engaged scientific team at NSF, argues for the need to reorient economic systems around scientific and ecological goals. He writes, "A scientifically informed government should lead the way in the invention of a culture which is sustainable perpetually. This is the only normative bequest to the generations to come. It is not adaptive to heavily damage the biosphere when our own offspring and all the generations to follow will need it . . . to survive" (Robinson 2005, 323–24). A scientific government, consequently, should focus on bringing to fruition an environmentally sustainable socioeconomic system that is most likely to lead to *permaculture*. Edgardo's memo goes on, in fact, to say, "Protection of the environment, therefore, along with restoration of landscapes and biodiversity, should become one of the principal goals of the economy" (324). The scientists at NSF become convinced that science itself needs to be more political, rather than more objective, due to the extreme consequences of inaction during abrupt climate change. They decide, as a result, to build from Edgardo's ideas to speculate exactly how a scientific government might operate, and put these theories into practice as they propose a type of shadow candidate during the presidential election—the virtual scientific politician with an appropriately passionate-scientific political platform.

In an earlier novel, *Antarctica*, Robinson explores a similar idea through a representation of "a continent ruled by scientists," as the Antarctic environment and its human communities undergo ecological and political challenges brought on by global warming. Several of his characters are fond of saying that "if it's true in Antarctica; it true everywhere!" (Robinson, *Antarctica*, 347). Carlos, who was actually born in an Antarctic outpost to Chilean parents, has subsequently spent most of his childhood and adult life on the frozen continent. Carlos consequently considers himself a native of Antarctica and this position offers him a certain credibility with his peers that goes beyond general knowledge of the local environment; rather, Carlos's consistent voicing of alternative systems of power and knowledge in opposition to the broader world's status quo is credited, by his peers, as a quasi-indigenous perspective that deserves a legitimate hearing. In many ways, Robinson constructs this very intriguing character as a voice speaking for both the global South in general and the frozen continent in particular. And, in so doing, Carlos's perspective highlights the connections between science, politics, and environmental justice.

Carlos explains the imminent environmental catastrophe to a co-worker, who simply goes by the nickname X, and a visiting U.S Senate staffer, Wade Norton, in no uncertain terms: "[Climate change is] an emergency situation. Governments have to guide us through this tight spot in history, if we are going to get through it without supercatastrophes. But how will they do it?" (349). Using the slang term for scientists in Antarctica; X answers that the leaders will most likely be the "Beakers" (349). Carlos clearly agrees and continues to explain this idea to Norton: "You [the government] make your decisions by consulting with a technical staff, the technocrats, and they make their decisions by consulting with the scientific bodies, the scientists. And so the scientists call the shots!" (349). Despite the clearly idealistic and rather oversimplified nature of this description, Carlos is quite convincing in arguing that science must extricate itself from the larger socioeconomic structures of capitalism. And that it should do this in order to engage with politics as a new passionate voice for action, rather than pretend to objectivity. Throughout the novel, in fact, Robinson seems to suggest the smaller scale of economic, political, and scientific activity on Antarctica possibly allows for a more fundamental critique of the current relationship between science and government, as well as a revolutionary vision of an alternative future.

While recognizing the issues involved in the modern professionalization of science, Carlos insists upon the idea of science as a potentially utopian organizational system. He argues that "the great outsider, the system that capitalism cannot conquer, is science. The two are actually at odds with each other, the one trying to defeat the other. This is the great war of our time!" (349). As if to underscore this claim, Wade Norton, as he is leaving the (for now) icy continent, dreams he is in conversation with the head of the National Science Foundation's Antarctic science team. "Wade said . . . in his dream, maybe technocrats have taken over the world, maybe scientists have taken over the world. Maybe the highest, driest, coldest, least significant of the continents would show the way" (630). The alternate present Wade dreamily imagines seems to point toward a "scientific government," but with the NSF at the lead it could not be a familiar type of technocracy (due to its foundations in situated knowledges and passionate science). Carlos's analysis of the relation between science and government in Antarctica, in which science engages from an emplaced, passionate, and political stance, is also a gesture toward a future of successor science based in positioned rationality and relational knowing. Rather than the current "post-truth" impulse of our contemporary political discourse, which increasingly ignores inconvenient science, the scientific politics for which Carlos advocates would depend upon material knowledge formation practices that understand scientific methods as embedded in, and fundamentally dependent upon, relational systems of human and nonhuman communities.[10]

Other than talks with Carlos and dreaming of passionate science, Wade Norton spends his time on the frozen continent as a political emissary of the environmentally focused Senator Phil Chase (whom we of course meet again in his successful bid for president in the *Science in the Capital* trilogy). Antarctica is ground zero for research into climate change, government-funded scientific research run by the National Science Foundation, and the first forays of private investment in energy resources and natural resource extraction. There is an international treaty generally being ignored and an icescape beginning to melt; Robinson's depiction of this continent of scientists is one in which politics is everywhere. This future successor science is embedded with the power to energize politics and offers a transformational opportunity for environmental and social justice on a continental scale. Yet whether such a government would be possible outside of Antarctica and, rather, within a developed, capitalist society, and exactly how a government based on passionate science might function, is not fully explored in *Antarctica*, the novel (outside of Carlos's postulations and Wade Norton's dreamworld). These questions do reappear, as we have seen, as a central problematic for the *Science in the Capital* trilogy.

The Unknowable Now

To this point, this chapter has outlined the distinctions between Frank's radical transformation on the level of the personal (optimodality) and professional (passionate science). Exploring this connection brings us to our central concern regarding the potential disruption, created by these new posthuman constructs of subjectivity and knowledge formation, of concepts of political agency and futurity. That is, the trilogy figures the crisis of futurity, which is wrapped up in the challenge to liberal humanist conceptions of subjectivity, agency, and the objectively knowable world, as in actuality also a question of knowledge formation and agency in the present moment. It is important to note the ways in which the broader societal transformations in the trilogy, the imagined sociopolitical and economic opportunities, often remain somewhat limited and predominantly reformist. As a case in point, President Chase, elected as a social and environmental reformer at the end of the second novel, embodies a type of somewhat familiar populist liberalism. And, not surprisingly, he strikes a cautious tone when it comes to the appropriate economic approaches necessary to mitigate climate change. As he firmly explains to his more radical aides, "Without conceding that private ownership of the public trust is right. . . . Right now we have to harness it [capitalism] to our cause, and use it to solve our problem. If we can do that, then the capitalism we end up with won't be the same one we began with anyway" (374). The capitalism Chase hopes to "end up with" is something along the lines of contemporary theories of eco-economics or natural capitalism. The process he foresees is very much a traditional step-by-step, D.C. insider politics style of reform. So what of a more radical revolutionary, or critical-utopian, political response?

Chase's own blog posts, appearing in a coda near the end of the final novel, do indeed foreground a new type of intense and radical focus on the present, namely *permaculture*. Chase predicts that there will be a series of experimental actions needed to determine what does and does not work. This is about more than simply climate change mitigation; rather it is broader, transformative social, economic, and political change with a goal of social justice as much as environmental sustainability. "While individual actions play an important role, Robinson also presents a vision of a wider political and societal change" (Mehnert 2016, 175). For instance, in an earlier blog post Chase writes, "Globalization has gotten far enough along that the tools are there to leverage the whole system in various ways. You could leverage it toward justice just as easily as toward extraction and exploitation. In fact it would be easier, because people would like it and support it" (Robinson 2007, 464). One aspect of this process is clearly a critical project; that is, societies must search out the contemporary problems before each can "experiment" with the cures.[11] Chase, by arguing that politics can be used to tilt the power of global capital toward justice, also echoes Frank's inclusion of "compassion and right action" into scientific practice. As Frank comes to contend that science should help make a more just and livable society, now Chase argues that politics must do the same through its power to incentivize and disincentivize particular types of capital investment and development. In fact, Chase asks both his political followers and critics to embrace experimental action as he simultaneously recognizes that decision makers are dealing with a fundamentally uncertain future and also an apparently inaccessible contemporary moment, a type of *unknowable now* that nonetheless demands action of some sort.[12]

Jameson has famously argued that the role of critical utopian fiction is to invite the reader to engage with their own inclination for, as well as objections to, particular aspects of utopia in a given narrative. In this manner, a critical utopia moves beyond the more traditional "monological" utopias where the transformation is based upon a singular event or reconfiguration of society, economics, etc. (Jameson, "One Good City," 410).[13] As a result, the expectation of reader engagement can be understood to last beyond the narrative itself as the aesthetic expectation of closure is postponed and the problematics of the text are left open-ended. This open-endedness also highlights the realities of inhabiting the present while facing an increasingly uncertain future. Critical utopian science fiction, in this reading, leaves an open space that invites the reader to get involved, and to imagine a continued narrative of which they might just be a part. As a result, Jameson explains, "The Utopian form itself is the answer to the universal ideological conviction that no alternative is possible, that there is no alternative to the system. But it asserts this by forcing us to think the break itself, and not by offering a more traditional picture of what things would be like after the break" (Jameson, "Future as Disruption," 232). While the trilogy gestures toward the critical-utopian possibility of permaculture, as Jameson would have us come to expect, it does not lay out a blueprint. It does, however, suggest the individual transformation that Frank undergoes in his personal and professional life is a "break" that might also be possible at the institutional and societal level, resulting in a systemic and lasting tilt toward social and ecological justice. This is the type of cognitive estrangement through "radical novelty" that Carl Freedman, building from Darko Suvin's definition of science fiction, has noted as fundamental to science fiction's ability to conjure utopia. Science fiction is "defined by its creation of a new world whose radical novelty estranges the empirical world of the status quo" (Freedman 2000, 69).[14] The culmination of the trilogy, rather than narrating the future utopia ahead, interrogates the "break" itself, one created by, more than even climate change alone, the linked challenges of (situated) knowledge and (distributed) agency in the contemporary moment.

Comparing the assessments of President Chase and Science Director Chang, whose marriage at the culmination of the trilogy rather clumsily symbolizes the integration of science and politics, draws our attention to an illustrative and integral point. First, Frank is persistently troubled by an expression Director Chang uses to explain the predicament of climate change: "We know but we can't act." This may sound quite familiar to climate scientists and activists alike in a political climate in which, not only can we not act, so many public figures will not even admit what we certainly by now know. Chang's truism, however, is indicative of a traditional understanding of the empirical and unassailable nature of scientific facts versus the dysfunctional and corrupt political system. On the other hand, in an intriguing twist on Chang's version of the problematic, President Chase argues something quite different. In his blog, he suggests that society has to act even if we do not know exactly what to do or fully understand all the consequences of these actions (Robinson 2007, 516–17). This is fundamentally different from Chang's more traditional construction that posits *We know but can't act*; in that for Chase, *We must act even if we do not know*. Of course, this means we need to "know" differently, rather than not know anything at all. We need to cultivate a new relation to knowledge, based in positioned rationality and passionate science, and agency, wherein all acts unfold in intra-active assemblages.

Director Chang's more traditional contention assumes both the power of empirical knowledge and, if it were only to be accepted by an undereducated public and/or dysfunctional political class, also assumes an unfettered human agency to act upon that knowledge. On the other hand, Chase presents us with a new, and I think more interesting, even if probably more difficult, problem. First, his construction of the task ahead highlights our lack of knowledge and, in so doing, brings to light an uncertainty in our ability to know the nonhuman environment and to act upon it with anything near real confidence regarding the results. Second, in terms of the relation between knowledge and agency, by arguing that even withstanding this uncertainty we must still find ways to act, Chase is suggesting a process of developing a more situated (positioned, contingent, and subjective) knowledge making process that recognizes both the limits of our abilities and their still yet powerful impact upon the planet. This approach would recognize, as Karen Barad has argued, "We are not outside observers of the world. Neither are we simply located at particular places in the world; rather, we are part of the world in its ongoing intra-activity" (Barad 2007, 184). Pressing the point further, she continues, "There is an important sense in which practices of knowing cannot fully be claimed as human practices, not simply because we use nonhuman elements in our practices but because knowing is a matter of the world making itself intelligible to another part. Practices of knowing and being are not isolatable" (185).[15] President Chase's experimental approach to climate policy emphasizes the complex relationship between knowledge production, policymaking strategies, and climate mitigation actions, while remaining fundamentally aware of the distributed qualities of subjectivity and agency, or the intense "intra-action" between human society, its systems and institutions, and the nonhuman world.

We must respond to the challenge of climate change, according to Chase, but do so with an approach founded in awareness of our limited knowledge and the unstable nature of the circumstances within which human acts will occur. We can still act, Chase suggests, but we must do so while consciously developing a new understanding of, and relation to, our agency generally and each action's consequences more specifically. While Zizek, in only a slightly different context in his book *Living in the End Times*, astutely warns us that this type of "openness to radical contingency is difficult to maintain" (Zizek 2010, 352), this appears to be exactly what Chase is attempting to call forth in his updated version of FDR's call for "radical and persistent experiment." He expands upon this point to the readers of his presidential blog:

> That's what we're doing in history; call it the invention of permaculture. By permaculture, I mean a culture that can be sustained permanently. Not unchanging, that's impossible, we have to stay dynamic, because conditions will change, and we will have to adapt to those new conditions, and continue to try to make things better—so that I like to think the word permaculture implies also permutation. We will make adaptations, so change is inevitable. (Robinson 2007, 516)

The keys to this "experimentation" are caution, flexibility, and a new type of passionate attention to the consequences and emerging developments that remain at least partially outside human control. A permaculture dwells in perpetual permutation (now say that aloud three times fast, and be happy I didn't use "persists").

The echoes of Frank's optimodality are clear in President Chase's articulation of permaculture, and the question remains whether such an individual transformation can be mapped onto these societal structures in some way. Furthermore, this disruption of current models of agency and linear history presses the problem, or the topic of speculation, ever closer to the present moment. The uncertainty is not just pertinent to the future existence of human and nonhuman communities, but also highlights the ways in which human social, political, economic, and scientific structures currently function in the absence of, to various degrees, the knowledge and intentional agency each purports to maintain.[16] This is not only a question of futurity in crisis, but of a fundamental reorientation of our understanding of the present; or, that is, the confidence in our ability to see and assess the present. As the character Fan in *On Such a Full Sea*, an unintentional political radical herself whom we met in the previous chapter, would probably suggest, Chase, Frank, and every one of us will have to start from where they, or we, are presently situated.

It is clearly not a given that this newly decentered subjectivity and experimental engagement with the inaccessible present, or unknowable now, will somehow automatically lead toward the justice-oriented transformative change that President Chase is promoting.[17] In many ways, Chase's final blog posts, outlining his plans to initiate a socioeconomic transformation toward permaculture, bring the individual transformations Frank has undergone throughout the trilogy to a societal level. However, it is not entirely clear that Chase's program will win the day; even as the trilogy closes, we find him hopeful, yet not convinced, that his fellow Democrats will win the majority in Congress after upcoming mid-term elections. This hope in itself, we should note, is indicative of the reformist approach of Chase and his allies: this is a political revolution that, for the most part, seeks to remain within the comfortable territory of electoral politics and liberal democratic practice. There is no question, however, that Chase's suggestive twist on the conventional truism of "We know but can't act" raises several extremely fundamental, and therefore quite challenging, questions. Is not the present moment, to some degree, as unknowable as the next? And, to the extent to which this is the case, what are the implications for our understanding of the causal link between the present and its future? The fundamental nature of these questions is indicative of the astounding challenges climate change poses for human society; coupled with the complications that come along when the autonomous and intentional Human is replaced by a *decentered human* and Nature by a *postnatural environment*. In other words, as sociopolitical strategy takes the transformative possibilities of distributed agency more fundamentally into account, the recognition of a profound limitation of human knowledge and agency calls for a rethinking of our very notion of creating change and what radical transformation might look like.

The unknowable now does not materialize due to some type of absolute lack of empirical knowledge but, instead, operates under the assumption that we do not know the nonhuman world in the manner in which mainstream conceptions of knowledge formation currently assume we do (that is, from the position of the objective and impartial observer). Rather than gaps in our knowledge that need to be filled, what we find necessary is an entire reorientation of our sense and practice of knowing, being, and doing as human subjects. According to the fictional President Chase, much as Haraway, Barad, and Braidotti have theorized in their scholarship on critical posthuman feminisms, we need a knowledge production process that is in practice more attuned to the embedded, partial, and fragmented quality of postanthropocentric subjectivity. This is exactly why, as I suggest here, recognizing the clear link between Frank's optimodality and Chase's permaculture is so critical; understanding this connection is central to developing a fuller understanding of the trilogy's radical critique of dominant humanist conceptions of science and agency.

As Thoreau once created a hybrid remapping of Walden, connecting the cabin, pond, and railroad in a shifting and rotating relationality, Chase now wants to remap our economic, scientific, and political systems as a hybrid-object. Chase's permaculture, as a gesture toward how to build an environmentally and socially just society within the agentic assemblage of distributed agency, accepts that, as much as we cannot predict the future in the age of climate change, neither can we actually know the present moment (without radically rethinking our account of knowledge). Meanwhile, Frank's optimodality attempts to reconceive what it means to exist and act within the entanglements of our material everyday. Rather than a crisis of vulnerability, therefore, the trilogy—via the links between Chase's permaculture and Frank's optimodality in particular (not to mention Thoreau's relational knowing)—tries to imagine what Braidotti would call an "affirmative politics" that is ready to practice both humility and hope from a radically posthuman perspective (2013, 54).[18] Ultimately, the trilogy suggests we must learn to navigate the turns along this path—away from a promissory future toward a radically uncertain one, while simultaneously grappling with the reality that humans are not the only agents whose *acts* matter. Chase's call for a permutating permaculture, in concert with Frank's engagement with optimodality and distributed ways of knowing, invites us to explore, evaluate, and, ultimately, act *with* a dynamic network of relations rather than *upon* a passive and objectified Other. We begin from a situated, entangled and decentered posthuman subjective position and we must recognize the consequences of our actions manifest within, and as the result of, a distributed agency always partially beyond our control.

Coda

President Chase's permaculture politics for the unknowable now of the Anthropocene bring to mind Thoreau's material remapping of Walden Pond. Thoreau's remapping of his temporary neighborhood, in which he places his house, the pond, and the railroad into rotating and speculative intra-relation, is based in his reconfiguring of knowledge formation processes (as relational and embedded in place). The intense focus upon relationality is indicative of an initial step toward a situated way of knowing (and seeing) that draws our attention to the distributed nature of agency and mixed-communities, our complex and entangled human and nonhuman worlds. Thoreau's open-ended and parabolic walks, brought to our attention by Patrick Chura in chapter 2, can be construed as a materialist approach to being and acting in the world, an essential aspect of his search for new ways of being and knowing in a remapped world of intimate relations, all the way down to its hybrid foundations. It is a fragmentary worldview that won't fragment, or, more accurately, that learns to exist—even possibly thrive—in the rupture. An open-ended experimentation is the very core of Thoreau's parabolic walks and President Chase's permaculture, and the very thing that makes these approaches flexible enough to openly and earnestly engage with seemingly vast and intimidatingly unchartered disanthropocentric modes of constructing subjectivity, knowledge, and agency.

As this book comes to a close, the way certain currents of the contemporary theoretical work in the New Materialisms call to mind Thoreau's Relational Knowing, so well chronicled and explained by Laura Walls and other leading Thoreau scholars, remains striking to me. Much of the contemporary theoretical work takes us way beyond, in terms of sophistication and depth, the disruption of subject/object and nature/

culture dualisms that we find in Thoreau's work, of course; however, the notion of a scientific practice based in a relational and ever-shifting field of local observation and limited (yet in-depth) subjective perspective of an embodied scientist (or poet-scientist in his case) is fascinatingly relevant for new materialist theories. Relational Knowing asks us to resist closure, hybridity is fluid and draws our attention to interchange, overlap, and rupture. As President Chase would ask us to engage in permaculture experimentation, Thoreau might invite us for a parabolic walk, if we had a free afternoon. Always open, the arc never closing. Working in the now, accepting the great challenge of our time and holding our gaze upon it, and sauntering toward a future we cannot and will not predict. Thinking anew, the Useful Ignorance of breaking with orthodoxy that Thoreau so cherished, we look back upon ourselves and remap our communities as hybrid-objects. On this parabolic walk, rather than keeping time with the causal relations of linearity, we find ourselves within the relational unfoldings of human and nonhuman assemblages. Drawing upon Marxist critical theory and millennia of Indigenous knowledges, Leslie Silko's Angelita La Escapia articulates a nonlinear revolutionary temporality based in a material, cultural, and political construct of time, which leaves us contemplating the contradictory juxtaposition of patience and urgency.

Exploring political agency that operates without intention and outside linear temporality, engaging with an unknowable moment that welcomes an uncertain future, simultaneously demands both stubborn persistence and radical flexibility. This is a deeply vexed and uncertain path with many more questions ahead for eco-theorists and activists for ecological, social, and economic justice, as the era of intensive climate change and tipping points appears to have arrived, and this type of experimentation provides me with hope that we might still invigorate a distributed environmental politics that is viable in these posthuman and postnatural times. Within these imaginative and transformative approaches to living, studying, and acting in the world in posthuman modes, we find the seeds of a disanthropocentric approach to the social, economic, and environmental crises we face two decades into the twenty-first century.

The difficulties abound here, certainly. The speculative, incomplete, and at times incommensurate nature of the ideas drawn from these literary narratives of more-than-human political agency, clearly do not lend themselves to straightforward pronouncements of strategy and tactics for an environmental politics of any recognizable type. Progressive politics without Progress? Political acts without intention? Patience in a time of global-scale environmental catastrophe? Thinking and acting our way through such apparent contradictions will undoubtedly be challenging. It appears, however, that the experimental paths these tensions invite us to explore are the best options available to us in this moment; that is, if we are serious about developing a justice-oriented environmental politics that accounts for the massive reconfiguration of causality that materialist theories of distributed subjectivity and agency foist upon us. To depend on the traditional Western subject—autonomous, rational, and intentional—as a still operable model for political organizing would in itself be a dangerous gamble, if not an outright fool's errand. The literature we have examined does not provide us with readymade answers, of course, nor a blueprint set for copying but, rather, exactly the opposite.

The speculative fiction engaged in this book acts in a similar vein, it helps us imagine the "ideological break" we need from long traditions of humanist thought, providing us glimpses of political subjects and movements that do not yet exist in our "real world." Like Fan's open-ended prescription "where you are" seeding the B-Mors' halting steps toward a politics of materiality, a distributed environmental politics must seek to reorient its sense of its own relation to place and time. Ways of knowing, seeing, and acting are deeply intertwined with temporality, of course, but we have been experimenting with events that unfold without the objective notion of causal relation. When we are hybrid-subjects in nonlinear time, the immediacy of our material presence is at once urgent and a call for a patient slowing-down; this invites a reorientation, a remapping, a regeneration.

The argument across these varied approaches to environmental literature's multifaceted yet inchoate depiction of a distributed environmental politics has been, at its core, twofold. First, new materialism and posthuman decentering of the human does not inevitably create an automatically ecological subject or society. Consciousness change at the individual, and even the societal level, is limited in its ability to translate into political power in the age of Carbon Democracy. Even if we successfully reorient the ethics—toward a decentered and materialist perspective—of a minority or a small majority of citizens, what is the resulting political substantiation of this change? A preponderance of mainstream political theory is based on the liberal humanist activist-subject, and environmental politics in the age of climate change finds itself mostly trapped in these modes of operation as well. We need to keep searching for the political agency that is possible, if certainly not inevitable, within distributed political entanglements. Second, literary imaginations of environmental and social justice politics provide a chance to explore the opportunities and challenges embedded in postanthropocentric material subjectivities, relational ways of knowing, and distributed agentic capacities, via the many imperfect yet eye-opening glimpses we catch of possible political subjects and movements that do not accord with existing notions of liberal Western democratic norms. Reading these speculative fictions defamiliarizes the all-too-familiar narratives of political progress, all the exhausted constructs we know are insufficient for the moment, prompting us to remain open to the unexpected and improbable potentialities of new formations, new relationships, new rhythms of posthuman and postnatural times and places. But defamiliarization is not sufficient, just as individual consciousness change loses its radical edge under the posthegemonic state power of Carbon Democracy, and we must now find ways to generate social movements as posthuman subjects entangled in the materiality of distributed agency, whose claims to sovereignty and recognition from the state do not still contain the power we assume, and maybe never did.

The distributed environmental politics we seek may lie beyond our current vision, but fictional narratives provide a window, each limited by the particulars of its situated perspective, but also, as vast and weird as the human scope of imagination, to peer through into the unknown, as we patiently and urgently acclimate ourselves to these fragmentary, uneven, shifting foundations of posthuman and distributed subjectivities, knowledge formations, and agencies. Like President Chase's call for permutation over prescription, the project of developing a distributed environmental politics is an ongoing process for a constantly mutating problematic; it is a process of (material) becoming that at once demands human engagement and rebuffs human direction. A process of transformation that requires urgency but defies linear timelines and humanist narratives of Progress. The distributed political subject will instead study the unknowable now for incipient opportunities to participate with—to join, resist, engage, influence, and generate—complex assemblages of unfolding momentum, complex and shifting amalgams of influence, and will learn to negotiate agency from an entangled and situated perspective within the material temporalities of distributed agency. More accurately, the distributed political subject is already a collective, not, then, an individual actor as construed within humanism; she finds herself within the wave of distributed agency and expresses her embodied reality by engaging and connecting with our more-than-human prospects and challenges from inside the mesh, the network, the rupture, and the hybrid map of mixed-communities. Just as the members of The People's Army in Silko's *Almanac of the Dead* hoped to be, will we be ready when the lights go out?

Notes

Introduction

1. In their introduction to *Material Ecocriticism*, Serenella Iovino and Serpil Opperman describe distributed agency as such: "Agency assumes many forms, all of which are characterized by an important feature: they are material, and the meanings they produce influence in various ways the existence of both human and non-human natures. Agency, therefore, is not to be necessarily and exclusively associated with human beings and human intentionality, but it is a pervasive and inbuilt property of matter, as part and parcel of its generative dynamism. From this dynamism, reality emerges as an intertwined flux of material and discursive forces, rather than as a complex of hierarchically organized individual players" (2014, 3).

2. Serpil Opperman, in her contribution to *Material Ecocriticism* entitled "Ecological Postmodernism to Material Ecocriticism," clarifies the ethical impact of new materialist theory as such: "Underlying this radical rethinking of human and nonhuman relations is the attempt to dehierarchize our conceptual categories that structure dualisms and to reconfigure our social, cultural, and political practices" (2014, 35). There is a clear goal articulated here that the decentered human should be a more ecological and ethical member of their community.

3. Rosi Braidotti, in her book *The Posthuman*, defines her version of critical posthumanism in an attempt to lay out an ethical, affirmative vision of posthuman subjectivity. Braidotti's work makes major strides toward theorizing the political potential of an "ecological posthumanism," and I find it compelling overall. Clarifying her version of the posthuman subject, she explains: "I define the critical posthuman subject within an eco-philosophy of multiple belongings, as a relational subject constituted in and by multiplicity . . . but still grounded and accountable. Posthuman subjectivity expresses and embodies an embedded and hence partial form of accountability, based on a strong sense of collectivity, relationality and hence communal building. . . . A posthuman ethics for a non-unitary subject proposes an enlarged sense of inter-connection between self

and others, including the non-human or 'earth' others, by removing the obstacle of self-centered individualism" (2013, 49–50).

4. In "Human and Non-Human Agencies for the Anthropocene," a 2015 article published in *Ecozon@*, Europe's main scholarly journal focused upon the intersections of environment and literature, co-authors Durbeck, Schaumann, and Sullivan call for environmental scholarship to engage with distributed agency and its consequences more deeply and intensely. The authors ask, "What if . . . we try to approach climate change not from the normative viewpoint of exclusive human agency (human exceptionalism), but rather from the perspective that we are a species living in conjunction with our co-species and interacting with—not just impacting or controlling—the weather, the water flows, the landscapes?" (120). This suggestion is timely, necessary, and a more difficult challenge than we may have as yet fully realized.

5. I am greatly indebted to Bennett's theorizing of agency without subjectivity and utilize the term *actant* in this book quite often, a term originally coined by Latour, which she has greatly and usefully expanded upon. As she explains here: "An actant is neither an object nor a subject but an 'intervener,' akin to the Deleuzean 'quasi-causal operator.' An operator is that which, by virtue of its particular location in an assemblage and the fortuity of being in the right place at the right time, makes the difference, makes things happen, becomes the decisive force catalyzing an event" (2012, 262). She offers a brief and clear expansion on these two terms that is helpful, as well, both "are substitute words for what in a more subject-centered vocabulary are called agents. Agentic capacity is now seen as differentially distributed across a wider range of ontological types" (9).

6. As Alaimo explains, "Transcorporeality is a new materialist and posthumanist sense of the human as perpetually interconnected with the flows of substances and the agencies of environments. Activists, as well as everyday practitioners of environmental . . . movements, work to reveal and reshape the flows of material agencies across regions, environments, animal bodies and human bodies" (2016, 112).

7. In his most recent short work *Down to Earth*, Latour elucidates, while discussing what he terms "climatic regimes" more broadly, how climate denialism is an intentional decision of elite powers and how it has become one of the major driving forces behind the State's continuing abdication of its responsibility to the public interest (2018, 9, 24–25).

8. In addition to these contemporary theoretical registers of the book's title, a historical echo is also drawn from Lawrence Buell's 1999 article in *New Literary History*, entitled "Ecocritical Insurgency," which outlined the emergence, and disruptive potential, of ecocriticism within the traditional discipline of literary studies at the turn of the century.

Chapter 1

1. The Sierra Club's first-ever official participation in civil disobedience was strangely, but also perhaps tellingly, invite only.

2. More details on the economic and environmental aspects of the pipeline (both practically and politically) is explored later in the chapter, with particular emphasis on its relation to environmental justice and global climate change environmentalism.

3. This sentiment is reminiscent of the fictional National Science Foundation's director Diane Chang, in K. S. Robinson's *Science in the Capital* trilogy, discussed in the final chapter of the book. Furthermore, the rift that emerges between the optimism of the Sierra Club's official statements on Keystone XL and the increasing pessimism from the nominal leader of the movement opposing that project, 350.org's founder Bill McKibben, are quite similar to the differences in approach between Chang and the fictional U.S president Chase in the trilogy.

4. This familiar rhetoric was reinforced by a *New York Times* opinion piece by Elizabeth Rosenthal, entitled "After Oil and Gas," which was circulated heavily across environmental organizations social media and email listservs in March 2013. Rosenthal argued that the United States already has the technical ability to transition to a "clean energy" economy but lacks the political and social "will" to do so. But again, what do we understand "political will" to mean exactly? If this simply means the courage of elected officials to "stand up" to the fossil fuel industry (and their lobbying power) and vote for legislation that undermines their economic dominance of the energy market, it seems to underestimate the power of carbon democracy (not to mention its deep infiltration into our social consciousness, what Lemanager calls petrotopia).

5. The event that had probably done the most to bring climate change back into public discourse in 2013, following a presidential campaign season in 2012 in which it went almost entirely unmentioned by both candidates, was the flooding and destruction wrought by Hurricane Sandy along the highly populated northeast coast in late October 2012 (in the weeks directly prior to election day on November 6).

6. For instance, Cronon argues, "Many popular ideas about the environment are premised on the conviction that nature is stable, holistic, homeostatic community capable of preserving its natural balance more or less indefinitely if only humans can avoid 'disturbing' it. This is a deeply problematic assumption" (Cronon 1995, 24). Ecocriticism, and eco-theory more broadly, have destabilized the nature/culture binary in an attempt to move beyond "appealing to non-human nature as the objective measure against which human uses of nature should be judged" (25).

7. Alaimo's trenchant critique of sustainability discourse is effectively articulated, in part, through a set of rhetorical questions that remain relevant: "Has

the term sustainability become too articulated to a technocratic, anthropocentric perspective? Is it possible to recast sustainability in such a way that it ceases to epitomize distancing epistemologies that render the world as resource for human use? Should biodiversity be one of the principal, or even the foremost, states to be 'sustained,' notwithstanding the fact that perpetual change, not fixity is the ungrounded ground for the survival of diverse species? Could sustainability be transformed in such a way as to cultivate posthumanist epistemologies, ethics, politics, and even aesthetics?" (Alaimo 2016, 177).

8. As possibly best shown in his essay "Can the Mosquito Speak," which I turn to later in chapter 3, Mitchell provides an extremely productive analysis of postanthropocentric agency and historical change.

9. Latour's most recent book *Down to Earth* is a welcome exception, as he incorporates Mitchell's theory of carbon democracy in his attempt to redefine the political framework of activism.

10. Karen Barad, in *Meeting the Universe Halfway; Quantum Physics and the Entanglement of Matter and Meaning*, explains her approach to distributed agency as such: "Crucially, agency is a matter of intra-acting; it is an enactment, not something that someone or something has. It cannot be designated as an attribute of subjects or objects (as they do not preexist as such). It is not an attribute whatsoever. Agency is doing or being in its intra-activity. Agency is about changing possibilities of change entailed in reconfiguring matter . . . particular possibilities for (intra-)acting exist at every moment, and these changing possibilities entail an ethical obligation to intra-act responsibly in the world's becoming, to contest and rework what matters and what is excluded from mattering" (Barad 2007, 178). My work is deeply indebted to Barad's theories of diffraction, intra-acting, and agential realism.

11. McKibben is the author of the first book, published in 1989, on climate change intended for a public audience: *The End of Nature*. In it he mourns the loss of, effectively, the Holocene: "Our comforting sense of the permanence of our natural world, our confidence that it will change gradually and imperceptibly if at all, is then, the result of subtly warped perspective. Change that can affect us can happen in our lifetime in our world. . . . I believe that without recognizing it we have already stepped over the threshold of such a change: that we are at the end of nature" (*The End of Nature*, 8).

12. The abstract for the 2008 paper, entitled "Target Atmostphere CO2: Where Should Humanity Aim," of which Hansen was the lead author, explains, "If humanity wishes to preserve a planet similar to that on which civilization developed and to which life on Earth is adapted, paleoclimate evidence and ongoing climate change suggest that CO_2 will need to be reduced from its current 385 ppm to at most 350 ppm, but likely less than that. The largest uncertainty in the target arises from possible changes of non-CO_2 forcings. An initial 350 ppm CO_2 target

may be achievable by phasing out coal use except where CO_2 is captured and adopting agricultural and forestry practices that sequester carbon" (Hansen et al. 2018).

13. 350.org had, until commencing the anti-Keystone campaign, mostly focused on rallying citizens from around the world to participate in small symbolic acts that bring attention to what they term the "climate crisis." For instance, on their website they have promoted the fact that "we coordinated a climate art project so large it had to be photographed from a satellite in outer space." The 350.org website also boasts: "In October of 2009 we coordinated 5200 simultaneous rallies and demonstrations in 181 countries, what CNN called the 'most widespread day of political action in the planet's history'" (Our Mission, 350.org).

14. Eilperin, Juliet. "Keystone Contractor Did Not Pose Conflict of Interest, IG Says." *Washington Post*, Feb. 9, 2012, washingtonpost.com/national/health-science/keystone-contractor-did-not-pose-conflict-of-interest-ig-says/2012/02/09/. Accessed July 1, 2020.

15. Steven Mufson and Juliet Eilperin. "Environmental Firm Writing U.S. Keystone Report Studied Pipelines for Landowners." *Washington Post*, Feb. 7, 2014, washingtonpost.com/business/economy.environmental-firm-writing-us-keystone-report-studied-pipelines-for-landowners/2014/02/07. Accessed July 1, 2020.

16. A January 18 *New York Times* article by John M. Broder and Dan Frosch, entitled "State Department to Put Pipeline on Hold," quotes Obama as having said: "I'm disappointed that Republicans in Congress forced this decision, but it does not change my administration's commitment to American-made energy that creates jobs and reduces our dependence on oil." Clearly, this decision was politics and not an indication of the Obama administration signaling a move beyond the carbon economy.

17. Gardner, Timothy. "U.S. Review Gives Boost to Keystone Oil Pipeline." *Reuters*, March 1, 2013, reuters.com/article/us-keyston/u-s/review-gives-boost-to-keystone-oil-pipeline. Accessed July 31, 2020.

18. Aranoff, Kate. "The Unlikely Alliance that Could Stop Keystone and Transform the Democratic Party." *In These Times*, Sept 26, 2017, inthesetimes.com/features/keystone_nebraska_climate_activism_jane_kleep.html. Accessed July 1, 2020.

19. Kevin Schaul and Kevin Uhrmacher. "How Trump Is Shifting the Most Important Courts in the Country." *Washington Post*, Sept. 4, 2018, washingtonpost.com/graphics/2018/Politics/trump-federal-judges/. Accessed July 1, 2020.

20. Kusnetz, Nicholas. "More States Crack Down on Pipeline Protestors, Including Supporters Who Are Not Even on the Scene." *Inside Climate News*, Mar. 28, 2019, insideclimatenews.org/news/28032019. Accessed July 1, 2020.

21. Eliza Barclay and Umair Irfan. "Why the Climate Protests that Disrupted London Were Different." *Vox*, April 26, 2019, vox.com/energy-and-environment/

2019/4/24/18511491/. Accessed July 1, 2020; See also Ella Nilson, "The New Face of Climate Activism is Young, Angry—And Effective." *Vox*, Sept. 17, 2019, vox.com/the-highlight/2019/9/1020847401/. Accessed July 31, 2020.

22. McKibben adds, "The people we consulted were helpful, but they were mostly veterans of an earlier era of social protest, and they kept talking about the need for a march on Washington. That seemed wrong, and not just because we lacked the chops to pull it off. . . . The architecture of the U.S. had changed . . . in a way that opened up new possibilities" (2010, 207). Though in coming years, 350.org would help organize this traditional tactic as well.

23. It is worth noting that 350.org, which has become a relatively well-known and influential environmental organization working on climate change, is the direct result of a senior seminar course at the elite and expensive liberal arts institution, Middlebury College. Additionally, in 2019, Middlebury was finally convinced to divest its endowment from fossil fuel companies.

24. Prior to the publication of this story, 350.org had tried traditional public outreach, petitions and letter writing to elected officials, legally sanctioned rallies and public events, acts of direct civil disobedience, instigated a campaign (inspired by the similar campaign targeting South African Apartheid) promoting institutional economic divestment from fossil fuel corporation, and the following year (2014) would organize a "People's Climate March" in New York City (drawing hundreds of thousands of people to the symbolic economic heart of the nation). The People's Climate March in 2014 is generally affiliated with the nonprofit environmental group People's Climate Movement. For our purposes, it's important to note that these marches come and go from the news cycle quickly, and it is not clear that bringing hundreds of thousands of people into the streets has much tangible impact on policy.

25. In the preface to *Eaarth*, McKibben writes, "It's true that we've lost that fight, insofar as our goal was to preserve the world we were born into. That's not the world we live on any longer, and there's no use pretending otherwise. But damage is always relative. So far we've increased global temperatures about a degree, and it's caused the massive change chronicled in chapter 1. That's not going to go away. But if we don't stop pouring more carbon into the atmosphere, the temperature will simply keep rising, right past the point where *any* kind of adaptation will prove impossible" (2010, xv).

26. The increasing likelihood of drastic climatic change is in large part due to the vast reserves of carbon the fossil fuel industry plans to burn in the future: "[T]hose 2,795 gigatons of carbon emissions are worth about $27 trillion. Which is to say, if you paid attention to the scientists and kept 80 percent of it underground, you'd be writing off $20 trillion in assets" ("Terrifying Math"). The divestment campaign has gone on to have quite significant success, and fueled a newly energized climate change environmentalism on U.S. campuses, but one

would not want to suggest that the carbon economy is yet willing to abandon those assets in the name of climate action.

27. Elsewhere, McKibben compares global climate change's impact on the planet to a disease's impact on the human body: "But between global warming and the end of oil and the economic backwash from both, it's as if we've come down with a chronic disease that slows us down, stoops us over. Now we have to engage in some triage, decide what from our previous life we most want to keep, and how we plan to do it" (2010, 124).

28. Di Chiro astutely points out that much of mainstream environmentalism is in its own way becoming co-opted into global capital. She coins the terms *neoliberal environmentalism* and *ecoliberalism* to denote the deployment of the "global commons" in such terms that reassert "cultural difference in the terms of making the world environmentally secure for unrestrained capitalist accumulation on a planet of finite resources and limited ecosystemic resilience (in the name of 'sustainable development')" (2008, 205). Therefore, "Ecoliberalism in this sense is about constructing an ideology of the 'global commons' in order to justify the enclosure of, and guarantee ongoing access to, more and more of the world's dwindling resources by multinational corporations and the national regimes that underwrite them" (205). For Di Chiro, the question becomes: "Can we fashion non-imperializing formulations of the global commons—those that retain its 'gathering together' impulse without obscuring real differences in livelihood and survivability, power, and environmental consequences?" (206).

29. Ursula Heise outlines a case for a justice-oriented, cross-cultural "eco-cosmopolitanism" in her book *Sense of Place, Sense of Planet*, as necessary due to the broader impacts of globalization's *deterritorialization*. She writes: "The challenge that deterritorialization poses for the environmental imagination, therefore, is to envision how ecologically based advocacy on behalf of the nonhuman world as well as on behalf of greater socioenvironmental justice might be formulated in terms that are premised no longer primarily on ties to local places, but on ties to territories and systems that are understood to encompass the planet as a whole" (Heise 2008, 10). I see Latour as trying to split the difference between Heise and something like McKibben's proposed localism, proposing *Terra* as a sort of third way.

30. Public figures and eco-political thinkers are probably correct to be concerned about fatalism, because allowing an acceptance of limited agency to slide into acute hopelessness is at the very core of an emerging conservative argument. That is, an increasing chorus of voices who suggest there is nothing that will work anyway, so let's not bother. For instance, writing in the conservative quarterly *National Affairs* in 2015, Jim Manzi, a senior fellow at the Manhattan Institute, and Peter Wherner, former member of the Reagan and both Bush administrations, argue that "the best models show us that global warming is a problem that is

expected to have only a limited impact on the world economy. Any attempt to do anything about those damages would be rife with unintended consequences and . . . is geopolitical fantasy" ("Conservatives and Climate Change"). Apparently, climate change can go from a hoax to a problem too big to fix, just like that. And, as a result, "Sober minds should select laissez faire as the best of imperfect options" ("Conservatives and Climate Change"). Manzi and Wherner represent a striking example of what law scholar Jedediah Purdy has pointedly called the "complacency mongers" who ask us to welcome the "neoliberal Anthropocene" and trust the market (Purdy 2015, 5, 46–47). Sober minds indeed.

31. The climate justice movement, embodying the opposite end of the spectrum from Purdy's "complacency mongers," is left to consider how exactly they might petition the state for their desired policy goals on climate change issues, especially considering the state appears unable or unwilling to regulate increasingly transnational corporations. Environmentalists' confidence in reformist and rights-based political strategies, particularly those activists concerned with the relation between environmental and social justice, is in crisis at the moment.

32. Estes expands on the potential impacts of Standing Rock on the future of Indigenous activism: "Though not without its faults, the reunification of the Oceti Sakowin reawakened an Indigenous movement intent on making and remaking, a world premised on Indigenous values, rather than on private ownership and heteropatriarchy. While Indigenous peoples committed themselves to caretaking relations, the police had also taken up their familiar role as caretakers of violence, attempting to snuff out the fires or resistance before they burned too hot or spread too far. But the fire of the prophesied Seventh Generation had been lit, and although the Oceti Sakowin campfire was ceremoniously extinguished to mark the end of one form of resistance (and the beginning of another), its warm coals went on to rekindle the fires of Water Protectors' home communities" (Estes 2019, 65).

33. Shelley Streeby also recounts the police response to the Water Protectors' acts of nonviolent civil disobedience on Oct. 27 and again on Nov. 20, 2016, where police in riot gear deploy "sound cannon" blasts, pepper spray in October, and "munitions, chemical agents, a water cannon, and hoses to blast water protectors on the reservation in subfreezing temperatures" (Streeby 2018, 49). This highlights the uniquely harsh treatment seemingly reserved for Indigenous minority protestors and denotes a sharp contrast from the treatment of the predominantly white protestors at Sierra Club protests discussed at the beginning of this chapter.

34. Jacey Fortin and Lisa Friedman. "Dakota Access Pipeline to Shut Down Pending Review." July 6, 2020, *The New York Times*, nytimes.com/2020/07/06/us/Dakota-access-pipeline.html. Accessed July 31, 2020.

35. For example, Estes highlights how the direct action was essential to the #NoDaPL campaign, drawing attention to how "the combination of direct action and the legal strategy to defeat DAPL in court . . . [worked because] direct actions drew media attention and thus amplified the messages of NoDAPL and

Mni Wiconi [Water is Life] . . . [and] also had the immeasurable psychological effect of empowering the powerless to action" (Estes 2019, 19).

36. See "Can the Mosquito Speak," in Mitchell's *Rule of Experts*, which is also discussed in detail later in chapter 3.

37. Shelly Streeby points out that, while there is an "irreducible particularity to the struggle at Standing Rock" that should not be dismissed in an attempt to universalize the experience, she does also argue, building from Edward Valandra, that "the water protectors push beyond environmentalist paradigms in a number of ways, including through understanding the river and the water as living persons" (Streeby 2018, 45).

Chapter 2

1. Thoreau rarely writes about his contributions to the Underground Railroad, understandably being discreet. But Walls finds three specific instances between 1851–53 where Thoreau's journals reference specific events in which his family housed escaped slaves overnight and/or he himself secretly transported slaves by wagon (Walls 2017, 318–19).

2. Kucich describes Thoreau's descriptions of the moose's butchering as nothing less than "gothic." And that across just a few pages, Thoreau's "revulsion" with the hunt's result changes his "view of the Moose . . . [from] tourist trophy to full personhood" ("Lost," 30).

3. Kucich conducts a detailed examination of the complex relationship between the Penobscot and Thoreau, and the white colonizers of New England more generally, but summarizes the cultural and historical context of it as such: "During the time of Thoreau's travels, two things are clear—the traditional knowledge of the Penobscot was very much intact, and such knowledge was carefully kept from white readers. The Penbscots had lost much political sovereignty over their tribal territory; indeed, surveying parties guided by the Penobscots themselves redrew traditional boundaries and apportioned land for lumbermen and settlers who cut trees, cleared farms, and built dams and mills that altered the riverine ecosystem. Yet the Penobscots held onto their cultural sovereignty" ("Lost," 33).

4. The essay "Walking" clearly does have its moments of transcendental universalism in which the romanticizing of nature often occurs right alongside a veiled instrumentalization of it. That is, the reader finds moments in which Nature serves as the awe-inspiring inspiration for the poet's art as well as symbol of the nation's strength and bedrock of its economic development. This includes a healthy dose of American exceptionalism and a variant of Manifest Destiny in which the poetry, culture, and religion of America soar to the forefront of the American nation's future as the City upon a Hill, rather than a political/economic

empire. For instance, this is more than evident in the exultation that "[a]s a true patriot, I should be ashamed to think that Adam in paradise was more favorably situated on the whole than the back woodsman in this country" (608).

5. Speaking of productive tensions in Thoreau's work, Lawrence Buell writes that, "To understand fully what nature meant to Thoreau, we need to examine . . . [his work] with the understanding that we shall arrive at an overall picture that is somewhat blurry, shifting, and pluriform, not tidily coherent or reducible to one or two sweeping statements" (Buell 1995, 126). I attempt to build upon Buell's argument, in which he rightfully points out the relationship between Thoreau's contradictoriness and the complexity of his ideas, to say that Thoreau's so-called failures might be instructive regarding the difficulties intrinsic to the critique of anthropocentrism.

6. Linda Vance's exploration of dualism and ecofeminism in her 1997 essay "Ecofeminism and Wilderness" remains foundational.

7. Of course, the recognition of nonhuman agency, nature's autonomous ecological systems, plays an important role in ecocentric critiques of anthropocentrism (it is often presented as one realization that "connecting to nature" offers the human a more humble realization of nature's vast and at least partially autonomous processes). A problematic nature/culture dualism remains evident, though, because of the construction of an either/or debate: anthropocentrism or ecocentrism (which becomes another dualism).

8. Interestingly, in her analysis of Thoreau's movement away from transcendental Romantic holism, Walls argues that Humboldtian science operates as a similar influence on Thoreau's thought and motivates his process of transformation into a type of passionate scientist in the latter stages of his career. This connection is intriguing in its potential to offer a reading of Thoreau that works to understand his critique of liberal humanism (anthropocentrism, etc,) as not fully, if at all, ecocentric. Essentially, Walls's argument suggests that Thoreau attempts to move beyond the ecocentric narrative; that is, the romantic tale of an eco-transformational process that relies upon a simple recognition of the "correct" relation to Nature that then naturally compels an appreciation for that same Nature from the human subject. It is in this attempt that we find Thoreau's attention to hybridity, chaos and liminal space becomes central to his thinking.

9. This serves as an alternative to the science of Louis Agassiz, for instance, which removes the agency of nature for a passive nonhuman world to be catalogued, classified, and explained through the agency of the professional and discipline-oriented scientist. From this perspective, with which Thoreau engages early on yet ultimately discards, Nature is unitary and divinely ordered. Therefore, humans, from their perch at the top of the pyramid, so to speak, can search for and ultimately determine the laws that together form that unified order.

10. In a long but helpful quote, Walls explains, "In the years after 1850, what Thoreau strove to create was, in a sense, a new form of science . . . that would be relational rather than objective. This 'relational knowing' extended and

applied the possibilities opened up by the disintegration of the subject/object dualism, which encouraged the subject to 'know' by seeing correspondence in the world's objects, as if they were the mirror of the self, or by 'reading' the book of nature as it were a text ready-made for decoding. By contrast, knowing as an active process in Thoreau's sense becomes no less than what H. Daniel Peck calls 'worlding,' the making of world 'by interaction—the dance—of the creative self and the world'" (Walls 1995, 147).

11. In particular, Walls notes the entries on November 25, 1850, August 5, 1851, and June 30, 1852, as particularly telling for Thoreau's refusal to accept the growing disciplinary rifts between poetry and science.

12. Walls emphasizes that Thoreau's later writing moves beyond traditional Transcendental concepts such as Correspondence Theory and approaching nature as a "mirror" of social facts, etc. At the same time though, Thoreau is attempting to create an alternative to objective knowledge-making practices at a time when empiricism is really at the earliest stages of its dominant role in the professionalization of Science. It is interesting then that Robinson returns to Thoreau in search of alternatives to empirical science in the early twenty-first century after it has been so fully institutionalized.

13. Walls contends that Thoreau makes "a sustained argument for and demonstration of relational knowing, out of which Thoreau proposed a kind of science that Humboldt would have recognized and honored but which in America was a novelty" (Walls 1995, 144).

14. Walls writes: "What energized him was his conviction that nature does not lie passive and ready-made, to be 'read' by his educated eye' rather, it is continually creative, improvising in front of his very eyes everywhere and at every moment" (Walls 1995, 147–48).

15. The close observation of details, place-based system of knowledge making, is central to Thoreau's way of interaction with and better understanding the nonhuman world. He does certainly look for larger cycles and unities in nature, but it often begins with what is reminiscent of, as Walls also points out, a commitment to what Haraway has since termed situated knowledge.

16. Karan Barad writes of agency and futurity in relation to the nature/culture binary and hybrid objects: "Rather, it is inherent in the nature of intra-activity [i.e., distributed agency]—even when apparatuses are primarily reinforcing, agency is not foreclosed. Furthermore, the space of agency is not restricted to the possibilities for human action. But neither is it simply the case that agency should be granted to nonhumans as well as humans. . . . What is at issue, rather, are the possibilities for the iterative reconfiguring of the materiality of human, nonhuman, cyborgian, and other such forms. Holding the category human (non-human) fixed (or at least presuming one can) excludes an entire range of possibilities in advance, eliding important dimensions of the workings of agency" (Barad 2016, 178).

17. This is not a Thoreau that easily lends itself to a "deep green" or simply ecocentric vision (in which it is often assumed that when humans simply "leave

nature alone" all will be well). The idea of natural balance and stable natural systems, though certainly present in some moments of Thoreau's writing, is not the impression that this layer of uncertainty, motivating his critique of the capitalist funding the ice-cutting enterprise, provides the attentive reader.

18. Stacy Alaimo, in *Bodily Natures*, writes of this interdependency: "[U]nderstanding the substance of one's self as interconnected with the wider environment marks a profound shift in subjectivity. As the material self cannot be disentangled from networks that are simultaneously economic, political, cultural, scientific, and substantial, what was once the ostensibly bounded human subject finds herself in a swirling landscape of uncertainty where practices and actions that were once not even remotely ethical or political matters suddenly become the very stuff of the crises at hand" (Alaimo 2010, 20).

19. This raises many pertinent questions for consideration: What is the water of Walden Pond in relation to the water of the Ganges River? Is it most notable that the waters of Walden and Ganges are brought (blended) together? Another hybrid-object such as the ice and the sandbank—nature and culture? East and West? Two aspects of nature—the commodity form and the spiritual ideal—are intermixed or even always already inextricable. What does this reimagining of globalism through this speculative journey following the circulation of Walden's ice in its commodified form accomplish here? What is this merging of nature, commodity, knowledge, and philosophy (in the form of Walden's ice) actually doing in terms of Thoreau's representation of (distributed) agency? What is the global exchange of ideas unfolding here, and how is it intertwined with the ice as commodity and/or its resistance to commodification (melting back into the pond to rejoin other systems of nature-culture exchange)?

20. Haraway's description of our task in the moment reminds me of Thoreau's willingness to dwell in liminal spaces and upon hybrid objects, even when it is uncomfortable or leads to contradictory emotions and ideas. She writes, "Our task is to make trouble, to stir up potent response to devastating events, as well as to settle troubled water and rebuild quiet places. In urgent times, many of us are tempted to address trouble in terms of making an imagined future safe. . . . Staying with the trouble does not require such a relation to times called the future. In fact, staying with the trouble requires being truly present, not as a vanishing pivot between awful or Edenic pasts and apocalyptic or salvific futures, but as mortal critters entwined in myriad unfinished configurations of places, times, matters, meanings" (Haraway 2017, 1).

Chapter 3

1. Di Chiro explains that Whitt and Slack "propose the term 'mixed communities' to signify the relations of interdependence that inhere in geographically diverse 'mixed species' (human and nonhuman) assemblages" (318).

2. Schlossberg and Caruthers make this connection to social reproduction in Di Chiro's work explicit. They explain, "The overall emphasis of such groups is on individual and community functioning—including the basics of health and safety, the preservation of local economies, and the preservation of local and traditional cultures and practices—what Di Chiro calls social reproduction" (18).

3. Karen Barad, contemplating distributed agency's impact on contemporary concepts of intention, writes: "Perhaps intentionality might better be understood as attributable to a complex network of human and nonhuman agents, including historically specific sets of material conditions that exceed the traditional notion of the individual. Or perhaps it is less that there is an assemblage of agents than there is an entangled state of agencies" (23). This ongoing destabilization of the assumed connection between human subject and intentional act demands that we consider the subsequent impact upon sociopolitical organizing strategies.

4. Wallace's and my own reading both mainly concentrate on the Matacao itself, while Heise's reading of the novel also includes an examination of the "metal cemetery" or rainforest "junkyard" discovered by scientists deep in the rainforest (99–100). I focus upon the Matacao due to what I see as its more complex representation of distributed agency. The "metal cemetery" presents an intriguing picture of co-evolving nature and technology but ultimately implies that the rusting machinery has invaded a previously natural space, compelling the flora and fauna to then adapt in return. While drawing attention to the interaction of nature and culture through this back and forth, the metal cemetery maintains an original separation of nature and culture in a way that the Matacao does not. That is, the Matacao further disrupts the nature/culture binary via a refusal to accept that original separation of agencies.

5. Braidotti, in "The Politics of Life Itself," discusses, more broadly, biocitizenship. Her engagement with hybridity through the lens of biopolitics overlaps in interesting ways with this discussion of hybrid-objects in the Brazilian rainforest of Yamashita's imagination. Braidotti explains that biocitizenship "marks a shift away from anthropocentrism, in favor of a new emphasis on the mutual interdependence of material, biocultural, and symbolic forces in the making of social and political practices" (2010, 203–204).

6. Heise offers a more extended reading of Kazumasa's satellite-ball in her work. Importantly for the purposes of this project, she points out how this is one of many ways in which the novel "invests a great deal of narrative capital in the blurring of the boundaries between biology and technology" (114).

Chapter 4

1. Over the course of the narrative, we also learn that "the almanac in Yoeme's possession . . . include[s] a fifth, undiscovered Mayan codex, one that has been kept secret from anthropologists and museum directors, and protected

for hundreds of years" (Adamson 2001, 139). The almanac's stories then play a fundamental role in the transformative shift that is predicted to move society beyond the era of the Destroyers; dominated as it is by a racialized (white) human exceptionalism. Adamson explains: "Their books provide them with many of the details of their ancient culture and systems of knowledge as well as a comprehensive interpretation of the past, thus giving them a solid foundation on which to view the present and a 'place to see' how they might move more intelligently in the future" (141). Admittedly, Adamson's depiction of how the sisters' knowledge in the present relates to their future actions does seem to harbor certain assumptions of linear temporality and intentional, rational agency.

2. Adamson is certainly correct to point out that Zeta and Lecha's personal relation to the almanac's contents inspires the twins to do more than simply hold onto the stories as cultural relics, as the stories become a hybrid catalyst for nothing less than the retaking of the Americas from the Euro-American colonizers.

3. This raises a few questions that resonate with the overall explanation of knowledge and agency in a posthuman context, as well as in terms of progressive temporality and its relation to social movement organizing: How does the knowledge of history—and its relation to the present and future—change when understood in a nonlinear context, or within a context that embraces the uncertainty of historical change? Can it be relied upon to facilitate a type of mistake-free human enterprise (as we so often fall back on that truism for "remembering" history so as to inform our present)? My argument throughout has been that these issues are made more complex in the process of decentering human subjectivity.

4. A related push for reorienting our relation to temporality has been taken up recently within the context of eco-theory conversations on geologic or deep-time. Jeffrey Jerome Cohen, in his brilliant book *Stone: An Ecology of the Inhuman*, suggests that thinking across geologic time productively disorients our more common, biological sense of temporality and challenges our collective narratives, whether biographical, spiritual, or scientific. He suggests that deep-time helps us see nonhuman agency more clearly, and "stone offers a perpetual invitation to think time and agency outside small category, to cease to force the world into diminished frames" (Cohen 2015, 27). Jeremy Davies, in *The Birth of the Anthropocene*, has also recently suggested that bringing geologic time to the fore of our thinking, as he contends the discussion around the Anthropocene is capable of accomplishing, has value for environmental politics. Davies further contends that a geologic temporality would allow environmental activists to articulate the transition from the Holocene to the Anthropocene as an opportunity for human society "to negotiate a way through the transition between these two epochs . . . with an urgent recognition of the need to respond in a radically new way to an earth system that has itself become something radically new" (Davies 2016, 148).

5. Both Cohen and Davies are careful to consider their discussions of geologic temporality in relation to distributed agency: for instance, *Stone* explores

a "disanthropocentric" subjectivity and agency, while Davies argues, "[T]he birth of the Anthropocene . . . redistributes agencies, reconfigures systems, and reorders the loops of consequence and assimilation out of which the working of the earth are made" (8). These explorations of geologic time are still based upon linear temporality, of course, as they are framed within Western scientific knowledge and discourses. As a result, the question of intentionality seems quite fraught in these scholarly works as well.

    6. Silko describes the subaltern subjects' ability to operate outside of the legalized capitalist system to some degree and their repurposing of mainstream political tools to further their own cause, as Angelita raises funds via the Cubans' and other nations' differently motivated desires to be seen as "friends of the Indians." But it must be understood that this is a means to an end as it becomes clear that, for these subjects, revolution, and not reform, is the only hope for a future of any kind—political, economic, or cultural.

    7. Adamson again seems attuned to this when she argues that Angelita's "organizing activities . . . will require her to search continually for new ways to express herself in a world dominated by national and international voices urging that she and her people be ignored or silenced" (153). Here, I think Adamson astutely points out that the Indigenous army's strategy and goals are depicted as an attempt to build a movement even as the political actors know the state is unresponsive. This sense of being conventionally powerless is an element of what allows Angelita and the other Indigenous leaders to think beyond and outstrip conventional environmental justice campaigns of the late twentieth century (which so often unfold within more conventional legal and political frameworks).

    8. Ultimately, the novel itself leaves questions regarding the efficacy of violent and nonviolent resistance to colonization an open question (refusing to present nonviolent resistance as the only ethical option, as liberal politics would suggest, but never quite depicting violent revolution as the only, or even the correct, path). The questions surrounding revolutionary political tactics and the ethics of violent resistance are essential and complex and should certainly remain a part of any examination of political agency in the novel; however, my analysis focuses more squarely upon the novel's presentation of subjectivity, agency, and temporality within the resistance movement (thus, leaving the debate about violent and nonviolent options within this new framework of distributed agency, at least in part, for a future discussion). This all does, however, raise a question that relates very closely to this project's preoccupations: that is, if the concept of distributed agency disrupts humanist concepts of intentionality significantly enough, what becomes of accountability? In other words, when the political subject's act is seen as the product of a complex network of distributed agency, then we need to reconsider to what degree each political act and its subsequent consequences are traceable back to a given traditional subject. And if this is no longer possible in

a distributed political network, the ethical debate surrounding social movement tactics is made even more complex.

9. It is true, as Romero points out, that "gusts of wind, floods, droughts, volcanic eruptions, and earthquakes, and other natural disasters killing people in the name of social justice is repeated throughout the novel" (Romero 2002, 635). And it is suggested that these natural disasters act in the "name of social justice," but we should be careful not to assume they remain distinctly separate from the human mobilizations for justice recounted in the novel. Still, Romero remains unconvinced: "Despite all the space in the text devoted to describing the material actions of Zeta, Angelita, and other people preparing for social revolution, the novel seems ambivalent about whether the prophesied revolution can really be waged by humans" (635). This approach to agency in the novel, however, might lead to some rather unhelpful questions, such as: Is natural or human agency more important? When do humans get to direct this revolution? And to where? These kinds of questions can quickly lead to a surreptitious reassertion of the traditional liberal humanist (or even radical revolutionary) political actor. Instead, it is imperative to develop a new method of evaluation that might better help us make sense of the political agency that would be wielded (albeit partially and imperfectly) by a distributed political subject.

10. Reluctant to follow the disruptive logics of distributive agency to their fullest ramifications, Romero's assessment of agency in the novel brings to light a key difficulty we face in thinking political efficacy within the framework of distributed agency. She worries, "Although the . . . [conclusion] suggests that people have the possibility of changing their world, *Almanac* expresses a profound ambivalence about the extent of human involvement in the revolution it prophesies" (635). Reminiscent of our discussion of *Through the Arc* in the previous chapter, Romero seems concerned that this emphasis on "natural disasters" means there is no role at all for humans to resist social and environmental injustice unless the humans become "natural forces" themselves. I try to approach the novel with a more nuanced approach to what Bennett calls "agentic assemblages" of the human and nonhuman.

11. Reed further argues that *Almanac* depicts a political form of resistance to global capitalism that blends environmental and social justice goals in such a way as to offer both a mode of critique and, importantly, a path toward an alternative society based on equality and justice. For Reed, "*Almanac* dramatizes the fact that current forms of free market fundamentalism have collapsed various kinds of economy (aesthetic, spiritual, textual, and environmental) in one: the commodity" (Reed 2009, 33). The commodification of all aspects of life, bringing each activity, institution or belief-set under the determination of the global market, creates a market-based evaluation system for the usefulness of any given human activity, or even humans themselves. After depicting this phenomenon in the American Southwest as well as urban and rural areas of Mexico (with an

emphasis on the permeability of the borders between), the novel spends a great deal of time imagining both a resistance to this process as well as the possible worlds that might succeed in its wake. "While the novel offers no easy way out of this situation, it is clear that this logic must be broken; the reduction of all things to their economic value in the market-place must be replaced by a process in which human and environmental needs are at the center" (33).

12. So, what are the most integral differences between "sustainability" and "social reproduction"? I would suggest that sustainability, in most manifestations and certainly in its deployment within mainstream green capitalism, is less critical of capitalism and its growth-based model. There are examples, such as the concepts of "slow" and "no-growth" economics, which move a bit more substantially into critiques of capital's externalization of costs, etc. On the other hand, social reproduction reemphasizes human relation to each other (community) and relation to nonhuman world (mixed-community). It changes the measurements for quality of life in significant ways and, at its best, provides a goal that is more difficult for capital to subsume into its own logics. Stacy Alaimo lays out an excellent critique of sustainability's problematic reliance on anthropocentrism in the final chapter of *Exposed: Environmental Politics and Pleasures in Posthuman Times*. I tend to agree with Di Chiro that the concept of social reproduction is a more nuanced and productive way of theorizing the goal of much environmental justice work due to its unromantic concentration upon a material, integrative, and systemic approach to quality of life.

13. Glen Coulthard, in his book *Red Skins, White Masks* describes grounded normativity as "place-based foundation of Indigenous decolonial thought and practice" (Coulthard 2014, 13), and goes on to explain that it is based upon the "the modalities of Indigenous land-connected practices and longstanding experiential knowledge that inform and structure our [Indigenous] ethical engagements with the world and our relationships with human and nonhuman others over time" (13). Grounded normativity is discussed in chapter 1 in the context of the #NoDAPL campaign.

14. An organizer and sometimes spiritual leader, known as the Barefoot Hopi, makes this reorientation of the human to radical political activism and historical change particularly clear. "[He] knew he might work to make preparations the rest of his life, yet never see the day when prisons and jails all over the U.S. were hit with riots and strikes simultaneously. But that didn't discourage the Hopi. One human lifetime wasn't much; it was over in a flash. Conjunctions and convergences of global proportions might require six or seven hundred years to develop" (618). A type of goal-oriented agency certainly remains a part of the revolutionary practice of Angelita, El Feo, and the Barefoot Hopi, however, it is a revolutionary goal of radical transformation of society based in non-Western concepts of temporality and historical change that I think are best understood as closely related to their sense of distributed agency.

15. Shelley Streeby makes an important connection between fiction and reality by noting: "Silko's vision of people of color coming together in response to Earth's crisis was partly realized in 1991, the year the novel was published, by the First National People of Color Environmental Justice Leadership Summit in Washington D.C., a major marker of people of color's significant role in imagining the future of climate change" (Streeby 2018, 55).

16. A November 27, 2019, article published in *Nature* by Timothy Lenton and his colleagues, entitled "Climate Tipping Points: Too Risky to Bet Against," sparked discussion and media coverage by arguing that the tipping points of runaway climate change are already here.

Chapter 5

1. Interestingly, the actual event of Hurricane Sandy occurred while Rich's book was in press with his publisher, Picador, drawing a bit more media attention to this work of speculative fiction than it may have otherwise expected and lending more credence to Lawrence Buell's suggestion that climate fiction is the "social realism" of our time.

2. As Schneider-Mayerson correctly points out, the selection of the neighborhood derails any possible broader value, particularly regarding issues of climate justice, in Mitchell's project right from the outset: "While Flatlands might seem like the end of the Earth from the vantage point of Manhattan's Upper West Side . . . it is (in the real world) a stable, middle-class neighborhood of 60,000. Home to African-Americans, Caribbeans, Latinxs, and Asian-Americans" (Schneider-Mayerson 2019, 952). And, highlighting the way Rich's novel problematically centers whiteness, Schneider-Mayerson continues: "To recapitulate: two white, wealthy, educated, twenty-somethings find a complicated financial means to profit off of climate disasters, then use these funds to settle a destroyed minority neighborhood where they discover themselves by working the land. The echo of settler-colonial land appropriation . . . is too loud to ignore" (952).

3. I draw here from scholar Adeline Johns-Putra, who discusses this unconventional narrator in her article "The Rest is Silence," and categorizes it as a "disembodied community spirit" (Johns-Putra, 36–37). While Amanda Page, on the other hand, has speculated, "Although the perspective of the novel often seems like one narrator using "we" to mean like-minded people, at others times it seems like a genuine "we"—the collective narration group of scholars of Fan, the legend and mystery. While an unusual formal choice, it does underscore the communal dynamic of B-Mor, a place where individuality does not matter and only the success and stability of the group are important" (Page 2017, 93). However one chooses to characterize this unusual narrative device, it is certainly the case that reader experience of the narrative is filtered through a relatively mysterious lens.

4. The physicality of the expression's resonance is pretty clearly explained, in a way that weirdly denies Fan interiority almost altogether, by the narrator: "And that's one of the funny things about Fan, as we think about her now, which is that when it mattered most she was an essentially physical being, rather than some ornate bundle of notions, wishes, dreams" (244).

5. One demand they do articulate is more upward mobility in the form of increased options for their children to enter Charter society (as they argue that the current testing model is too limiting and unfair). This would be a step toward economic upward mobility, but certainly not democratic rule. However, the goals of the movement do seem to move beyond the purely economic, as at one point late in the novel the narrator declares, "This is not about the price of fish anymore" (292). And, just a bit later, the narrator speculates, "Where we are does not wholly comfort us. And perhaps never truly has" (296).

6. As to how difficult it is to think agency without intention, or temporality without progress, Tsing is again very helpful in her articulation of forethought as integral to dominant expressions of human exceptionalism: "Progress is embedded, too, in widely accepted assumptions about what it means to be human. . . . [W]e learn over and over that humans are different from the rest of the living world because we look forward—while other species, which live day to day, are thus dependent on us" (Tsing 2015, 21).

7. Tsing explains: "It suggests that any gathering contains many inchoate political futures and that political work consists of helping some of those come into being. Indeterminacy is not the end of history but rather the node in which many beginnings lie in wait. To listen politically is to detect the traces of not-yet-articulated common agendas" (254).

Chapter 6

1. The first novel begins during the second half of a Republican president's first term, clearly meant to be reminiscent of George W. Bush's administration, complete with corporatist perspective and antiscience climate skepticism.

2. Gib Prettyman, for instance, has described the trilogy as a "liberating crisis." Later in the chapter I address the ways in which I do and do not agree with Prettyman's broader assessment of the novels.

3. The gendered aspect of this contradiction between professional objectivity and subjective passion is intriguing and worthy of further consideration. Does Frank insist on objectivity as part of a performance of his at times hypermasculinity? He admits to seeing the inclusion of passion into science as in some way "feminine" and the emphasis here is on Anna's ability to integrate the two perspectives. This gendered construction of professional life also connects

to Robinson's depiction of Anna and her husband Charlie's domestic roles, in which Charlie has embraced the role of stay-at-home dad while Anna works full time (*Sixty Days*, 48–49). In this case, the internal debate and struggle between a career as environmental policy analyst and the domestic labor of childrearing is represented through Charlie rather than Anna (depicted as a work-first career scientist putting in 60+ hour weeks).

4. Wark explains the strength of Haraway's and feminist studies' critique of objectivity and the value in her commitment to situated knowledges as successor scientific practice in this way: "Feminist science studies persistently recasts the objectivity claims of the sciences, and does so, to make it worse, without dismissing the scientific endeavor. It is so much harder to dismiss a critic who takes a knowledge practice seriously, who wants not to abandon objectivity, but wants a stronger one, grounded in making a more extensive series of mediating links in the production of knowledge available for scrutiny" (2013, 134).

5. For a thorough overview and critique of the lack of engagement with climate justice initiatives in the trilogy, as well as climate fiction's overall deficiency in this important arena, see Mathew Schnieder-Mayerson's recent article "Whose Odds? The Absence of Climate Justice in American Climate Fiction Novels," in *Interdisciplinary Studies in Literature and the Environment*.

6. Robinson's depiction seems to be a fictional representation of what many second-wave ecocritics have argued in regard to the relationship between traditional views of Nature and a progressive environmental movement. That is, as Morton has articulated it, "Ironically, to contemplate deep green ideas deeply is to let go of the idea of Nature, the one thing that maintains an aesthetic distance between us and them, us and it, us and 'over there.' How deep does deep ecology want to go? In a truly deep green world, the idea of Nature will have disappeared in a puff of smoke, as nonhuman beings swim into view" (*Ecological Thought*, 204). The key is to see both the *naturalness* of the city and the social production of wilderness at once. As Morton aptly depicts it, they are at once distinct and inextricably intertwined.

7. Along with further discussions with Anna and the Tibetan Buddhist exile Rudra Cakrin, Frank also turns, quite predictably, to recent scientific research on the human decision-making process. What he finds surprises him, as he notices "all the new research was adding up to a new understanding of the roles played by the various elements of human thought, consciousness, behavior; a new model or paradigm, in which emotion and feeling were finally understood to be indispensable in the process of proper reasoning" (*Fifty*, 447). And he comes to realize: "The definition of reason as a process that abjured all emotion had been wrong" (448). And, for that matter, "Descartes and most of Western philosophy since the Greeks had been wrong. It was the *feel* one was looking for" (448). Both Sax and Frank, quite clearly then, operate as symbols of a wider change in scientific thought and practice and their personal transformations are indicative

of the potential for the more systemic, institutional, and societal shifts postulated in the novels.

8. Braidotti explains her affirmative approach to the posthuman: "My focus is on the productive aspects of the posthuman predicament and the extent to which it opens up perspectives for affirmative transformations of both the structures of subjectivity and the production of theory and knowledge" (66).

9. Braidotti very clearly places an emphasis on the process itself as productive: "My posthuman sensibility may come across as visionary or even impatient . . . but it is . . . affirmative. Affirmative politics combines critique with creativity in the pursuit of alternative visions and projects . . . the challenge of the posthuman condition consists in grabbing the opportunities offered by the decline of the unitary subject position upheld by Humanism" (54).

10. McKenzie Wark, in *Molecular Red: Theory for the Anthropocene*, makes the important point that Haraway's proposed successor science, far from abandoning rigorous scientific practice, productively complicates objectivity in order to strengthen and improve our systems of knowledge production.

11. In actuality, this is an ongoing process performed throughout the trilogy as various characters hold sporadic yet persistent conversations that assess the current state and groundbreaking work in their respective fields of science, economics, and politics.

12. Morton's concept of hyperobjects is helpful here as well. For instance, he writes, "The ecological thought that thinks hyperobjects is not one in which individuals are embedded in a nebulous overarching system, or conversely; one in which something vaster than individuals extrudes itself into the temporary shapes of individuals. Hyperobjects . . . present us with scalar dilemmas in which ontotheological statements about which thing is the most real (ecosystem, world, environment, or conversely, individual) become impossible" (hyperobjects, 19). Additionally, as he has argued persuasively elsewhere, for instance in his *The Ecological Thought*, under these circumstances scholars can no longer afford to leave intentionality and causation unexamined (ch. 2).

13. In *Archaeologies of the Future*, Jameson writes, "This is why it is a mistake to approach Utopia with positive expectations, as though they offered visions of happy worlds, spaces of fulfillment and cooperation, representations which correspond generically to the idyll or the pastoral rather than the utopia . . . the Utopians, which, like those of the great revolutionaries, always aim at the alleviation and elimination of the sources of exploitation and suffering, rather than at the composition of blueprints for bourgeois comfort . . . these are however maps to be read negatively" (12).

14. Freedman expands on science fiction as critical utopia: "It is the transformation of actuality into utopia that constitutes the practical end of utopian critique and the ultimate object of utopian hope . . . the cognitive rationality . . . of science fiction allows utopia to emerge as more fully itself, genuinely critical and

transformative. In this way, the dynamic of science fiction can on one level be identified with the hope principle itself" (69).

15. McKenzie Wark provides the absolute clearest summary of the import of Barad's theory of diffraction, her expression of intra-active knowledge-making processes, that I have come across: "It [diffraction] does not take as given what is object and what is subject, or what is nature and what is culture. It is about their joint production. Diffraction is about how things pass through and produce differential patterns" (154). Consequently, she continues, "Diffraction, at its best, does not look for the way science is just a mirror of culture, as the social constructivists might. Nor does it take science to be a mirror of nature, as scientific realists might. Rather, it's a question of taking apparently separate things, passing them through each other and seeing how they interact, how they might in part be mutually produced . . . yet not alike" (155).

16. As one of Frank's colleagues at NSF so blithely puts it to his fellow scientists: "I told you, we're stupid! We're going to have a tough time getting out of this mess, we [humanity] are so stupid!" (*Sixty*, 149).

17. Interestingly, this aspect of the trilogy is indicative of Neil Easterbrook's argument concerning the increasing amount of science fiction set in the present in his article "Alternate Presents: The Ambivalent Historicism of Pattern Recognition," published in Science Fiction Studies in 2006. Increasingly science fiction writers do not feel the need to turn to the past or possible futures in order to depict/uncover the unusual and the unknown; they're writing science fiction in a science fiction-y world. It is also clear that this is simply a more obvious manifestation of the claim that science fiction, whether alternative futures or alternative histories, is in actuality always about its contemporary moment. In fact, David Ketterer makes the "science fiction as present" claim as early as 1974 in his *New Worlds for Old: The Apocalyptic Imagination, Science Fiction, and American Literature.*

18. Braidotti explains her use of the term in this way: "Affirmative politics combines critique with creativity in the pursuit of alternative visions and projects. As far as I am concerned, the challenge of the posthuman condition consists in grabbing the opportunities offered by the decline of the unitary subject position upheld by Humanism, which has mutated in a number of complex directions" (*The Posthuman*, 54).

Works Cited

Adamson, Joni. *American Indian Literature, Environmental Justice, and Ecocriticism: The Middle Place.* U of Arizona P, 2001.

Alaimo, Stacy. *Bodily Natures: Science, Environment, and the Material Self.* Indiana UP, 2010.

———. *Exposed: Environmental Politics and Pleasures in Posthuman Times.* U of Minnesota P, 2016.

———. "Sustainable This, Sustainable That: New Materialisms, Posthumanism, and Unknown Futures." *PMLA,* vol. 127, no. 3, May 2012, pp. 558–64.

Arsic, Branka. *Bird Relics: Grief and Vitalism in Thoreau.* Harvard UP, 2016.

Bahng, Aimee. "Extrapolating Transnational Arcs, Excavating Imperial Legacies: The Speculative Aspects of Karen Tei Yamashita's *Through the Arc of the Rainforest.*" *MELUS,* vol. 33, no. 4, Winter 2008, pp. 123–34.

Barad, Karen. *Meeting the Universe Halfway: Quantum Physics and the Entanglement of Matter and Meaning.* Duke UP, 2007.

Bennett, Jane. *Vibrant Matter: A Political Ecology of Things.* Duke UP, 2012.

Braidotti, Rosi. "The Politics of 'Life Itself' and New Ways of Dying." *New Materialisms: Ontology, Agency, and Politics,* edited by Diana Coole and Samantha Frost. Duke UP, 2010, pp. 201–18.

———. *The Posthuman.* Polity, 2013.

Brown, Wendy. *Undoing the Demos: Neoliberalism's Stealth Revolution.* Zone Books, 2015.

Brune, Michael. "The Day We Move Forward On Climate." *Coming Clean: The Blog of Executive Director Michael Brune.* February 6, 2013. Sierraclub.typepad/michaelbrune/2013/02. the-day-we-move-forward-on-climate.html. Accessed July 31, 2020.

———. "From Walden to the White House." *Coming Clean: The Blog of Executive Director Michael Brune.* January 22, 2013. blogs.sierraclub.org/michaelbrune/. Accessed July 31, 2020.

Buell, Lawrence. "The Ecocritical Insurgency." *New Literary History*, vol. 30, no. 3, 1999, pp. 699–712.

———. "Ecocriticism: Some Emerging Trends." *Qui Parle*, vol. 19, no. 2, 2011, pp. 87–115.

———. *The Environmental Imagination: Thoreau, Nature Writing, and the Formation of American Culture*. Harvard UP, 1995.

———. *The Future of Environmental Criticism: Environmental Crisis and Literary Imagination*. Blackwell, 2005.

Canavan, Gerry, and Kim Stanley Robinson, eds. *Green Planets: Ecology and Science Fiction*. Wesleyan UP, 2014.

Chakrabarty, Dipesh. "The Climate of History: Four Theses." *Critical Inquiry*, vol. 35, no. 2, Winter 2009, pp. 197–222.

Cherniavsky, Eva. *Neocitizenship: Political Culture after Democracy*. New York UP, 2017.

Chin, Allison. "Today We Take Part in Civil Disobedience for the Climate." *Compass: Pointing the Way to a Clean Energy Future*. February 13, 2013. Accessed April 1, 2019.

Chura, Patrick. *Thoreau the Land Surveyor*. U of Florida P, 2010.

Cohen, Jeffrey Jerome. "Introduction: Ecology's Rainbow." *Prismatic Ecology: Ecotheory beyond Green*, edited by Jeffrey Jerome Cohen. U of Minnesota P, 2013.

———. *Stone: an Ecology of the Inhuman*. U of Minnesota P, 2015.

Coole, Diana, and Samantha Frost. "Introducing the New Materialisms." *New Materialisms: Ontology, Agency, and Politics*, edited by Diana Coole and Samantha Frost. Duke UP, 2010, pp. 1–43.

Coulthard, Glen Sean. *Red Skin, White Masks: Rejecting the Colonial Politics of Recognition*. U of Minnesota P, 2014. Indigenous Americas Series.

Cronon, William. "The Trouble with Wilderness; or Getting Back to the Wrong Nature." *Uncommon Ground: Rethinking the Human Place in Nature*, edited by William Cronon. Norton, 1995, pp. 69–98.

Davies, Jeremy. *The Birth of the Anthropocene*. U of California P, 2016.

Di Chiro, Giovanna. "Living Environmentalisms: Coalition Politics, Social Reproduction and Environmental Justice." *Global Environmental Politics* vol. 17, no. 2, 2008, 276–98.

———. "Nature as Community." *Uncommon Ground: Rethinking the Human Place in Nature*, edited by William Cronon. Norton, 1995, pp. 298–320.

———. "Beyond Ecoliberal 'Common Futures': Environmental Justice, Toxic Touring, and a Transcommunal Politics of Place." *Race, Nature, and the Politics of Difference*, edited by Donald S. Moore et al. Duke UP, 2003.

Dillon, Grace. *Walking the Clouds: An Anthology of Indigenous Science Fiction*. U of Arizona P, 2012.

Donahue, Brian. *The Great Meadow: Farmers and the Land in Colonial Concord*. Yale UP, 2004.

Durbeck, G., Caroline Schaumann, and Heather I. Sullivan. "Human and Non-Human Agencies in the Anthropocene." *Ecozon@, vol, 6, no. 3,* 2015, pp. 118–136.

Easterbrook, Neil. "Alternate Presents: The Ambivalent Historicism of Pattern Recognition." *Science Fiction Studies,* vol. 33, no. 3, November 2006, pp. 483–504.

Estes, Nick. *Our History Is the Future: Standing Rock versus the Dakota Access Pipeline, and the Long Tradition of Indigenous Resistance.* Verso, 2019.

Fishel, Stefanie R. *The Microbial State: Global Thriving and the Body Politic.* U of Minnesota P, 2017.

Freedman, Carl. *Critical Theory and Science Fiction.* Wesleyan UP, 2000.

Ghosh, Amitav. *The Great Derangement: Climate Change and the Unthinkable.* Penguin Books, 2016.

Gilio-Whitaker, Dina. *As Long as Grass Grows: The Indigenous Fight for Environmental justice, from Colonization to Standing Rock.* Beacon Press, 2019.

Golden, K. C. "The Keystone Principle: Stop Making it Worse." *Grist.* February 16, 2013. https://grist.org/climate-energy/the-keystone-principle/. Accessed December 15, 2020.

Hansen, James, et al. "Target Atmospheric CO_2: Where should Humanity Aim?" *The Open Atmospheric Science Journal,* Vol. 2, 2008, pp. 217–231.

Haraway, Donna. *Primate Visions: Gender, Race, and Nature in the World of Modern Science.* Routledge, 1989.

———. *Simians, Cyborgs, and Women: The Reinvention of Nature.* Routledge, 1991.

———. *Staying with the Trouble.* Duke UP, 2017.

———. *When Species Meet.* U of Minnesota P, 2008.

Heise, Ursula. *Sense of Place and Sense of Planet: The Environmental Imagination of the Global.* Oxford UP, 2008.

Iovino, Serenella, and Serpil Oppermann. "Introduction: Stories Come to Matter." *Material Ecocriticism,* edited by Serenella Iovino and Serpil Opperman. Indiana UP, 2014, pp. 1–17.

Jameson, Fredric. "The Future as Disruption." *Archaeologies of the Future: The Desire Called Utopia and Other Science Fictions.* Verso, 2005, pp. 211–33.

———. " 'If I Find One Good City, I Will Spare the Man': Realism and Utopia in Kim Stanley Robinson's Mars Trilogy." *Archaeologies of the Future: The Desire Called Utopia and Other Science Fictions.* Verso, 2005, pp. 393–416.

———. "The Utopian Enclave." *Archaeologies of the Future: The Desire Called Utopia and Other Science Fictions.* Verso, 2005, pp. 10–21.

Johnson, Rochelle. " 'This Enchantment is No Delusion': Henry David Thoreau, the New Materialisms, and Ineffable Materiality." *ISLE: Interdisciplinary Studies in Literature and Environment* vol. 21, no. 3, Summer 2014, pp. 606–635.

Johns-Putra, Adeline. "The Rest Is Silence: Postmodern and Postcolonial Possibilities in Climate Change Fiction." *Studies in the Novel.* vol. 50, no. 1, Spring 2018, pp. 26–42.

Kucich, John. "Lost in the Maine Woods: Henry David Thoreau, Joseph Nicolar, and the Penobscot World." *The Concord Saunterer: A Journal of Thoreau Studies*, vols. 19/20, 2012, pp. 22–52.

Latour, Bruno. *Down to Earth*. Translated by Catherine Porter. Polity, 2018.

Leane, Elizabeth. "Chromodynamics: Science and Colonialism in the Mars Trilogy." *Kim Stanley Robinson Maps the Unimaginable; Critical Essays*, edited by William J. Burling. McFarland, 2009, pp. 144–56. Critical Exploration in Science Fiction and Fantasy, 13.

Lee, Chang-rae. *On Such a Full Sea*. Riverhead Books, 2014.

LeMenager, Stephanie. *Living Oil: Petroleum Culture in the American Century*. Oxford UP, 2014.

Luckhurst, Roger. "The Politics of the Network: The Science in the Capital Trilogy." *Kim Stanley Robinson Maps the Unimaginable; Critical Essays*, edited by William J. Burling. McFarland, 2009, pp. 170–80. Critical Explorations in Science Fiction and Fantasy, 13.

Manzi, Jim, and Pete Wherner. "Conservatives and Climate Change." *National Affairs*. Vol. 44, Summer 2015, nationalaffairs.com/publications/detail/conservatives-and-climate-change. Accessed July 1, 2020.

Markley, Robert. *Dying Planet: Mars in Science and the Imagination*. Duke UP, 2005.

Marx, Karl. "On the Jewish Question." *The Marx-Engels Reader*, edited by Robert Tucker. Norton, 1978, pp. 26–46.

McGown, Brian. "Whatever Happened to the Dakota Access Pipeline?" *Forbes*. June 4, 2018, forbes.com/sites/what-ever-happened-to-the-dakota-access-pipeline/. Accessed July 1 2020.

McKibben, Bill. *Eaarth: Making a Life on a Tough New Planet*. St. Martin's, 2010.

———. *The End of Nature*. Random House, 1989.

———. "Global Warming's Terrifying New Math." *Rolling Stone Magazine*, July 19, 2012, Rollingston.com/politics/politics-news/global-warmings-terrifying-new-math-188550/. Accessed July 1, 2020.

Mehnert, Antonia. *Climate Change Fictions: Representations of Global Warming in American Literature*. Palgrave MacMillan, 2016. Literatures, Cultures and the Environment Series.

Mitchell, Timothy. *Carbon Democracy: Political Power in the Age of Oil*. Verso, 2011.

———. *Rule of Experts: Egypt, Techno-Politics, Modernity*. U of California P, 2002.

Morton, Timothy. *The Ecological Thought*. Harvard UP, 2010.

———. *Hyperobjects*. U of Minnesota P, 2013.

Newman, Lance. *The Literary Heritage of the Environmental Justice Movement: Landscapes of Revolution in Transatlantic Romanticism*. Palgrave Macmillan, 2019.

Nixon, Rob. *Slow Violence and the Environmentalism of the Poor*. Harvard UP, 2012.

Opperman, Serpil. "Theorizing Ecocriticism: Toward a Postmodern Ecocritical Practice." *ISLE: Interdisciplinary Studies in Literature and the Environment*, vol. 13, no. 2, Spring 2007, pp. 103–28.

———. "From Ecological Postmodernism to Material Ecocriticism." *Material Ecocriticism*, edited by Serenella Iovino and Serpil Oppermann. Indiana University Press, 2014, pp. 21–36.

"Our Mission." www.350.org. Accessed March 1, 2019.

Page, Amanda. *Understanding Chang-rae Lee*. U of South Carolina P, 2017.

Prettyman, Gib. "Living Thought: Genes, Genres, and Utopia in the Science in the Capitol Trilogy." *Kim Stanley Robinson Maps the Unimaginable: Critical Essays*. McFarland, 2009. pp. 181–203. Critical Explorations in Science Fiction and Fantasy, 13.

Purdy, Jedediah. *After Nature: A Politics for the Anthropocene*. Harvard UP, 2015.

Reed, T.V. "Toxic Colonialism, Environmental Justice, and Native Resistance in Silko's *Almanac of the Dead*." *MELUS*, vol. 34, no. 2, 2009, pp. 25–42.

Rich, Nathaniel. *Odds Against Tomorrow*. Picador, 2014.

Robinson, Kim Stanley. *Antarctica*. Random House, 1998.

———. *Blue Mars*. Random House, 1996.

———. *Fifty Degrees Below*. Random House, 2005.

———. *Forty Signs of Rain*. Random House, 2004.

———. *Green Mars*. Random House, 1994.

———. *Red Mars*. Random House, 1993.

———. *Sixty Days and Counting*. Random House, 2007.

Romero, Channette. "Envisioning a 'Network of Tribal Coalitions' in Leslie Marmon Silko's *Almanac of the Dead*." *The American Indian Quarterly*, vol. 26, no. 4, 2002, pp. 623–40.

Rosenthal, Elizabeth. "Life After Gas and Oil." *New York Times*, March 23, 2013. nytimes,com/2013/03/24/Sunday-review/life-after-oil-and-gas/. Accessed July 1, 2020.

Schlosberg, Eric, and David Carruthers. "Indigenous Struggles, Environmental Justice, and Community Capabilities." *Global Environmental Politics*, vol. 10, no. 4, 2010, pp. 12–35.

Schneider-Mayerson, Matthew. *ISLE: Interdisciplinary Studies in Literature and Environment*, vol. 26, no. 4, Autumn 2019, pp. 944–967.

Silko, Leslie Marmon. *The Almanac of the Dead*. Simon and Schuster, 1991.

Simpson, Leanne Betasamosake. *As We Have Always Done: Indigenous Freedom through Radical Resistance*. U of Minnesota P, 2017. Indigenous Americas Series.

Streeby, Shelley. *Imagining the Future of Climate Change: World-Making through Science Fiction and Activism*. U of California P, 2018. American Studies Now.

Szeman, Imre, and Maria Whiteman. "Future Politics: An Interview with Kim Stanley Robinson." *Science Fiction Studies*, vol. 31, no. 2, 2004, pp. 177–88.

Thoreau, Henry David. *The Portable Thoreau*, edited by Carl Bode. Penguin, 1982.

———. *The Journal; 1837–1861*, edited by Damion Searls. New York Review of Books Press, 2009.

Tillett, Rebecca. "'The Indian Wars Have Never Ended in the Americas': The Politics of Memory and History in Leslie Marmon Silko's *Almanac of the Dead*." *Feminist Review*, vol. 85, 2007, pp. 21–39.

Tsing, Anna. *The Mushroom at the End of the World: On the Possibility of Life in Capitalist Ruins*. Princeton UP, 2015.

United States Department of State. "Keystone XL Project Environmental Report." n.p., November 2008. Accessed May 1, 2013.

———. "Keystone XL Pipeline Project: Draft Supplementary Environmental Impact Statement." n.p., March 2013. Accessed May 1, 2013.

Vance, Linda. "Ecofeminism and Wilderness." *NWSA Journal*, vol. 9, no. 3, 1997, pp. 60–76.

Vint, Sheryl. "Archaelogies of the Amodern: Science and Society in *Galileo's Dream*." *Configurations*, vol. 20, no. 1–2, 2012, pp. 29–51.

Wallace, Molly. "A Bizarre Ecology: The Nature of Denatured Nature." *ISLE: Interdisciplinary Studies in Literature and the Environment*, vol. 7, no. 2, Summer 2000, pp. 137–53.

Walls, Laura Dassow. "'And As You Are Brothers of Mine': Thoreau and the Irish." *The New England Quarterly*, vol. 88, no. 1, March 2015, pp. 5–36.

———. "Believing in Nature: Wilderness and Wildness in Thoreauvian Science." *Thoreau's Sense of Place: Essays in American Environmental Writing*, edited by Richard J. Schneider. U of Iowa P, 2000, pp. 15–27.

———. *Seeing New Worlds: Henry David Thoreau and 19th Century Natural Science*. U of Wisconsin P, 1995.

———. *Henry David Thoreau: A Life*. U of Chicago P, 2017.

Wark, McKenzie. *Molecular Red: Theory for the Anthropocene*. Verso, 2015.

White, Damien F., and Chris Wilbert, eds. *Technonatures: Environments, Technologies, Spaces, and Places in the Twenty-first Century*. Wilfred Laurier UP, 2009.

Yamashita, Karen Tei. *Through the Arc of the Rainforest*. Coffee House Press, 1990.

Zizek, Slavoj. *Living in the End Times*. Verso, 2010.

Index

actant: definition of, 210n5; *see also* distributed agency

Adamson, Joni: on *Almanac of the Dead*, 105, 109, 221–22n1, 223n7

affirmative politics: *See* Braidotti, Rosi

agency: *See* distributed agency

agential realism: 4–5; *see also* Barad, Karen

Alaimo, Stacy: on precarity, 40; on sustainability, 21, 211–12n7; on "transcorporeality," 21, 210n6, 220n18

the Anthropocene, 36–37, 222n4, 222–23n5

anthropocentrism, 4–5; *see also* postanthropocentrism

Arsic, Branka: Thoreau and relationality, 75

Barad, Karen: "agential realism," 4–5, 85; distributed agency, 212n10, 219n16, 221n3; intra-action, 88, 199; relating to Thoreau, 68, 72, 82

Bennett, Jane: "agentic capacity," 7–8, 210n5

"blockadia," 43

Braidotti, Rosi, 3, 88; affirmative politics, 189–90, 201, 229n8, 229n9, 230n18; "biocitizenship," 221n5; on death, 146; posthuman subject, 185

Brown, Wendy: on neoliberalism, 151–52, 158–59

Brune, Michael, 33–34

Buell, Lawrence: on *Odds Against Tomorrow*, 138; on Thoreau, 57, 59, 218n5

Canavan, Gerry, 189

capitalism: and carbon democracy, 20–27; in climate fiction, 138–39, 147–49, 158–59, 190–96; and colonialism in *Almanac*, 115–22; and commodification in *Through the Arc*, 80, 86–92; and commodification in *Walden*, 60–70; and pipeline politics, 30–36; *see also* Brown, Wendy and "Carbon Democracy"

Carbon Capitalism, 42; *see also* "Carbon Democracy"

Carbon Democracy (Mitchell): and activism, 24–26, 46–47; introduction of, 21–22; politics of, 23

Carruthers, David: on socio-environmental injustice, 82–83

causality: *See* intentionality

Cherniavsky, Eva: neocitizenship, 10–11, 24–25; on Occupy Wall Street, 45–46; political agency, 166

Chin, Allison: on Sierra Club's climate activism, 17–19
Chura, Patrick, 73–75
citizen: *See* Brown, Wendy and Cherniavsky, Eva
climate change environmentalism: Keystone XL, 18–19, 28–29; mainstream tactics 17–20; #NoDaPL, 43–47; theoretical and practical challenges, 5–11
Cohen, Jeffrey Jerome: "agentism," 5; geologic time, 222n4
contingency: *See* distributed agency and "unknowable now"
Coole, Diana, 2–3
Coulthard, Glen: *See* "grounded normativity"
crisis: politics of, 188–90
Cronon, William: on social construction of nature, 20, 211n6

Dakota Access Pipeline, 43; and Indigenous activism, 46–47; racial politics of, 44
Davies, Jeremy, 222n4, 222–23n5
decolonizing environmentalisms: *See* Reed, T.V.
Di Chiro, Giovanna: "ecoliberalism," 199–201; "social reproduction," 81–83, 118, 215n28, 225n12
diffraction (Barad), 230n15
Dillon, Grace, 103, 109
"disintentional politics": implications of, 166–68; introduction of, 15, 133–35; in *Odds Against Tomorrow*, 148–49; in *On Such a Full Sea*, 161–68; *see also* distributed agency and distributed environmental politics
distributed agency: in *Almanac of the Dead*, 106–12, 124–30; definition of, 1, 209n4; and intentionality, 2, 4–5; in *Odds Against Tomorrow*, 138–40, 144–48; in *On Such a Full Sea*, 150, 159–61, 163–64; politics of, 5–8, 85, 210n4; and revolutionary politics, 123–30, 127–31; in *Science in the Capital*, 186–87, 200–202; and temporality, 102–104, 106–108, 110–12; in *Through the Arc*, 86–92, 97–99; in *Walden*, 63–73; *see also* "optimodality"
distributed environmental politics: and climate change, 42; meaning of, 8–9, 26–27; in *Science in the Capital* 199–202; *see also* "disintentional politics" and "distributed agency"
distributed knowledges: Thoreau, 60–62, 66–69; *see also* "passionate science" and "situated knowledges"
dualism, 20, 58–60; disruption of 86–88, 90–91; *see also* "optimodality"

Easterbrook, Neil, 230n17
eco-cosmopolitanism (Heise), 215n29; *see also* Heise, Ursula
entanglement, 5–6; *see also* distributed agency
environmental justice, 80–83; and climate change, 179; and decolonization, 119–21; in *Through the Arc*, 81, 94, 98–99
environmentalism: *See* climate change environmentalism and distributed environmental politics
Estes, Nick: on #NoDAPL, 43–44; Indigenous activism, 109, 216n32, 216–17n35; on Indigenous futures, 45–46
exceptionalism: humanist, 210n4; *see also* distributed agency

Index

fatalism: and climate change, 36–37; political implications of, 13, 215n30
Fishel, Stefanie: "microbial politics," 9–10
Freedman, Carl: critical utopian fiction, 229n14; see also "radical novelty"
Frost, Samantha, 2
futurity: and agency, 170; in *Almanac of the Dead*, 114–15; Jameson, Frederic, 189; and justice, 80–83; in *Odds Against Tomorrow*, 137–39, 142–44, 148–49; in *On Such a Full Sea*, 155–56, 165; politics of, 40–43; and Progress, 133–34; in *Science in the Capital* trilogy, 196; see also "material temporalities" and "unknowable now"

geo-engineering, 175, 188
Ghosh, Amitov, 3–4
Gilio-Whitaker, Dina, 121
governmentality (Foucault), 10–12
"grounded normativity" (Coulthard), 43, 119–20, 122, 225n13

Hansen, James, 35, 212n12
Haraway, Donna: on activism, 220n20; "positioned rationality," 174, 183; "situated knowledges," 88, 173
Heise, Ursula: "eco-cosmopolitanism," 41, 215n29; on *Through the Arc*, 87, 95, 221n4, 221n6
holism, 172–73
human exceptionalism: critique of, 210n4; see also distributed agency
hybrid-agency (Mitchell): See distributed agency and Mitchell, Timothy
"hybrid-objects": in *Through the Arc*, 87–89; in *Walden*, 69–73

"hyperobjects," 170; see also Morton, Timothy

indeterminacy: politics of, 168
individualism: disruption of, 4–5; see also distributed agency and "optimodality"
"insurgent bacteria": meaning of, 86; politics of, 90–92, 96–99
intentionality, 20–21, 27; and accountability, 223n8; in *Almanac* 127–32; disruption of, 2, 4–5; in *Odds Against Tomorrow*, 144–49; in *On Such a Full Sea*, 166–68; in *Science in the Capital* trilogy, 186–87; in *Through the Arc*, 88, 94, 96–98
"intra-activity": See Barad, Karen
Iovino, Serenella: on distributed agency, 209n1

Jameson, Frederic: critical utopian fiction, 197, 229n13; on fear, 189
Johnson, Rochelle, 56
Johns-Putra, Adeline, 226n3

Ketterer, David, 230n17
"Keystone Principle," 31
Keystone XL Pipeline, 18–19; and colonialism, 45; history of, 28–29
Klein, Naomi, 24, 43
knowledge production: 2–3, 49–52; see also "distributed knowledges," "passionate science" and "situated knowledges"
Kucich, John, 55, 217n3

Latour, Bruno, 26, 79; climate denialism, 210n17; *Terra* politics, 40–41
Leane, Elizabeth, 186

Lee, Chang-rae: *On Such a Full Sea*, 136, 149–58, 161–68
LeMenager, Stephanie, 24
Luckhurst, Roger, 170–71, 184, 187

Markley, Robert, 185
Marx, Karl, 23
"material temporalities": introduction to, 102–103; political implications of, 104–105, 131–32, 166; *see also* futurity and "unknowable now"
McKibben, Bill: climate change activism, 34–36, 38; distributed politics, 33; fatalism, 36–37; feedback loops, 38–39; 350.org, 27–28, 32–33
Mehnert, Antonia: on *Odds Against Tomorrow*, 138, 141; on *Science in the Capital* trilogy, 196
Mitchell, Timothy: hybrid-agency, 83–86; *see also* "Carbon Democracy"
"mixed-communities": definition of, 220n1; relation to environmental justice, 82–83, 87, 89–90, 96–97, 119
Morton, Timothy: on hyperobjects, 170, 228n6, 229n12

nature: as construct, 211n6; in crisis, 34–35, 37–39; and culture, 3–4; as postnatural, 20–22, 58–63
neoliberalism: in *On Such a Full Sea*, 151–52, 154, 158–59; *see also* capitalism
New Materialism: and agency, 2; politics of, 5–9
Newman, Lance: Thoreau and social justice, 53–54
#NoDAPL campaign, 43–47; *see also* Estes, Nick

nonlinear temporalities: *See* "material temporalities" and "patient urgency"

objectivity: alternatives to, 49–52, 57–62; *see also* Barad, Karen, Haraway, Donna, "passionate science," and "situated knowledges"
Opperman, Serpil: ethics of new materialism: 209n2
optimism: politics of, 189–90, 200–202; *see also* Braidotti, Rosi
"optimodality": and crisis, 187–90; definition of, 172; disrupting humanism, 180–82; as "split" subjectivity, 177

Page, Amanda, 150, 162, 226n3
"passionate science": as knowledge production: 174, 176, 180, 194–95, 199; *see also* "situated knowledges"
"patient urgency": in *Almanac of the Dead*, 102–103, 126; and climate activism: 127; political implications of, 131, 166–67; *see also* "material temporalities"
permaculture, 193, 196–97, 199, 200–202
pessimism: *See* fatalism and McKibben, Bill
petrotopia (Lemenager), 24
political agency: *See* disintentional politics, distributed agency and distributed environmental politics
positioned rationality: *See* Haraway, Donna, "passionate science" and "situated knowledges"
postanthropocentrism: and agency, 4–8; and intentionality, 134–36; in *Odds Against Tomorrow*, 144–45; in *On Such a Full Sea*, 160–61,

163–67; and scientific practice, 183–84; in *Walden*, 57, 77; *see also* "optimodal"
posthuman subject: definition of, 209n3; politics of, 85–86; *see also* Braidotti, Rosi and postanthropocentrism
postnatural, 20–22
Prettyman, Gib, 175, 186
Purdy, Jedediah: on complacency, 215–16n30; Thoreau for the Anthropocene, 56, 63; Thoreau and relationality, 77; Thoreau and rupture, 73; Walden pond, 74

radical novelty (Freedman), 197
rationality: alternatives to, 176; critique of, 174–75; and subjectivity, 171–72
Reed, T.V.: on *Almanac of the Dead*, 224–25n11; decolonizing environmentalisms, 117–18
"relational knowing," 59, 76–77, 88, 97–98, 166; *see also* Walls, Laura
relationality: posthuman perspectives, 185
Rich, Nathaniel: *Odds Against Tomorrow*, 135–36, 137–49, 168
Robinson, Kim Stanley: *Antarctica*, 193–95; *Fifty Degrees*, 170–71, 177–82, 190–91; *Forty Signs*, 175–76; *Mars* trilogy, 172–73, 185–87; *Sixty Days*, 169, 191–93, 196–98; Thoreau connection, 49–52
Romero, Channette: on *Almanac of the Dead*, 106–107, 224n10, 229n9

Schlosberg, Eric: socio-environmental injustice, 82–83, 221n2
Schneider-Mayerson, Matthew: on *Odds Against Tomorrow*, 144, 226n2; on *Science in the Capital* trilogy, 228n5
Sen, Amartya, 82
Sierra Club, 17–19
Silko, Leslie Marmon: *Almanac of the Dead*, 101–104, 127–31; the Homeless Army in *Almanac*, 115–17, 121, 124–26; the People's Army in *Almanac*, 108–15, 120, 123–24
Simpson, Leanne Betasamosake, 119–20, 167
"situated knowledges" (Haraway): as passionate science, 50; Thoreau connection, 57–60, 62; *see also* Haraway, Donna
Slack, Jennifer, 82; *see also* "mixed-communities"
"social reproduction": in *Almanac of the Dead*, 109, 118, 122; capitalism, 86; definition of, 81–83; *see also* Di Chiro, Giovanna and "mixed-communities"
Standing Rock: *See* Dakota Access Pipeline and #NoDAPL
Streeby, Shelly: on *Almanac of the Dead*, 226n15; on Standing Rock protests, 43, 216n33, 217n37
subjectivity: *See* distributed agency, "optimodality," and postanthropocentrism
sustainability: critiques of, 21, 225n12
Suvin, Darko, 197

temporality: *See* "material temporalities" and "patient urgency"
Thoreau, Henry David: for the Anthropocene, 56; in climate fiction, 49–52, 183–84; distributed agency, 63–69; hybrid-objects, 69–73; and knowledge formation,

Thoreau, Henry David *(continued)* 58–61, 75–77; and privilege 52–56; as subversive surveyor, 73–75

Tillett, Rebecca: on *Almanac of the Dead*, 106, 121–22

Traditional Ecological Knowledges: in *Almanac of the Dead*, 105–106, 110–14, 118–19; and #NoDAPL, 45–47; in *Through the Arc*, 87, 90

transcorporeality, 21; *see also* Alaimo, Stacy

Tsing, Anna: agency and temporality, 166–67, 227n6; on justice without progress, 135; on "latent commons," 168, 227n7; "salvage rhythms," 148–49

"unknowable now," 169–71; political implications of, 197–202

Vint, Sheryl, 173

vulnerability: politics of, 189–91, 201; *see also* "unknowable now"

Wallace, Molly, 87; *see also* "hybrid-objects"

Walls, Laura Dassow: Humboldt, 218n8; relational knowing, 59–61, 76–77, 218–19n10, 219n13, 219n14; *Seeing New Worlds*, 58; Thoreau and abolition, 53; Thoreau and savagism, 55

Wapner, Paul: on "postnature politics," 20, 26–27

Wark, McKenzie: on diffraction, 230n15; on situated knowledges, 175, 228n4, 229n10

White, Damian: environmental justice, 179

whiteness: denial of privilege, 180; as privilege, 177–79

Whitt, Anne, 82; *see also* "mixed-communities"

Wilbert, Chris: environmental justice, 179

Yamashita, Karen Tei: *Through the Arc of the Rainforest*, 80, 86–92, 94–99, 130

Zizek, Slavoj, 169, 180, 199

www.ingramcontent.com/pod-product-compliance
Lightning Source LLC
Chambersburg PA
CBHW020647230426
43665CB00008B/343